The Liberation of the African Mind

The Key to Black Salvation

VOLUME I

By

Adisa Franklin

authorHOUSE

1663 LIBERTY DRIVE, SUITE 200
BLOOMINGTON, INDIANA 47403
(800) 839-8640
www.authorhouse.com

First published by AuthorHouse 01/21/05

ISBN: 1-4184-0465-9 (sc)

Library of Congress Control Number: 2004107085

Printed in the United States of America
Bloomington, Indiana

This book is printed on acid-free paper.

This book is dedicated to the ancestors, all spiritual warriors who labor for the freedom of Africans in America and the world, and especially to the generations which are to come.

Table of Contents

Chapter 1: Black Man, How Did You Fall 1

Chapter 2: The Benefits of Slavery 39

Chapter 3: Judging the Tree by the Fruit 53

Chapter 4: What Euro-Christianity Stole 83

Chapter 5: What Euro-Christianity Added 103

Chapter 6: What Euro-Christianity Misrepresents 125

Chapter 7: Upon Whose Authority 135

Chapter 8: Reversing the Reversal 159

Chapter 9: A Declaration of Religious Independence 185

Chapter 10: Open Letter to the Pimps in the Pulpit 193

Chapter 11: Taking a Stand for the Truth 215

BELOVED GOD
CREATOR OF THE HEAVENS AND THE EARTH
GIVE ME THE STRENGTH AND CLARITY
TO CONVINCE MY PEOPLE
THAT IT IS MUCH LATER THAN THEY THINK

<u>Acknowledgements</u>

I acknowledge first of all the Creator who was the source of inspiration and who provided the will to persevere for over twenty five years in the accumulation of information and experience necessary to write this book. I especially would like to acknowledge my children, Trevious, Shamika, Michael, Eboni, Noah, Kamaal, Joshua, and Jordan for their inspiration, for this work is about them, my grandchildren and the generations of Black youth to come. I would like to thank Dr. Althea Armstrong for demanding that I at least began to write. Lastly I would like to thank my family and friends that have been there for me through the years.

Introduction

"Surely the Light is in the world and the world knows it not"

The very "Cornerstone of the Temple" was rejected by those who claimed to be the builders and keepers of the Temple. Surely the light was in Africa and Western man knew it not. In ancient times the Light of the World was in Africa. This fact was covered up and denied and a false picture has been presented to the world concerning the origin of Western mans religious system. It is time that the truth is told.

> "The reason is simple. The early apostolic fathers of Christianity have long known that what they call Christianity today is nothing more than a reincarnation of Ancient Egyptian religious doctrines and practices of faith. If they acknowledge that Ancient Egypt was a black civilization, it would mean they also have to acknowledge that the concepts and doctrines of Christianity are ancient black African creations."

> "Secretly, Christian Europe has been fighting off the name and image of Ancient Egypt that have loomed rather too largely over the history and practice of Christianity for over two thousand years. This is because it would be inconsistent with early Christian leader's pronouncement of African religion as "pagan," and it would be inconsistent with European socio-political perception of itself as the superior one and Africans as the inferior ones. How would it sound to hear that Christian Europe adopted "pagan" Africa's concepts and doctrines of religion, or superior and civilized Europe merely redesigned inferior and primitive Africa's ancient civilization into modern civilization?"—*From Africans Who Wrote The Bible,* Nana Banchie Darkwah, Phd, pg. 141

Yet this is what happened and its time that African American Christians learned this truth. This book has a "Prophetic" message. Please do not reject its message until you have examined all of the testimony. This book is presented as a beacon of light in a land grown dark with the stench of materialism. Despite the numerous churches on every corner, the people still walk in spiritual darkness and confusion. Too many are ignorant of the Laws pertaining to Life and are worshiping God on an instinctual level. It is a dark time because man is out of tune with these laws, nature and the universe. This is true because he is operating with a faulty knowledge base and belief structure. A corrupted version of the truth has been substituted and accepted as authentic. The truth has been compromised. As in the sphere of philosophy, education, and history, the truth has been altered and corrupted by and in the Religious world. Western (European) thought has its base in Judeo-Christian beliefs, values and dogmas. These beliefs, values and dogmas have been accepted and internalized as valid by African Americans. These are the invisible chains and shackles that blind our minds, and limit our spiritual growth and development.

It is time we took a stand against this "flood of false-hood" and set a new standard in the land. A Spiritual "Matrix" must be established to replace the Matrix of materialism. Materialism is the world outlook of the natural man who has not discerned the "hidden man" of the heart as him-self. To stand for the truth is to stand for God the Creator and His master plan for man. This book reflects the authors efforts to take that stand and sound the call and invitation to all that read to do likewise. This is the real solution because it addresses the real problem; the root cause of the illness in our world is spiritual ignorance. Inability to discern this is the reason for our failure to heal ourselves and create a sane and humane world.

I must address an apparent contradiction in this work. My reason for quoting the Bible as a type of authority on certain matters and at other times appearing to be critical of it. First of all the moral teachings of Christianity are correct, there is no one who would argue with teaching people not to steal or kill. It is the doctrines or theories and interpretations that must be questioned today.

The Bible has undergone considerable change since it was introduced to the world. It is presented to the world as the Word of God. The New Testament is written by Europeans and presented as God's final revelation and authority. When the fact that the Bible is not original but a version of earlier sacred text with some additions is uncovered, many eyes will be opened. The Bible in its present form is a book that has been tainted by much revision and the overlay of another people's world outlook over the world view of people that were the originators of the first sacred writings.

The original contributors of sacred text were of a dark hue and they lived in Africa. Their sacred writings have provided the foundation for all other sacred writings including and especially the Christian Bible. For this reason even the Bible itself can bring clarity to the dark doctrines created by the ones who where not dark in hue but in character.

We acknowledge such contributions as Augustine and other men of color that impacted on Christianity's early development. Augustine is given credit for developing the "Doctrine of Depravity". He can be considered one of the founding Fathers of Christianity. But we must recognize that the dominant force in the shaping and promoting of Christianity however has been Western man. This is easily recognized in the attempt to make the Jesus of Scripture of European descent.

The ability to "rightly divide" the Bible begins with much study of the Bible but must end with the study of Ancient African Spiritual knowledge and understanding. In order to understand the Bible it is required that one has knowledge of metaphysics as well as an understanding of ancient signs, symbols and terms. Metaphysics would include numerology, astrology and the knowledge of the meaning of colors. The Bible uses all these to teach the spiritual and prophetic lessons we all need to learn.

Having spent over thirty years in the study of these various subjects including the study of Orthodox Christian scripture and beliefs I hope to contribute to bringing some clarity to what has been accepted without question, namely Christian doctrines and beliefs. In doing so I shall use the language that is most familiar. There is no other book as well read among Blacks as the Bible. Eighty percent is a conservative estimate of the numbers of Blacks that have embraced Christianity's perspective of God and his plan for man. For this reason I have chosen to use some Biblical quotes as an authority.

This is not a book that supports the status quo. We should all recognize that what we've been doing isn't working. This is a book by an African man in America who loves and honors the truth. This is therefore first a book for all seekers of Truth. It is a book for all those who sincerely seek to heal, unite, elevate, and liberate African Americans and the world.

"If you have ever driven through thick fog, you know how it restricts the view and distorts familiar objects along the roadway; how it closes in and circumscribes the range of vision, concealing the beauties of vista and perspective. Even your headlights do not pierce it indeed their light is often reflected back upon you and increases your difficulty. Until the fog lifts there is no clarity of vision.

It is just so with ignorance and by ignorance I do not mean illiteracy. The most learned person may still be ignorant of many things. Our knowledge of the objective world may be accurate, systematic, and to a certain degree complete. But without wisdom we propel our lives through a fog of ignorance that accepts the limitations of evil and error and that cannot get beyond the petty personal point of view. Until the fog is dispelled the ignorant mind faces an incomplete universe". *Know Thyself,* Richard Lynch, P.164

In conclusion, all men are created equal by the Creator and by necessity are endowed with the Creator's divine nature. In addition to our divine natures we each have a human nature. The crisis we face is a spiritual crisis. At present, the natural man is "The god of this world". It is incumbent on all men to "Put on immortality and incorruptibility" which means to let the spirit man, the divine man reign in this life. This is worshipping God "in Spirit and in Truth". Each race must address this critical issue. This is the only solution to our many problems! The "human race" is all about the race to spiritual perfection in this life.

This book should be read by every person interested in the empowerment and liberation of Africans in America. It is my hope that it will contribute to the cause of Spiritual freedom for many African Americans. The three volumes comprise a comprehensive review and analysis of the cause of; (1) The current crisis in race relations; (2) Self-hatred and Self-destructive behavior among blacks; (3) Moral decay; (4) Drug addiction and related crime; (5) The crisis in black leadership; (6) Black disunity; (7) Economic underdevelopment; (8) Political impotence; and most importantly; (9) The reason the Black Church has failed to address this 'crisis' and demonstrate they are the 'Light of the World'. In addition, and this is critical, together the three volumes provide a comprehensive plan of action for the solution to the problem. Together, indeed, they represent the illusive but powerful, "Key to Black Salvation" and the "Liberation of the African Mind".

"To this end was I born, and for this cause came I into the world,
that I should bear witness to the Truth.
Every one that is of the Truth hears my voice" **John 18:37**

Chapter 1

BLACK MAN, HOW DID YOU FALL

WE'VE FALLEN BUT WE CAN GET UP

Black man how did you fall from such a high estate
when did it happen, what far and distant date
in Africa long ago, you had built great pyramids
yet, your knowledge of how you did it has been cleverly hid
Black man how did you fall from such a high estate
you were made a slave that others love to hate
it is you that gave light to the human race
yet today you can't even keep pace
look at all you've given; you gave meaning to the word civilized
yet today you are despised, looked down upon and often criticized
Black man how did you fall from such a high estate
what caused this tragedy, who engineered this dark fate
Black man how did you fall from such a high estate
when will you rise again, how long must we wait?
before you, Black man, take a stand
and act like you know that you are a man
there are inside of you all the answers you seek
to make you strong again instead of so weak
so when your woman calls and says, where are you my dear
you can say with confidence, the mans right here

poem by adisa

1

PART 1

Africa was not a Dark Continent

The ancient African ancestors were highly regarded as great vessels of wisdom. Their country was reverently referred to as "the Holy Land". Africa's pre-Roman era is blatantly overlooked in the curriculum of public schools. This era was perhaps the greatest and most significant period in the history of mankind. This was the cradle or birthplace of true civilization. The light of wisdom was flowing in the land. Yet this perception of Egypt is held by too few African Americans, considering the fact that these ancient people were their ancestors. This lack of awareness is directly related to the fact that the public school system tenaciously avoids mentioning Africa's pre-Roman era. Most African Americans consider these ancient people as primitive people who worshipped many gods. This attitude can be traced directly to the teachings of the Orthodox Christian Church. According to the European Christian scholars, the Africans worshipped everything from animal deities to sun gods. In addition, there is no mention of the significant contributions to religion made by the inhabitants of ancient Africa.

Too few African Americans identify ancient Egypt's history as a part of their history. Indeed, to most African Americans, Africa and its history is truly a "dark subject". This is a direct result of the Euro-centric Educational System which misrepresents the history of African people and it's own.

"It would be better not to know so many things than to know so many things that are not so." –Felix Okaye

Euro-centric Schools Handicap and Poison Youth's Minds

So much of what we are taught in school is false and misleading that America's youth are beginning life mentally handicapped. This includes youth of all races. While the Truth heals and sets free, lies and distortions bring destruction and bondage. This is the real source of the pain and suffering of "mans inhumanity to man." And this is the reason it must be addressed today.

"American history textbooks promote the belief that the most important developments in world history are traceable to Europe." *The Lies My Teacher Told Me*, **James W. Loewen, pg. 51**

For most of us, our knowledge of history only dates back to ancient Greece and Rome. The reason for the obvious slant is that history is written from the perspective of the conquering and ruling class. It is evident that the major aim of this group is to paint the picture of their historical pursuits in the finest of lights possible and by "any means necessary." In the American public schools the glorious years of the African dynasties pre-dating the era of the Roman Empire, is systematically eliminated and distorted at best.

Such a curriculum causes White youth to have a distorted view of their African American classmates and peers. It causes them to view them as less valuable and a people to feel only distain for. Contrarily, such a curriculum causes Black youth to feel inferior. Euro-centrism is unhealthy for America. For that reason, any curriculum that does not teach the truth should be unacceptable.

> **"It is painful to advert to these things. But our forefathers, though pious, and sincere, were nevertheless, in respect to Christian charity, under a cloud; and, in history, truth should be held sacred, at whatever cost…especially against the narrow futile patriotism, which, instead of pressing forward in pursuit of truth, takes pride in walking backwards to cover the slightest nakedness of our forefathers. –Col. Thomas Aspinwall, *The Lies My Teacher Told Me,* James W. Loewen, pg. 76**

Speaking of nakedness, while we are pulling the covers on America's educational system, we must not neglect to shine the light of truth on America's religious system as well. It is the author's contention that together the past and present "sins" of the Church and School are responsible for the ills of our society today. Both the education system and the "Orthodox" churches, or the church that is accepted, has presented a false view of the Ancient Africans.

Too few Christians and especially African American Christians are aware that it is the Orthodox Church that created and perpetuated the misnomer that Blacks were a cursed race and therefore only fit to be slaves. It is the church that is responsible for the cloud around Africans and their early relation to their God. The Orthodox Christian church promoted the idea that Africans worshipped many gods and therefore were heathen and pagans. Because of the Church, White America deemed it right in the sight of god to proclaim that Africans were only two-thirds human. The most critical issue of the 21st century is the telling of the Truth.

The Truth must be told

Today, fortunately, the truth is being revealed in many areas kept in the dark for centuries. Unethical government practices, inside trading and deceiving the public by the business sector, and the recent bringing to the light of "some" of the sins of the Church has provided the news with lots of good Front page news. Yet, too few have undertaken the task of critically examining our major institutions. Today, in light of the death and destruction faced by Americans specifically and the world in general, we must begin to look for the source and cease attempts to correct the problem on the symptom level. **The symptoms are merely indicators of the depth of spiritual depravity and signs of a failing educational system. Therefore we shall limit our in depth analysis to the two institutions that directly impact on the mind and spirit of man, namely, the Church and School. The truth must be told about why these two vital institutions are failing us.**

If we would truly educate our youth, much of the conflict between the races would be minimized. Problems of self esteem among African American youth would begin to vanish, and young peoples disregard for the sanctity of life would be uplifted directly impacting youth on youth violence.

FOR THE HEALING OF AMERICA AND THE WORLD THE MOST CRITICAL NEED IS THE NEED FOR TRUTH TELLING IN OUR INSTITUTIONS THAT IMPACT THE MINDS OF THE PEOPLE, AND PARTICULARLY THE YOUTH. THE TWO KEY INSTITUTIONS ARE THE CHURCH AND SCHOOL.

With these facts in mind let us go on to correct the situation by some truth telling. Now let us take a look at how far Blacks have fallen and how they fell by examining the facts about Africa's true history. According to Anthony T. Browder in *Nile Valley Contributions to Civilization*; "Indeed, history has been kind to Europeans because they have written it in many instances, it has been the fiction (lie) agreed upon."

> **"Because of a global system of miss-education which currently exists, the average person honestly believes that civilization began in Europe, and the rest of the world waited in darkness for the Europeans to bring them the light". Mr. Browder also reminds his readers that "The Egyptians of today are not the same people as the ancient Kemites of 5,000 years ago, just as the Americans today are not the same as the Native Americans of 500 years ago".**

Nile Valley Contributions To Civilization, Anthony T. Browder, pg. 37

According to Mr. Browder, **"There is every indication that the Egyptians or Kemetics, who built the advanced civilization of Egypt, were indigenous African people of a dark hue and having wooly hair."** This fact has actually been established by the science of archaeology, anthropology, artwork, and through the many documents which have been discovered, as well as by documented testimonies of contemporary historians of that time. Many of these facts were even written on stone in the Egyptian temples by the Nubian people who built them.

Unfortunately, the deliberate and organized attempt to keep the truth about this glorious period in the history of humanity obscure and hidden, has been extremely detrimental to African Americans. Because of it, it is necessary to make all Americans aware of the importance of both recognizing the achievements of the Ancient Africans and the true cause of their demise. For this reason, considerable attention needs to be taken to assure that for once, African Americans and White Americans are able to pierce the dark veil that has kept them disconnected from the truth about the culture and wisdom that exemplified the life of the ancient people of Africa. It is important to recognize that Africa was not considered the "Dark Continent" until the Europeans turned out the lights by destroying that glorious African culture and civilization.

> "The study of the history of the blacks must begin in Egypt because more of their indestructible monuments are there; and, further, because many of the artifacts archaeologists have been uncovering during the past seventy-five years as 'Egyptian' are in fact 'African'". *The Destruction of Black Civilization*, Chancellor Williams, pg. 1

Racial Identity of Egyptians is no Mystery

Much has been lost or more particularly, destroyed, and the rest has been presented in a corrupted version, but the truth is being revealed. The records still exist however of both the accomplishments and the identity of the ancient Egyptians/Africans. The Egyptians took considerable effort to make the record of their contributions last even to the 21st century.

Initially, the orthodox Christian view was of the opinion that the ancient Egyptians were African; consider this quote by Arthur C. Custance, a Canadian who studied toward a Ph.D. in Anthropology from the University of Toronto. His Ph.D. studies were interrupted just prior to the presentation of his thesis by a move to Ottawa. Subsequently, the degree was granted by the University of Ottawa in

Education. Mr. Custance agrees with McGhee that the Egyptians were Black and the originators of civilization.

Mr. McGhee was widely respected as a pastor, teacher, lecturer, and author. McGhee implicitly admitted that historically an inaccurate view of race has been taught in the American school system. He taught that, "The first two great civilizations headed by the Black man are Sumer (Mesopotamia) and Egypt". Obviously, Custance shares with McGhee his belief that people of color were the originators of civilization. Listen to this quote:

> **"The Hamites according to my thesis include virtually all the people who in the ancient times were the originators and creators of civilization in both the old and the new world. It is this fact, for which we now have massive evidence that comes as such a surprise to most Indo-European readers, and which, in the words of one high Canadian Government authority, came almost as a 'revelation'.**

> Out of Ham have been derived all the so called colored races-'the yellow', 'red', 'brown', and 'black'-the Mongoloid and the Negroid. Their contribution to human civilization in so far as has to do with technology has been absolutely unsurpassed...The Canaanites and the Sumerians (both descendants of Ham) refer to themselves as 'black headed' people-a designation which seems more likely to have reference to skin color rather than color of hair, since all people in this area have black hair anyway; a hair-color distinction would be meaningless...**The evidence which does exist, for all its paucity at times, strongly supports a cradle of mankind in the Middle East from which there went out successive waves of pioneers who were neither Indo-Europeans nor Shemites.**

> **These were Hamitic pioneers, either Mongoloid or Negroid in type with some admixture, who blazed trails, and opened up territories in every habitable part of the earth and ultimately established a way of life in each locality which at a basic level made maximum use of the raw materials and resources of that locality...The black people have a quite remarkable series of high cultures to their credit,** and are almost born metallurgists...Almost every African community of any size has its own smelting furnace and smithy. No part of this iron working has been borrowed from Europe". *Beyond Roots, A Deeper Look at Blacks in the Bible,* William Dwight McKissic, Sr. & Anthony T. Evans, p. 42

Bible Declares Egyptians are Black

"Religious broadcaster, New York Theological Seminary and Yale Law School graduate, Pat Robertson, who hosts the 700 Club television program leaves no doubt about what he believes about the origin and identity of the races of mankind. In response to the question 'Where did all the races come from'? Robertson answers:

> ...Ham became the father of the Egyptians, the Ethiopians, and the other black races, as well as the Canaanites who once lived in the land now occupied by Israel. Japheth was the father of the Greeks, the people who lived in the islands of the sea and who settled Europe and Russia; Shem was the father of the Semitic people-the Jews, Arabs and Persians". *Beyond Roots, A Deeper Look at Blacks in the Bible,* William Dwight McKissic, Sr. & Anthony T. Evans, p. 47

First and foremost the Egyptians own testimony support what their art and language both reveal; that is they were African. The "Egyptians themselves-who would surely be better qualified than any one to speak of their origin, recognize without ambiguity that their ancestors came from Nubia and the heart of Africa". *The African Origin of Civilization*, Cheikh Anta Diop. In addition, a most trusted contemporary historian of the Greeks confirms, that the Egyptians were of African stock.

> "The 'Father of (European History)', Herodotus, states: "The...Ethiopians and the Egyptians have thick lips, broad nose, wooly hair, and they are burnt in 'skin'".

Many people do not associate Egypt with Africa for primarily three reasons; (1) The current race inhabiting Egypt as its rulers are not indigenous Africans. (2) The "white-washing of African history by European scholars, educators and clergymen. (3) The image of the Egyptians portrayed by Hollywood. Therefore the task must be undertaken to first put Egypt back in Africa and authenticate they were African people in the minds of African Americans. This necessity only demonstrates the degree of the success of Europeans efforts to destroy the memory of African Americans and their connection to these ancient fathers of civilization in the minds of African Americans.

Considerable effort was expended in making the recalling of the memory, both painful and undesirable. Yet, recalling the experience can and should be both pleasant and medicinal for the sons and daughters of Africa. It is equally important that White America is made aware of these facts even though it may be painful to their innate sense of superiority fostered by the lie.

Religion was Life

Having answered that basic but critically important question, "Who were the real Africans of antiquity, let us move on to take a close look at what these ancient Africans left for posterity to ponder. The first fact that must be appreciated is that their culture and society were centered on the priesthood and their "Mystery" teachings. The Priest were the pillars of Ancient African society and their activities formed the foundation for and gave direction to their entire society. For Africans, religion was not a part of their life, it was life itself. The scholar Chancellor Williams in *The Destruction of Black Civilization* states it this way; **"Religion to the Africans was far more than ritual reflecting beliefs, but a reality reflected in their actual way of life, religion from the earliest times became the dynamic force in the development of all the major aspects of black civilization".** p. 35

"More has been learned about ancient Kemet (Egypt) within the last hundred years than any other time within the past two millennium. No other nation on earth has had the privilege of 3,000 years of cultural and historical continuity, nor has been the object of such intense international scrutiny. Based upon their findings, it is certain that the length and breadth of this great civilization is yet to be fully realized". *Nile Valley Contribution To Civilization*, Anthony T. Browder, p.67

Righteousness Reigned in Africa

It has been said that "power corrupts and ultimate power corrupts totally", yet to the African priest of Egypt, this axiom did not apply. Their purpose was to bless the society with the wisdom necessary to live fruitful lives in harmony with each other and the natural world around them, and to that charge they remained true.

"The priest was in the most strategic positions to acquire great economic and political power for themselves naturally and without any particular efforts to do so. They **were the first men of learning-scribes, historians, scientist, architects, physicians, artists, mathematicians, astrologers, and especially chemist.** Many temples, therefore, were colleges as well as places of worship. The temples were also places through which flowed much of the national revenue". *The Destruction of Black Civilization*, Chancellor Williams, P. 52

Though they had ultimate control of what was taught and the finances, the priests used the wealth to build and sustain a righteous society. **The connection between the Church and State is fundamentally correct if it is modeled after the Egyptian system of the King/priest.** As we shall see later in this chapter, the ancient Africans would never consider separating education from religion or the church from the state. Certainly, this is the reason politics is a dirty word, it is void of any spirituality.

The funds coming into the first Black Church belonged to a national treasury, which in turn belonged to the people. This is in stark contrast to the type of Churches we have today where the bucks stop (and stay) in the church treasury, to be used mostly to build bigger churches and to help each local pastor outshine his peers in material possessions. **The power of God to transform natural men and women into true spiritual men and women, is lost as the Churches argue over which is the right form (outward, appearance) of faith.**

Righteousness must once again be the standard in the Church, then the Church will demonstrate to the unbelieving the true power of God. Surely, God's people have not turned from their wicked ways and sought God, for we would have heard from heaven by now. For once again, God's people would be the light of the world that cannot be hidden.

PART 2

Africans Were The Light of the World

The priest of yesterday instilled life and infused light into the culture and lives of the African community. All learning proceeded from the wisdom, knowledge and understanding possessed by the priest. This fact is illustrated by Chancellor Williams; "The ancient religion that gave birth to science and learning, art, engineering, architecture, the resources for a national economy and political control-that same religion was the mother of history, of writing, of music, the healing art, the song and the dance". *The Destruction of Black Civilization*, Chancellor Williams, P. 37

With these facts taken into consideration, we can better understand the success of the Africans in building a true model of civilization and for their success in the above mentioned areas. It is important that we examine these achievements individually to fully appreciate their contribution. The key to their success was the African educational system called today, the Mystery Schools. To this day the true worth and meaning of what they taught remains a 'mystery' to Europeans and Africans Americans as well.

RELIGION & EDUCATION

According to African tradition, religion provides the foundation for learning, therefore, these two must be considered together. This fact contributed to the success of what has come to be called the African Mystery System. "Numerous records exist which show that the Africans in the Nile Valley, particularly those in ancient Kemet (Egypt), had created such an educational system, the likes of which have yet to be duplicated.

> "Every temple in Kemet had vast libraries equipped with thousands of papyrus scrolls which contained dissertations on law, medicine, philosophy and numerous other subjects". *Nile Valley Contributions To Civilization*, Anthony T. Browder pg. 123

From this we can glean that not only was religion important, but the transfer of that understanding and the wisdom which it supplied, to the people was also a priority with these people. All knowledge had a practical application. Much of the success of the educational system could be attributed to the fact that the Egyptians had created a system of writing and a form of paper called papyrus to record their accumulated wisdom for sharing with succeeding generations. Because of their importance these two contributions will be considered separately. However, the primary factor for the success of the African Mystery system is that it was based in, and grew out of, the religious knowledge of the priest. It was they who were the instructors in all of the temple schools.

In 1984, at the Nile Valley Conference, Dr. Asa Hilliard presented a paper on the Kemetic Concepts in Education and cited the significance of Ipet-Isut as a center of learning during the Eighteenth Dynasty (note: Ipet-Isut is in Africa):

> **"It was both a center of religion and education, since the two could not be separated in the minds of the Kemetes.** It housed an elite faculty of priest-professors. It has been estimated that at one time there were more than 80,000 students at all grade levels studying at Ipet Isut University (Abdullah, 1984). Temples were at the center of religion, politics, and education. The faculty were called Hersetha or 'teachers of mysteries', and were divided into departments."

Purpose of Education is to Establish Harmony

Much has been written about the 'Mystery Schools' of the Nile Valley, but one important factor must be remembered; these schools, and the subjects taught within them, were a mystery only to those who were unfamiliar with that system of education. **"The purpose of education in the Nile Valley was to create a society where the citizens would understand the relationship, which existed between them-selves and the universe (all of which was understood to be a manifestation of their Creator).** In the truest sense of the word, the educational centers in the Nile Valley were the first 'universities". *Nile Valley Contributions To Civilization,* Anthony T. Browder pg. 124

TO THAT I WOULD ADD FOR THE SAKE OF CLARITY, THAT THEY ALSO ESTABLISHED THE FIRST CHURCH.

In chapter 7 we will examine in more depth the contrast between the character of the early African priest and the class of priest that replaced them. **The purpose of religion and education is to establish harmony between man and his Creator, as well as between man and man.** Both of these are dependent on harmony being present in individual men. This required knowledge is totally neglected in today's learning institutions.

WRITING & PAPYRUS

It is important to remember that it was the African and not the Greeks, which were responsible for these important contributions to civilization. Without these contributions there could not have even been any recorded history, for it is these inventions that enabled man to pass on the accumulated wisdom of the ages.

This fact also dispels any notion that Africans were "oral" people only. As a result of the Africans being the originators of written language, the origin of all other languages can be traced back to them. Consider these statements regarding the importance of writing and the paper to write on, both African contributions.

"In the ultimate sense it is therefore true that the Egyptian alphabet was the parent of every other that has ever been used in the Western world". Edward McNall Burns and Phillip Lee Ralph, *World Civilizations, 5th Ed.* W.W. Norton & Co., N.Y. p. 21-22

Professor Walter A. Fairservis, Associate Professor of Anthropology at the University of Washington State Museum wrote: "One of the most important contributions made by ancient Egypt was paper making. Paper was made from the papyrus. Before the Egyptians invented paper, writing was done on clay tablets". He goes on to say that: "unlike the rest of the ancient world, the Egyptians required only a brush and some ink, and they could easily carry these materials anywhere they went".

> "It is not the proud Aryan or his elder brother the Semite who claim the honor of the invention (the first alphabet). It belongs neither to Japhet nor Shem, but to the despised Ham, with whom they are unwilling to acknowledge kinship". *Paleography*, by Bernard Quaritch, London, 1994, p. 5

The Egyptians invented three different alphabets, one of which was exclusively for sacred material. This alphabet was called Hieroglyphics. Can you imagine schools without the benefit of paper and no one able to write? How would the instructors teach? I have seen on bumper stickers the slogan, "If you can read this bumper sticker thank a teacher". With all due respect to this noble profession, it would have been more accurate and perhaps more appropriate if it had read, "If you can read this bumper sticker, thank an African"!

GOVERNMENT

The African system of government was truly of the people and for the people. Everything functioned to support the life and the needs of the society. It is true that much was centered on the will of the King/priest. Yet, the will of the Creator and the will of the people, gave direction to the ruler-ship of these King/priest. Their character was not evil as in the extensive list of European despotic dictators. There were even times when the African societies functioned without a king. **Contrary to the current position of today's governments which declare all would be chaos and anarchy if not for the existence of a powerful government with the military capabilities to in-force its will, Africans remained civilized and lived in harmony without a king.** There are still places in Africa, believe it or not, where people live in peace and harmony. These places have no police or prisons.

Godly Kings

In ancient African society the people believed that they would be blessed or cursed according to the character of the king and his relation to the Deity (God). Anything less than a character that was almost God-like was unacceptable. His behavior had to please the gods and particularly the Most-High God. In fact, in many instances, he was believed to be the earthly incarnation or "son" of the Most-High God. The African king, therefore, worked for the welfare of his people. Compare this to the kings and presidents of today. When there was a king, he adhered to a constitution and policy that benefited the people. For this reason the character of the king was without blemish. This fact is illustrated in the following quote by Peter J. Paris:

> **"In traditional African societies, it was necessary for the king to be a person of exemplary moral integrity because a direct correlation existed between his character and the community's well-being. He was permitted no moral blemish lest it diminish the efficacy of his mediating powers".** *The Spirituality of African Peoples*, Peter J. Paris, pg. 58

Consider this description of the state treasury by Chancellor Williams; "The state's income from religion stemmed from the requirement of sacrificial offerings from the people. **But where traditional constitutional law of the blacks prevailed the people contributed of their means willingly for a quite non-religious reason: The central treasury belonged to the people and was maintained for the people's welfare;** and not only for public projects but for the relief of each and every individual in distress whose needs could not be met by his family or clan".

During those times the people were united in one purpose. The welfare of the entire society was the priority of each individual no matter what his function or role. They did not function under the misconceived notion of 'the rugged individual' which 'does it his way'. The rights of the individual did not supercede the welfare of the community. The Africans willingly adhered to the wisdom of the priest/guides. **The people had good reason to trust the guidance of the priest and King/priests. They were righteous!** They had lived for generations in the most fertile Valley in the world, trusting their King/priest. The Nile Valley afforded its inhabitants an almost "Eden-like" existence. In addition, the priest adhered to and taught the mysterious way of harmony with the universe through harmony with the laws governing the universe. This assured that, withstanding outside influence, their life as it was would continue.

A True Democracy

As mentioned above, there were times in which the African society did not always require kings or dictators. Consider this quote by Chancellor Williams:

"Many writers refer to the 'kingless' periods before centralized states as the rule of nobles, oligarchies or hierarchies, etc. From the very beginning, therefore, the Westerners applied Western concepts to quite different African Institutions. Later they described the same kind of societies as 'chief less' or, worse, 'stateless'.

They did not understand the African constitutional system of real self-government by the people through their representatives, the Council of Elders". (*The Destruction of Black Civilization,* by Chancellor Williams, pg. 41) This prejudiced position, cannot change the fact that what the Africans had worked.

Our system would prove to be the world's first truly democratic society, and perhaps the "only" example. With or without a king our ancestors flourished in the Nile Valley. "These facts are set forth at the outset because both the constitutional system and its offspring, African democracy, originated in 'chief less societies'. **And, what is even more significant, democracy reached its highest development here where the people actually governed themselves without chiefs, where self-government was a way of life, and 'law and order' were taken for granted".** *The Destruction of Black Civilization,* Chancellor Williams, pg. 92

In the work *The Black Man's North and East Africa,* Professors ben-Jochannan and George Simmons make the following observation: **"The only perfect government recorded by man occurred in Egypt around 2500 B.C.E. What is meant by a 'perfect government'? One in which there is no bribery or corruption"**

Because of the wisdom of the ancient Africans, they enjoyed a level of civilization unparalleled in history. This was accomplished without any police and without building a single jail. Only in a righteous society (one free from corruption) can such achievements be made. Today we must ask why there is even a need for such a system. Even though it has been labeled a "correctional system", there is nothing "corrective" about it.

Besides, if they could do it, why can't we? Perhaps, the answer lies in the fact that these are not the true goals of the institutions of American society and other European dominated societies. **The people today never stop to consider, that maybe the "expressed" interest of the government and the church for that matter, is not their true intentions.**

One thing is for certain, the spirit of brotherhood and the desire to govern our-selves could truly benefit the African in America today. Unfortunately, this spirit is sorely lacking in too many African Americans and especially African American so called leaders. It must be concluded that as a people, Blacks need to learn more about the wisdom of the ancient Africans and the system they had established by which the people truly governed them-selves. This knowledge must then be systematically passed on to each new generation. This would necessitate Blacks building their own schools as well as financially sustaining them. Then Blacks could control the agenda, the curriculum and the outcome.

SCIENCE AND ARCHITECT

Though Europeans take the credit for this contribution, the Egyptians combined religious knowledge, science and architect to create monuments that still astound the world today. The Egyptians were not seeking to impress the world with the construction of the world's largest and tallest building. The dimensions and purpose of the Great pyramid reflected their knowledge of "sacred science". It needs to be noted here that the pyramids served functions other than merely to house the bodies of the Pharaohs upon their deaths. The Egyptians went through a great deal of trouble to construct these mysterious monuments according to precise astrological and engineering calculations. Even though it was not their purpose, these colossal monuments, continue to mystify and create awe in all who witness their majestic presence. Let us observe some of the reasons for this admiration and interest.

"**There is more stone in the Great Pyramid than in all the cathedrals, churches and chapels in England since the time of Christ.** In more contemporary terms, the Great Pyramid was built to a height equaling a 45-story building and with enough stone to build 30 Empire State buildings. So vast is this structure that, if all of its stones were cut into one-foot blocks and laid end to end, they would stretch two-thirds of the distance around the Earth at the equator. **The cement used to bind these stones in place is 1/50 of an inch, the thickness of two sheets of paper, and it is nearly invisible when compared to the one-half inch of mortar used in traditional brick construction**". *Nile Valley Contributions To Civilization*, Anthony T. Browder pg. 110

"Through a skillful interpretation of the Kemetic (Egyptian) Medu Netcher (hieroglyphics) and symbolism, **the Lubicz family discovered that the architectural forms in Kemet embodied a level of knowledge they describe as *sacred science*.** This sacred science was regarded as the grand synthesis of Kemetic art, science, religion, philosophy and architecture whose expression was unique with each pharaonic temple that was constructed". *Nile Valley Contributions To Civilization,* Anthony T. Browder pg. 120

Professor Piazzi Smyth made very careful measurements of the Great Pyramid; and his results were summarized by Dr. Alfred Russell Wallace in an address before the British Association for the Advancement of Science, at Glasgow in 1876, as follows:

"-That the pyramid is truly square, the sides being equal and the angles right angles".

"-That the four sockets on which the first four stones of the corners rested are on the same level".

"-That the directions of the sides are accurately aligned to the four cardinal points (of the earth)".

"-That the vertical height of the pyramid bears the same proportion to its circumference at the base as the radius of a circle does to its circumference".

"Now all these measures, angles, and levels are accurate, not as an ordinary surveyor or builder could make them, but to such a degree as requires the best modern instruments and all the refinements of geodetical science to discover any error at all.

In addition to this we have the wonderful perfection of the workmanship in the interior of the pyramid, the passages and chambers being lined with huge blocks of stone fitted with the utmost accuracy, while every part of the building exhibits the highest structural science". (*British Association Report*, Glasgow Meeting, 1876, *Part II, Notices and Abstractions*, p. 117) *What They Never Told You*, Indus Khamit-Kush, p. 93

"A classic study on how the pyramids were built was written by Somers Clarke and R. Engelbach who said that these ancients were: "perhaps the best organizers of human labor the world has ever seen". *Ancient Egyptian Masonry, What They Never Told You*, Indus Khamit-Kush, p. 94

Since it has never been figured out just how these majestic and colossal structures were built, this remains speculation. Until it is determined how they accomplished this amazing feat, the number of workers involved must remain a mystery as well.

Professor Pappademos (An outline of Africa's Role in the History of Physics, Blacks and Science) reflects a similar view regarding the work of these ancient people: "It is a small wonder that the achievements of the Egyptians would excite the admiration of the ancients. They still do today; the scope and precision of their monuments and pyramids would challenge the abilities of today's engineers, 5,000 years later". *What They Never Told You*, Indus Khamit-Kush, pg. 92

Africans Possessed Sacred Science

The fact that these people have been labeled primitive and had their culture and religion degraded by falsely being labeled as polytheistic, heathen, pagan, animistic, and other labels with similar negative connotations is indeed unfortunate and totally unjustified. It made identification by African Americans with these people undesirable. Obviously, their wisdom was such that it should be coveted and fully appreciated for the contribution it could make even to today's society. Their wisdom and understanding was "sacred knowledge". They were extraordinary people because they possessed an extraordinary wisdom and knowledge. Let us consider another of their marvelous contributions.

ASTRONOMY

Today we look up at the multitude of stars on a clear night and a few of us are able to identify a couple of constellations, but most of us simply stare in awe. What little knowledge we have is usually taken for granted. For that reason, the majority of us have never stopped to consider that; there was a people which had named the stars and constellations, calculated their distance from the earth and each other, and more or less given man a chart of the heavens, complete with the names of the constellations, and the course of their annual and regular trek across our skies.

"The ancient Greek writer Lucian wrote: 'The Ethiopians were the first who invented the science of the stars, and gave names to the planets". *Ruins of Empire*, Count Volney

"Summary: The complex knowledge of the Dogon of Mali about the Sirius star-system is sending shock-waves around the world. The West African people have not only plotted the orbits of stars circling Sirius but have revealed the extraordinary nature of one of its tiniest companions-Sirius B-which they claim to be one of the densest and tiniest of stars in our galaxy. What is most astonishing about their revelations is that Sirius B is invisible to the unaided eye. Euro centric scientists have attributed this knowledge to the presence of space-men...".

So incredible is this feat that as the French anthropologist Grianule and Dieterlen authors of the article: *'A Sudanese Sirius System'* and the book of *The Pale Fox* said:

"The helical rising of Sirius was so important to the ancient Egyptians (as indeed to the Dogon as well) that gigantic temples were constructed with their main aisles oriented precisely towards the spot on the horizon where Sirius would appear on the expected morning. The light of Sirius would be channeled along the corridor (due to the precise orientation) to flood the altar in the inner sanctum as if a pin-pointed spotlight had been switched on". *What They Never Told You, Indus Khamit-Kush*, p. 103

"The problem of knowing how, with no instruments at their disposal, men could know the movements and certain characteristics of virtually invisible stars has not been settled nor even posed"! *Journal of African Civilizations, Vol. 1, No. 2*, Nov. 1979

Without contributions in this area, it is doubtful that the U.S.A. would have the NASA program, which puts a huge drain on the national budget and waste so many hard-earned American dollars. **Ironically, we have not learned to live in harmony on earth together, yet we spend billions attempting to find life on other planets.**

"Professor John Pappademos cites the work of Richard S. Westfall, Never a Rest: A Biography of Isaac Newton which says that: 'Newton himself... believed that the most significant astronomical beliefs of the ancient Greeks were derived from the Egyptians". *(The Newtonian Synthesis, In Physical Science* and, *Its roots in the Nile Valley, The Nile Valley Civilizations)*

It is critically important to awaken the African in America to the reality of the truths being revealed about their own history. This is their history and these are their ancestors! Therefore literature such as the one you're reading must find its way into the curriculum of the schools that wish to truly empower our youth.

MEDICINE

European scientist and those in the medical profession remain quite arrogant regarding Western medicine. Even in the face of the knowledge that much of the wisdom of the Oriental race has proven to be both effective and inexpensive. These facts are ignored at the expense of astronomical increases in the cost of medical treatment along the lines of traditional Western methods and technology. Let's take a look at the African contribution and while we do, simply imagine where we might be if the records of the advancements made by these people had not been destroyed by racist scholars.

In public education, our children are taught the Euro-centric view of Hippocrates as being the Father of medicine. Hippocrates was Greek. Apparently, he attempted to plagiarize what he had learned in the Mystery schools, during his lifetime. Herodotus felt it necessary to remind the Greeks of where he (Hippocrates) had obtained his knowledge, with these words, "For Hippocrates, ancient medicine was Egyptian medicine…Hippocrates knew of the priority of Egyptian medicine and its emphasis on dietetics being the first medical knowledge: Galen (200 A.D.), who devotedly continued Hippocrates teachings, is simply expressing the belief of his Master when he writes 'the invention of medicine was the experience of the Egyptians". — they said

> **"The Edwin Smith Papyrus is the oldest medical treatise in existence,** and it is believed to have been written in the Eighteenth Dynasty (ca. 1550 B.C.E.). Many regard this papyrus as a copy of an original document that was created as early as the First Dynasty. Depending on what time line one uses to date the First Dynasty of Kemet, **this medical text could have been written as early as 4200 or as late as 3100 B.C.E.**
>
> **In any event, the appearance of a highly sophisticated text had to have been preceded by hundreds of years of observation, research and refinement.** The ancient physician/priests of the Nile Valley were said to have been instructed in temples, which were called 'Per Ankh'. In today's language they would be called the **'House of Life'. Of the thousands of medical papyri originally written, less than a dozen have been discovered,** and of that number, the Ebers Papyrus and the Edwin Smith Papyrus are deemed the most profound.
>
> The Edwin Smith Papyrus was published in 1930 by James Henry Breasted, who had spent ten years translating the document. **This papyrus describes 48 different injuries to the head, face, neck, thorax and spinal column**

and the appropriate surgical methods for attending to them. It is suspected that the Eighteenth Dynasty scribe who was responsible for copying the original text only wrote the first 48 cases dealing with the upper third of the body. **There are more than 90 anatomical terms referenced in the Edwin Smith Papyrus,** and there are more than 200 terms listed in various Nile Valley medical literatures. **This papyrus is also of great importance because of its use of the word 'brain' and neurological relationship between the brain (spinal cord and nervous system) of the body.**

The Ebers Papyrus (ca. 1500 B.C.E.) explores a broad range of medical science and includes chapters on the pulse and cardiovascular system, dermatology, dentistry, gynecology, ophthalmology, obstetrics, tumors, burns, fractures, intestinal disorders and much more. There is also considerable evidence that physicians in Kemet practiced circumcision, brain surgery and were extremely well versed in gynecology and obstetrics.

By 2000 B.C.E. physicians in Kemet had already created an effective organic chemical contraceptive. This product consisted of acacia spikes, honey and dates, which were mixed in a specific ratio, and inserted in the vagina. Modern science has since discovered that acacia spikes contain lactic acid, which is a natural chemical spermicidal". *Nile Valley Contributions To Civilization*, Anthony T. Browder pg. 125

Summary: Black Contributions to the Early History of Western Medicine, Frederick Newsome, M.D.: **"During several millennia, Blacks in ancient Egypt made numerous contributions to medicine and were acknowledged as the inventors of the art of medicine. They produced the earliest physicians, medical knowledge, and medical literature".**

"Herodotus (450 B.C.) writes that they (the Egyptians) have a persuasion that every disease to which men are liable is occasioned by the substance whereon they feed". *What They Never Told You*, Indus Khamit-Kush, p. 111

"Egyptian priest always regarded the preservation of health as a point of the 1st importance indispensably necessary to piety and service to the gods". *The Ruins of Empire*, Count Volney, P. 119

Professor John Henrik Clarke, Research Director of the First African Heritage Exposition, presents Sir William Osler, author of the book, *Evolution of Modern Medicine*, who refers to: **"Imhotep as 'the first figure of a physician to stand out clearly from the mists of antiquity".**

Professor Clarke further adds: "Imhotep, the Wise, as he was called, was the Grand Vizier and Court Physician to King Zoser…He became a deity and later a universal God of Medicine, whose images graced the first Temple of Imhotep, *MANKIND'S FIRST HOSPITAL*".

Europeans were still using bleeding as a method for treating seriously ill patients during the 1600's. As late as during the time of the infamous witch hunts they still believed that sickness was caused by little demons, the devil's minions. This belief is still fostered by many fundamentalist Christian Churches.

As we examine these "facts" about the early so called primitive African society we must come to the conclusion that we have been gravely misinformed and much to our detriment. Consider how much further medical science could be if all of the information had not been destroyed or otherwise hidden from the world. Though the medical contributions of the early Africans are ignored, their symbol the "caduceus" has been adopted as the universal symbol of medicine. *(Nile Valley Contributions To Civilization*, Anthony T. Browder, P. 168).

That which was not destroyed was stolen and plagiarized. Of course as in many other areas, that which was stolen was never reported as stolen. Sigmund Freud, for instance, did not discover his theory of psychology without help from the advances contributed by these ancient people. His home was a literal museum of African art and artifacts and the language he used can be traced to the information on psychology discovered by these people. Psychological terms such as the "id" and the "ego" have African origins. **The question is what prevents us from once again building true "Houses of Life" today, hospitals that actually cure and heal the sick.**

IRON SMELTING

This particular contribution and product of African science most often goes unnoticed by contemporary scholars and historians, and for that reason, the general public remains almost completely unaware. As in other areas, the Africans far surpassed any development among Europeans.

"It seems likely that at a time when the European was still satisfied with rude stone tools, the African had invented or adopted the art of smelting iron". Atlanta University Leaflet No. 19, cited by W.E.B. Dubois, *The Negro, The Home University Library, N.Y., 1979*

"Independent Origins of East African Iron Smelting is an article written by Clyde Ahmad Winters for the Journal of African Civilizations, Vol. I, No. 2, Nov. 1979. Winters, a specialist in African and Islamic history, presents evidence for the native origin of iron smelting in East Africa. He examines archaeological and other data which suggest an independent origin for iron smelting technology in East Africa in northern Tanzania within the Great Lakes area around Lake Victoria-more than 2,000 years ago". *What They Never Told You,* Indus Khamit-Kush, P. 107

"Visitors to various Egyptian museums found throughout the world often marvel at the priceless treasures that were created in ancient times. Aside from the numerous papyri, monumental architecture and phenomenal paintings, the artisans of the Nile Valley were also skilled jewelers who fashioned works of art made of gold, silver and semi-precious stones. One area that is often overlooked is the development of mining precious metals in Kemet and Nubia". *Nile Valley Contributions To Civilization*, Anthony T. Browder pg. 129

MATH & GEOMETRY

Most people were taught in school that Pythagoras was the "father" of mathematics and Geometry. Our children are still taught this "little white lie" today. Interestingly, they are taught all about so called Greek contributions, neglecting entirely, the pre-Greek era of glorious African dynasties. This is very misleading, and one wonders how in the face of the tremendous evidence demonstrated by the accomplishment of pyramid building, such deception could succeed. The Africans had to have had advance knowledge of these subjects long before the time of Pythagoras.

The Europeans claim to the possession of original mathematical and geometrical knowledge is therefore denied. For those of us who have any doubts that the ancient African civilization possessed superior knowledge of these subjects, listened to these statements regarding who may have been the originators of the knowledge of math and geometry, so that any and all doubts can be eliminated.

"Evidence of a mathematical system was discovered in Africa over eight thousand (8,000) years ago…The Ishango bone found in Zaire (Congo). Note well: Europeans had not even learned to read or write until well over two thousand (2,000) years later". Professor Claudia Zaslavshy illustrate proof of this fact in the *Journal of African Civilizations* (Vol. 5, No. 2, Nov. 1979) *What They Never Told You,* Indus Khamit-Kush, P. 95

"I have also known that Herodotus and others ascribe the origin of geometry to the Egyptian, but the period when it commenced is uncertain. Anticledes pretends that Meoris was the first to lay down the elements of that science, which he says was perfected by Pythagoras: but the latter observation is merely the result of the vanity of the Greeks, which claimed for their countrymen the credit of enlightening a people on the very subject which they had visited Egypt for the purpose of studying". Sir J.G. Wilkinson, *THE ANCIENT HISTORY, Vol. II*, P. 319

Indebtedness to Ancient Egypt for contributions to Mathematics is shown in the book *A Short History of Mathematics* by W.W. Rouse Ball:

"We are able to speak with more certainty on the arithmetic of the Egyptians. About forty years ago the hieratic papyrus, forming part of **the Rhind collection** in the British Museum, was deciphered, which has thrown considerable light on their mathematical attainments.

The manuscript was written by a scribe named Ahmes at a date, according to Egyptologist, considerably more than a thousand years before Christ, and it is believed to be itself a copy, with emendations, of a treatise more than a thousand years older. **The work is called, 'directions for knowing all dark things',** and consists of a collections of problems in arithmetic and geometry; the answers are given, but in general not the processes by which they are obtained. It appears to be a summary of rules and questions familiar to the priests'…knowledge of geometry was derived by the Greeks from Egypt…" *What They Never Told You*, Indus Khamit-Kush, p.97

"On the other hand, 'Greece has always poverty as her companion', according to the Greek historian Herodotus. A fact which generally discourages high mathematical development". *What They Never Told You*, Indus Khamit-Kush, p. 99

This fact actually discourages academic excellence in any other area for that matter. **As a result of possessing such advance knowledge in so many of these** critical areas of civilization, the Africans enjoyed an "Eden-like" existence in the fertile Nile Valley. Their knowledge of the universe facilitated a society blessed with true harmony and prosperity.

ETHICS AND MORALS

Highly Evolved Beings

The Africans lived in an "enlightened" culture. "Sharing was an aspect of African culture that was stressed at every level of society. No one ate unless all could eat. **The needs of the individual were the needs of the society as a whole.** Offense by an individual against an individual was considered an offense against the entire society. It was the duty of every member of society to see to it that the welfare of everybody was taken care of."

> "The old African society was therefore governed by strong traditions and customs. Crime was despised and the need for it reduced. Land and property were regarded as belonging to all humanity and bestowed upon man by the good grace of God. That everything man owned ultimately belonged to God therefore to steal or damage property was regarded as an act of offending God. **Man was the extension of God on earth, so the African believed. Harm to fellow man constituted harm to God the Creator. The woman was God's gift to man and earth, and on her shoulders God placed the responsibility of reproduction and continuity.** This belief is still widely held in many parts of Africa". *No More Lies About Africa*, Chief Musamaali Nangoli, pg. 19

Life in Paradise

Whether the Garden of Eden spoken of in scripture was in Africa can perhaps be debated. It is true however, that all indications are that it was. The fact remains however, that before the coming of the Europeans, life in Africa was anything but dark. It was more like an oasis, the African's own paradise, ruled by godly kings and a righteous priesthood.

> **"Those were the days when Africa belonged to Africans. Those were the days of proud kings, emperors, and chiefs ruling over flourishing kingdoms and empires! Those were the days. The ancient African societies then were highly organized and sophisticated.**

Each kingdom or empire was governed by laws that were for all intents and purposes, products of African culture. Each law embraced every aspect of the African culture and was re-enforced according to the custom of that kingdom or empire. **The rulers of the time were for practical purposes dictators, but the benevolent kind. Their power though absolute, had non-the-less to reflect the wishes of their subjects".** *No More Lies About Africa*, Chief Musamaali Nangoli, pg. 19

"…the developments in this favored land during the thousand or more years before the pyramid age represents a series of **creative advances unrivaled in human experience…the fourth millennium before Christ is like some talented, unnamed ancestor in a family tree whose genes send valuable but unacknowledged donations to descendants now alive".** *What They Never Told You*, Indus Khamit-Kush, pg. 33

"The same sort of talents that brought together a centralized government in Ancient Egypt, that constructed the vast network of irrigation canals, that developed the first phonetic writing and imbedded an alphabet into beautiful picture writing, that wrote the first medical treatises, composed a body of literature and phenomenal art that we still admire today, that invented the first ciphers to represent numbers-these were the talents that underlay the ability to create the awe-inspiring pyramids, obelisk and temples". *What They Never Told You*, Indus Khamit-Kush, pg. 90

This was perhaps the only time in the history of man when men were truly civil, there was peace and good will toward each man from his fellow man. This is the true meaning of the word civil and its offshoot, civilization. It implies a world of peace, something most of can only dream of today. Theirs were not a time of wars and rumors of wars typical of this European dominated era.

Other aspects of the African culture, in particular the African family will be discussed in more detail in chapter eight, "Reversing the Reversal".

SCOPE OF INFLUENCE

Righteous Rulers

Because of the wisdom embodied in their teachings, acceptance by the priest, and admittance in the Mystery schools, was highly sought by neighboring Greeks seeking enlightenment. **The dominance of the known world by the Africans was a wholly benevolent exercise in dominion. The Africans were not hostile and**

fear was not used as a weapon of control. People from other countries were graciously extended the same benefits provided for the Africans themselves by their government. Just as the Egyptian food storehouse fed the African and his neighbors, so did the Africans willingly give out of their treasury of wisdom, the light that could have possibly made the entire world a paradise, even as life in Africa.

> **"The new age…was marked at first by the world-wide dominance of Ethiopian representatives of the black race. They were supreme in Africa and Asia…and they even infiltrated through Southern Europe…"** *The Adventure of Mankind*, Eugene Georg, p. 121-122

> "Keith Irvine, author of, The Rise of the Colored Races, was the first White pupil to attend Achimota College in Ghana. He completed his education in Britain, studying at Edinburgh University and later at the Sorbonne in Paris. Since 1969 he has served as African Affairs editor for *Encyclopedia Britannica*.

Irvine quoted Ibn Battuta, a fourteenth century Berber writer regarding the African kingdom south of the Sahara; he reported:

> 'Perfect security reigns: one may live and travel without fear of theft or rapine. They do not confiscate the goods of those white men who die in their country; even when they place the heritage in the keeping of curators chosen from amongst the white men". *Beyond Roots, A Deeper Look at Blacks in the Bible*, William McKissic, Sr. & Anthony T. Evans, p. 48

> **"It was, in fact, the Golden Age in the history of the blacks, the age in which they reached the pinnacle of the glory so dazzling in achievements that Western and Arab writers felt compelled to erase it by sheer power of their position and begin black history over 3,000 years later,** limiting such as they allowed to 'Africa south of the Sahara". *The Destruction of Black Civilization*, Chancellor Williams, pg. xx, preview

> "Furthermore, Edward Schure believes that at one time, **"The black race dominated on the globe…"** *Sex and Race*, J.A. Rogers, Vol. I

The ancient writer Ephorus says that: "The Ethiopians were considered as occupying all the south coast of both Asia and Africa", and he adds that "this is an ancient opinion of the Greeks". *What They Never Told You*, Indus Khamit-Kush, p.130

The Scriptures Declare the Greatness of Ham's Descendants

Finally, the Christian scriptures, testifies to the greatness of the early African Empires. **"What better witness can we call to the stand to testify about the Black man other than God who said that the Ethiopians (descendants of Ham) were great from their beginning** (Is. 18:1,2)". *Beyond Roots, A Deeper Look at Blacks in the Bible*, William Dwight McKissic, Sr. & Dr. Anthony T. Evans, p. 58

"And the sons of Ham; Cush, and Mizraim; and Phut, and Canaan. And Cush begat Nimrod; he began to be a mighty one in the earth. He was a mighty hunter before the Lord; wherefore it is said, Even as Nimrod the mighty hunter before the Lord. And the beginning of his kingdom was Babel, and Erech, and Accad, and Calneh, in the land of Shinar. Out of that land went forth Asshur, and builded Neneveh, and the city of Rehoboth, and Calah, and Regen between Nineveh and Calah: the same is a great city". **Genesis 10:6, 8-16**

The Way it Was

There was a time when the Black community was a real community. We often quote but are yet to live the philosophy expressed in the African adage, "It takes an entire village to educate one child." Such a philosophy is necessary to establish the "unity" necessary to make a comm-unity a reality. The old Africa was not overflowing with drugs and drug addicts. Relationships were well defined, harmonious and stable. Children honored their parents and parents loved their children. The land was filled with peace and good will.

> **"Once upon a time in Africa, we paid no taxes, there was no crime, there was no police, there was no inflation, there was no unemployment, men did not beat or divorce their wives, then the white man came to improve things".** *No More Lies About Africa, Chief Musamaali Nangoli*, pg. 18

This glorious age of light in Africa continued for thousand of years! And then something happened! It is suggested by many European scholars and clergy-men, that the great African dynasties fell because they fell from grace. The record does not bear this out to be true. African civilization did not fall it was overcome or conquered by foreigners. **By contrast, the Roman Empire fell because it was built on corruption. Unlike the African empire, the Roman Empire was not**

built on principles in harmony with the laws of life and the universe. Our ancestors obviously were in tune with the universe, within and without. Yet, apparently, there was a flaw.

In chapter two, we will present the spiritual and scriptural reasons for the destruction of Egypt and the great civilization built by the Africans. But first let us view the external causes. At this time let us begin to take a look at those who came to conquer, and the reason for the ultimate demise of this; the grandest exhibition of a truly righteous kingdom, ruled by the true "holy men of old", the "Sons of Africa". These were the people that were "chosen" of God to be the "Mother of Civilization." Out of these people came the one blood that runs through the veins of "all" of us. It is out of this one people that many nations have come. There will be more on this subject in later chapters.

PART 3

THE INVASION OF AFRICA

Unlike the current borders of America, Africa had an open door policy. It is ironic that after coming to America and taking America from its rightful owners, a dominant European government now indulges in limiting admission by people (especially Africans and other people of color) who want to come to America for peaceful purposes. The Africans initial response to the arrival of the barbaric European was much like the generous but naïve Native Americans. Their presence was accepted in Upper Egypt (Southern) and many of their needs were met by their host. In return that which the Africans had and in which they willingly shared was coveted and lusted after. The European initially sought trade and enlightenment, later when their numbers increased they began to consider taking the wealth of these people from them. Because of their peaceful natures they seemed an easy target to the violent and aggressive Europeans. So the Europeans began to over-run them with violence, and the once peaceful and beautiful land of the Blacks was wounded and misery and suffering began to ooze out of the wounds inflicted by the aggressors.

"Perhaps the African's abstemious habits and his open handed welcome and acceptance of the white man was to be his first undoing! It certainly made him an easy target. Maybe he should have been less trusting and more questioning as to the white man's intentions in Africa. His hospitality was abused by the Europeans and mistaken for inferiority. The European believed that the reason the Africans went to great lengths to play host to them was because they (the Africans) felt inferior to them, the Europeans.

How mistaken they were"! *No More Lies About Africa*, Chief Musamaali Nangoli, pg. 65

The European that had been allowed to co-habit the African land began to consider the possibility of conquering these people and taking their great wealth for themselves. This was largely because of what they observed about the Africans, which perhaps could be summed up in this way:

1. The Africans were largely a peaceful people engaged in agriculture, mining, trade, fishing, the arts, crafts of various kinds and manufacturing such things as pottery, furniture, building materials, boats, weapons of war, etc.
2. That these settled states and their generally highly developed social and political systems indicate their advance civilization.
3. But that these are ill-prepared for war, except against their neighbors who also use the kind of spears, bows and arrows which we abandoned long since.
4. In general, they have no swiftly moving mounted soldiers.

"The first military and foreign occupation of Kemet was the Hyksos invasion, 1783-1550 B.C.E. The Hyksos were foreigners from Palestine and surrounding areas who immigrated into Lower Kemet and gradually seized control. The word Hyksos is of Kemetic origin and means 'chieftains of foreign countries'.

After approximately 233 years of ruler ship, the Hyksos were driven out of Kemet by native African forces from the south, which not only moved the seat of government back to Waset (Thebes/Luxor), but extended their boarder into Asia to minimize the possibility of further invasion from the north. The wonderful temples at Luxor and Karnak are a living testament to this grand epoch in human civilization.

For the next 500 years Kemet experienced unprecedented growth and development, which was followed by 300 years of internal turmoil and political instability. While teetering once more on the brink of uncertainty, the ruling body of Kemet looked to the south for leadership. Salvation came in the personage of the Nubian King Piankhi, who secured the northern boarders and once again unified the two lands, thus paving the way for Kemet to experience what would inevitability be her final years of glory.

In 525 B.C.E., Kemet experienced the first of two devastating invasions by the Persians. The Persians rulers were merciless and after a brief defeat by the army of Kemet in 380 B.C.E., they returned with a vengeance in 343 B.C.E. From that fateful day onward, Kemet would never again be ruled by an indigenous African population". *Nile Valley Contributions To Civilization*, Anthony T. Browder, P. 66

"This tremendous victory of the white man was not achieved by conquest. It was achieved by default on the part of a race too preoccupied with the immediate present and less with its future- and a race whose centuries of blind trust in the white man passes all understanding". *The Destruction of Black Civilization,* Chancellor Williams, pg. 110

Despite these facts Africans in America continue to trust the "white man" to make life better for their community. Such behavior can only be defined as naïve, neurotic and dangerous. Everyone knows, as the Native Americans so aptly declared, "The white man speaks with a fork tongue".

I would like to make it perfectly clear, when such references are made to the "white man" it is only to the ruling class of Whites that make the critical decisions that affect all our lives, the average white person as well as all people of color. I would not compare the suffering of the privileged race to that of the underclass, however, the quality of life for the average white family is being destroyed as well. I am of course not referring to the material side but the spiritual aspect of each ethnic group in America is negatively impacted by the decisions of the few who rule.

After conquering Egypt the heart of African civilization, the foreigners began to seize the best lands of Africa for themselves. This proved to be quite detrimental to the Africans as trade was now regulated by the Europeans because of their strategic position near the coast of Africa. It was as if they had put a hanging-noose around the neck of the Africans.

"This meant that even after nature had damned three-fourths of the land mass as impossible to support human life, the Asians and Europeans came in to seize and hold the best of the one-fourth that was left. The blacks found themselves cut off from all seacoast that then mattered, hemmed in from all directions, and confined within narrower and narrower limits.

Thus they became a wandering people, forever migrating in their own vast homeland, fragmenting from great united nations into countless little splinter societies, becoming so isolated from each other that each formed a new language of its own, considered itself quite different from its original brothers-now regarded as strangers and enemies in the endless tribal wars that ensued over the habitable land". *The Destruction of Black Civilization*, Chancellor Williams, pg. 7

As in America, where the indigenous people greeted the Europeans in peace, only later to be subjected to a cruel and vicious attack for the complete take-over of their land, so did the Africans. The Native Americans and the Africans alike who resisted were labeled renegades and heathen. It would appear that it was the Europeans and not God who is responsible for the scattering of the great citizens of that high culture; the Babylon Empire.

Today Europeans come on TV sitting in Africa, surrounded by children devastated by the actions of their brothers and which his white brothers continue to aggressively pursue. They con African Americans and others into sending money that seldom truly benefit the Africans. The construction of the Aswan Dam has caused the lands inhabited by blacks to become totally uninhabitable. The European, as in South Africa, has taken all the "fertile ground" and inhabitable land and as with the Native Americans, made the Africans wanderers in their own land, fighting each other over the scraps left over from the theft of a continent. The largest heist operation in history is the carving up of Africa by the European invaders. The second largest was the invasion and theft of the America's.

THE DESTRUCTION OF A CULTURE AND RACE

To Destroy a People, Destroy their Culture

A people without their culture are like fish on dry land…destined to die. When the culture of African people was all but destroyed, the destruction of the people was inevitable. The dominant class or conquerors in this case despised all that which was African. Europeans began to systematically disconnect Africans from all remnants and vestiges of their original culture and replace it with one that more resembled their own. This they did by making African culture seem undesirable and European culture the ultimate model. Once separated from his culture, the African was dead out of the water.

"The Persians were driven from Egypt by Alexander of Macedonia in 332 B.C.E. Following an age old custom, these Greek rulers married into the Egyptian royal families in an attempt to maintain dynastic ruler ship, which was passed on by the queen to her offspring. The last of the Ptolemy's to rule Egypt was Cleopatra VII, who wooed both Julius Caesar and Marc Antony in an attempt to prevent Roman control and occupation of Egypt. Cleopatra was unsuccessful in her attempts to maintain Egypt's sovereignty, which became a colony of Rome in 30 B.C.E. after her death."

"Perhaps the only time that the African and his culture nearly parted company, was with influences from without. **Tragically, these influences were not only about conquest and domination; they were also about the attempt to *kill* to *death* the African culture.** As evidenced by the goings on in present day Africa, these outside influences have succeeded in contaminating hence diluted this rich culture. There is tragically the tendency in Africa in her quest for so called modernization, to run away from this rich culture". *No More Lies About Africa*, Chief Musamaali Nangoli, pg. 15

CHRISTIANITY CONQUERED AFRICA

Most African Americans do not realize that to accept another's religion is to accept another's culture, religion and world view and constitutes rejection of their own culture and religion. This is vital, because as we have seen, the Africans were empowered by their religion and culture. This is the reason the European found it necessary to attempt to erase every vestige of both from the memory of the African captives. At least the Africans held on to their name for awhile, now, the African in America, who has been Christianized, despises his rich African heritage.

A rejection of your people is a rejection of self. This is the ultimate conquest! For the black man, the badge of Christianity identifies him as "the conquered". It also is a sign that he is still a mental slave. In truth to embrace Christianity, for an African American is to commit the ultimate act of treason, the rejection of self. Contrary to popular "belief" among African American Christians, Christianity has not set African Americans free it has only promised them that they would not have to "remain" in hell after they die. The truth is that it was used to put Blacks in mental bondage. Christianity is the White mans "Trojan Horse". It has allowed them to sneak past our mental guards and penetrate our minds and imprison our spirits.

32

The Romans, like the Greeks before them, saw great value in the civilization of Kemet and incorporated those elements most easily discernable into their culture. **But in the final analysis it was not the Roman army that ultimately brought Egypt to her knees and destroyed her, it was the newly emerging religion of Christianity".** *Nile Valley Contributions To Civilization*, Anthony T. Browder pg. 67

"Other invaders found penetration easy under the banners of religion. **Full advantage was taken of the fact that Africans are a very religious people. But what happened in the process of converting the blacks to Islam and Christianity was the supreme triumph of the white world over the black. Millions of Africans became non-Africans. Africans who were neither Muslims or Christians were classed as 'pagans' and therefore required to disavow their whole culture and to regard practically all African institutions as 'backward' or savage".** *The Destruction of Black Civilization*, Chancellor Williams, pg. 11

"It was during the same period that Europe established her firm grip on Africa, and that the white man established his so called 'supremacy' over the black man. It was during the same period that the Africans had their mind impregnated with ideas which rendered him helpless and split his personality right down the middle. Ideas which were intended to make him aspire to the white man's culture and traditions which were represented by the missionaries as superior"! Among many things, what also spurred on missionaries to come to Africa was the grand idea of converting the 'pagan' African to Christianity. To make him turn away from his 'primitive' ways and seek salvation through Christianity". *No More Lies About Africa*, Chief Musamaali Nangoli, pg. 71

"Here, then, is another case where the 'external influence' school can have a field day, since nothing is better known (and nowhere denied) than the fact **that the Africans who adopted European or Asian institutions, such as Islam and Christianity, for example, were not only 'influenced' by them, but often transformed into 'black Arabs', 'black Portuguese', 'black Frenchmen', 'black Englishmen' and so on. In fact, it was this very transforming external influence that played a decisive role in first destroying the best in African civilization".** *The Destruction of Black Civilization*, Chancellor Williams, pg. 162

Ironically, today, most Africans in American prefer to be called, "Black Americans" rather than Africans. This is because they have embraced the

attitude of their conquerors toward themselves. **In the eyes of the conquering Christians, the culture of the African is seen as pagan and backward. Many African Christians have a similar attitude toward their own culture. They believe that Africans and Africa are lost without Euro-Christianity and its worship of Jesus.** They would say, "I am first a Christian and then an African, even though they were first born African and later were made Christian. Rev. William D. McKissic, Sr., author of Beyond Roots, believes the Africans were Christians already upon being brought to America. Apparently, this theory is inaccurate.

> **"...this change of identity from traditional African religionists to African American Christians was a complex process that took place very gradually and was completed at a considerable price".** *The Spirituality of African Peoples*, Peter J. Paris, pg. 73

> "Nevertheless, whenever conquest did occur, full legitimation was not achieved until the conquerors had persuaded the conquered by the interweaving of their respective cosmogonies". *The Spirituality of African Peoples*, Peter J. Paris, pg. 69

> **"The coming of the Caucasian, whether from Asia or Europe, or whether in the name of peace, trade, an 'integrated society' or in the name of the Allah of the Arabs or the God and Jesus Christ of the Christians-no matter under what pretext they came it meant the destruction of the highly advanced civilization of the blacks and their total degradation as a people".** *The Destruction of Black Civilization*, Chancellor Williams, pg. 85

SYMPTOMS OF DESTRUCTION

Loss of Primary Identity

Because of the destruction of their culture and the subsequent loss of memory, the experience of having it savagely beaten and ripped from their hearts, and the daily degrading of the image of blacks by the media industry; today's African Americans do not identify with Africa. **Among blacks you find people who ignorantly declare that, "I ain't from no Africa, I'm from Alabama". Many, consciously or unconsciously, seek approval from whites and acceptance into their culture and lifestyle. Many of these same Blacks are unaware that their need to be accepted by Whites is seen in their embracing of the Whites religious beliefs. Many of the earlier slaves that embraced Christianity "thought" that such an act would gain them acceptance by Whites...unfortunately this proved a** fruitless theory then and now. Rejection breeds a need to be accepted in those who are rejected.

Because of Blacks self-hatred, their ears remain deaf to the drum call of their mother-land. They have no love for their own people, their own ancestors who gave them life. This "deafness", or the lack of having *"ears that hear"*, is the reason for the apparent position of last place in the human race, of the African American. However, spiritually, the black man is ahead of the game. We will continue with this important subject of the difference between where we as a people "appear" to be, and where African Americans really are in the human race toward a higher evolved man, in the next chapter. As the world judges progress, today, African Americans are considered to be in last place. Without an open mind to hear the Truth about themselves Black America will remain in last place as a nation of people within a nation.

> "For here a whole continent is involved, and on that continent a people who in one period of time were among the foremost people on earth, and in a later period the farthest behind". *The Destruction of Black Civilization*, Chancellor Williams, pg. 5

> "The loss of such memory, however, destroyed the retrospective longing. Hence, the eventual loss of their native languages, beliefs, and customs constituted the loss of tribal specificity, which was tantamount to the loss of primary identity. **For Africans such a loss constituted the most devastating aspect of slavery because it affected an irrevocable break with their homeland".** *The Spirituality of African Peoples*, Peter J. Paris, P. 70

> **From that standpoint, Africans who rejected such a valorization of the race rejected themselves, and self-hatred became the primary evidence of their pathological condition".** *The Spirituality of African Peoples*, Peter J. Paris, pg. 73

This is not a matter of no consequence, please do not pass over it lightly, here we see the condition of the vast majority of Africans being described as pathologically characterized by the loss of primary identity.

The Roots of Self Hatred and Self Rejection

The root cause of self-hatred and self-rejection by African Americans is the loss of primary identity. Blacks lose their identity as they pass through

35

America's education system and sit in America's Churches. It is caused by the change of identity and reinforced by the distorted pictured of the history of African people by primarily Euro-Christian scholars. However, the fundamental cause of self-hatred among African Americans is rooted in the acceptance and wholehearted embracing of Euro-Christianity. It is the reason Blacks seek to be a part of the White culture and push for integration with Whites. Unfortunately integration means assimilation for Blacks as they seek to be like White's. It is also the real reason nothing has really changed since the days of captivity. It is the reason Blacks remain in a fallen condition. It is the reason mental bondage exists today in the Black community. It is the reason for the lack of real spiritual fruit. African Americans have been made docile, and made to look to the "Great White Hope" for the solution to "their" dilemma. It is the reason Blacks trust Whites with their spiritual salvation, when Whites cannot even be trusted to resurrect the material lives of Black people. We are thankful that many White Spiritual Leaders such as Marrianne Williamson and Dr. Dwayne Dyer are helping many whites today to find their way back to God and humanity the African way.

People who reject their natural identity and the Truth about themselves show the signs of the destructive affects of embracing another's way of thinking. It causes the people eventually to view themselves through the eyes of the other people. And since the other people think very little of their human value, they soon began to think the same way. This reinforces the need to be like and with someone else, instead of ones own kind. Ironically, Blacks are asking to be loved by the very race that denigrates them and harbors the greatest contempt for them.

> "Throughout history, we have had the same types and classes of 'Negroes' who have always pushed frantically for integration and amalgamation with whites. They were generally the people who did not want to be classified as members of the African race". *The Destruction of Black Civilization*, Chancellor Williams, P. 206

This matter can be easily resolved by Blacks laying claim to their history, their culture and their religious knowledge and wisdom. This will be the most liberating and empowering step ever taking by Africans in America. Euro-centric education does not empower African Americans nor does Euro-Christianity. Euro-Christianity will not produce Spiritual freedom for African Americans. When God has made us free, we shall be free indeed. Christianity conquered the people of Africa and it continues to prevent Africans from claiming their true spiritual freedom! Together, Euro-centric education and Euro-Christian doctrines serve as the invisible chains that bind Blacks to inferiority. The doctrines of Euro-Christianity will not help African Americans to experience manifesting the fullness of the stature of the Christ. Conversely, Euro-centric education will not empower Blacks politically and economically.

> "The early disruption of African Civilization, as we have seen, was followed by a long series of absolute blockades to progress". *The Destruction of Black Civilization,* Chancellor Williams, pg. 199

Black America must purpose to break this stranglehold. First, Blacks must understand that the decline of the Black race was engineered and not a result of flaws in their form of religious worship.

Today, those who were once highly regarded now suffer the degradation of the badge of slavery. We can overcome these symptoms by first recognizing that they are merely symptoms. **The heart of the problem is that they are the result of imposing Euro-centric values and systems of thought on an African mind by those who created America's institutions. We overcome the symptoms secondly by accepting and embracing the Truth. Self hatred, self degradation, and other neurotic behavior (Pathologies) are symptoms. There are a multitude of symptoms, but there is one cure for them all…the Truth.**

A Vision of Victory

In spite of the current situation, as the "King" once declared, "We shall overcome". In order to do so, we must have a "Vision of Victory". The key to our success is the recognition that the wisdom of our Ancient Ancestors was and is valid and relevant. We can learn from our history the perils of disunity and of not considering the future for our seed. We can come together and work today for the generations to come.

THIS! THIS! THIS!

To accomplish this mighty task merely requires a sufficient number of conscious Africans in American and the world to recognize the key is to set the African mind free by re-introducing it to its own culture and the wisdom by which that cultured was shaped and formed. For African Americans this renewing of their minds is 90% of the battle. It takes only a sufficient number to awaken to the possibility of building another great nation of people that once again glorify their Creator on earth by keeping the "Garden" called earth and making the world a beautiful place to live again, to make this "vision" a reality.

When Blacks regain the wisdom that was lost, they can regain the means to be a people that greatly contribute to the advancement of humanity again. Blacks can take that wisdom, knowledge and understanding and build institutions that empower African American youth instead of hindering them. The primary impetus for this work is to inspire people with a "Vision of Victory". We can change our destiny. It is not the end of the world. Black Church, stop crying the sky is falling and began to prepare people to live not die. Black America must learn anew to truly live for God and worship their Creator in Spirit and in Truth. Whether it recognizes it or not, America needs the Black man to rise above the limitations of what he has learned by truly renewing his mind with the Truth, the whole Truth, and nothing but the Truth.

Chapter 2

THE BENEFITS OF SLAVERY

A PREPARED PEOPLE

"All things work together for good"

W hen the Black Man fell, he fell all the way. In street jargon, it could be said he "hit rock bottom". Slavery was indeed a gutter experience. However, there is another side to the negative impact of the slave experience and post slavery trauma. In our Christian fellowships we often refer to the scripture that says, *"All things work together for good, for those that love God and are called according to his purpose".* This chapter asserts that even slavery is subject to this divine dictate. Certainly the experience of slavery has left its scars on African Americans; traumatic experiences always leave wounds. Even today, much of the division, pathological behavior and self-hatred displayed by African Americans can be attributed to the traumatism of psychological and emotional damage experienced by their forefathers during slavery. Although someone else was responsible for the atrocities and the subsequent dysfunctional behavior, it is entirely the responsibility of African Americans to correct the problem. **The fortitude, compassion and of supreme importance, the humility, all spiritual insight gained during slavery can provide a foundation for recovery.** In fact, the recovery of African people is a major motivation for the writing of this book.

> **"The devastating experience of slavery indelibly bruised the consciousness of Africans throughout the Diaspora.** By no fault of their own, they had been permanently uprooted from the security of their communal and familial belonging and exposed to an alien environment of

humiliation and deprivation. **Given the centrality of community in their lives, no one can possibly imagine the intense pain they must have experienced in being cut off from their tribal solidarity and familial identity. Undoubtedly the conditions of slavery nullified the structural arrangements for viable family life.** Viewed and treated as property, slaves were afforded none of the conditions that contributed to the moral development of human beings. Rather, their entire life was proscribed by the arbitrary dictates and odious interest of their owners". *The Spirituality of African Peoples*, Peter J. Paris, p. 89

"African peoples have always tended to be disinterested in remembering sorrow and pain unless it pointed to some good and the only good relative to slavery was its end". *The Spirituality of African Peoples*, p. 67

There is a valid reason for the remembrance of the experience of captivity. **Often, Blacks today blame each other and refuse to even consider the effect that slavery has had on the black family. They consider making any references to the effects of slavery as making excuses. They call it blaming the white-man for what they do to themselves. Though on the surface this may appear to be true, this is only upon surface examination.**

If one were to probe deep for the root cause of the condition, they would find lurking in the darkness, a connection between the conditions of the black community and family today, and the destructive impact of captivity on the black culture and family. **"It ain't our fault", however, it is our responsibility to change it.**

From Men to Boys

One particular disruptive aspect of the effects of captivity is the affect it had on black "manhood". Captivity imposed on former African men the status of "boys". This was to affect black manhood for generations. During slavery, black mothers, out of fear for the lives of their black male children, assisted the Europeans in cultivating a submissive attitude in their boys. This also, would affect generations. Even today, some black women "train" their sons to not rock the boat, for fear that it will cause them to be injured or killed. Being conditioned to accept the role of "black boys", in contrast to "white men", is one of the main reasons black men do not take full responsibility for their own lives nor the lives of those they father. It is the reason the black man does not take full responsibility for protecting the women, elders and children in his community.

In reality, the black man has had a short period to relearn the art of manhood. This he is doing without the aid of any rehabilitation assistance, few examples, and institutionalized racism to ascertain that the road is rocky and steep. In addition, he has not re-learned how to trust his brothers. Most black men stand, alone.** The sisters have not had to overcome the same type of conditioning and therefore have established a multitude of support groups where they are able to help one another to buffer the effects of institutionalized racism and sexism. In a sense, the sisters face double jeopardy; however they are not viewed as possessing the same potential threat as the black man, and are therefore allowed to succeed in many areas restricted to black men.

There is no doubt that the imposing of the European culture on African people has had a destructive affect on the black family. Nor should there be any doubt as to its connection to the destruction of the black family, and the appalling condition within the black community. **We must face the fact that slavery did bruise the African psyche and destroyed a sound family structure in order to get on with the business of reconstruction and liberation.** This is the one valid reason for bringing up the subject of slavery; that is, in order that we may heal and get on with the business at hand. It is time for African Americans to take back what was stolen and claim their *inheritance* and *birthright*. **Understanding both the positive and negative aspects of slavery will go far in placing that claim within their grasp.**

"But as for you, you meant evil against me; but God meant it for good, in order to bring, it about this day, to save many people alive". **Genesis 50:20**

The "Saviour Race"

There should also be very little doubt that White people *"meant evil against"* Blacks. But, the Creator had other plans. **Because of the work the Creator is doing within the "souls of black folk", many lives will be saved. Black People are a "Messianic" race; they are of the "Savior Race" if such a term can be used.** Saving the human race will involve a collective and unified effort; however it is the opinion of many that Blacks will have to lead that effort.

One very positive aspect of captivity is that Black people survived! Not only did they survive, but in spite of the intense odds against the average black man, still they rise. Captivity has by its very nature, caused African Americans to grow mighty in spiritual fortitude. It has strengthened the very constitution of every survivor of its horrors.

41

The Creator "Made" us Black and Beautiful

The Creator took all the ugliness and created something very beautiful. African Americans are truly a people that are both "Black and Beautiful". Some may take such valorization of their race as a indictment against white people or of catering to the "black ego". Here, and throughout this writing, the objective is not to tear down the image of the European, it is the building up of African Americans by telling the truth about what has happened to them. Our purpose is to strengthen and build up the inner man and not the "ego" of the black man. This motivation provides a valid reason for candidly reviewing the painful past. This is the only reason for such an honest and raw look at the historical actions of white people.

> "But the primary aim was never that of highlighting the evil of slavery as an end in itself but only as a means for demonstrating how the African American race survived and progressed in spite of centuries of oppression" (*The Spirituality of African Peoples*, Peter J. Paris, p.68)

**In the darkness of the womb,
life is conceived.
In the darkness of the soil,
seeds germinate.
In the darkness of the inner mind,
ideas are born.
Darkness is nature's time of rest,
formation, incubation,
rejuvenation, and secret rendezvous
of invisible powers
and unseen realities.**
The Spirituality of African People,
Peter J. Paris, p. 87

A Prepared People

In the darkness of the inhumanity of a savage and brutal economic system called slavery, a new African was conceived. In the darkness of injustice, was born an even greater thirst for righteousness. It was during captivity, that I believe Black people were being prepared to lead the world back to righteousness, and back to God. Invisible powers worked to form a new creature with unseen possibilities and realities. Despite its appearance today's Black race will be a new and improved model when the Creator is finished.

Even the horrors of the slave experience, had its benefits. The intense pressure of the experience provided the seed for the spiritual re-birth of African men and women. As Maya Angelo so eloquently put it, "And still we rise". **African Americans can achieve even greater accomplishments than the Africans of ancient times. Today's African American is the seed of the Ancient Africans, the potential for greatness lies within the heart of every black man, women and child.**

African Americans know first hand what the fruits of unrighteousness taste like. They can easily identify unrighteousness because its picture has been before their face since their coming to America. And for that reason, most blacks prefer righteous living to a life without morals and ethical behavior.

The Rise of the Black Man

The black man has shown the desire and ability to rise above; the centuries of negative conditioning; the decades of miss-education, the continuous assassination of his image by the media; a justice system tailor made to assure that a disproportionate number of black men find their way behind bars; and economic barriers that are designed to guarantee that he remains financially handicapped. He is asserting himself, and demonstrating that he is ready to put away childish things and be a man. The Million-Man-March was a demonstration of that desire. This desire is yet to be harnessed and given a comprehensive plan of action and consistent direction, yet, it is seething within the soul of many black men.

Captivity was a unique experience, and it has made African Americans a unique people. I say because of it Blacks are a better people, a "Prepared People". Not a People that's better than others, but a race of People that are being redeemed. During and after slavery many invaluable lessons have been learned by African Americans. It is true, much is taught even by negative examples i.e., racism, sexism and materialism. Because of the experience of slavery, Black people are perhaps the most compassionate, sensitive and forgiving people on the planet. These are priceless virtues.

To experience what Black people experienced and yet to harbor little or no malice toward those who inflicted the pain is remarkable. Black people know what it means to be treated unjustly like no other people. Yet, most Blacks have no desire for vengeance only for reconciliation. This moral aptitude, a direct gain from slavery has prepared African Americans, to play a key leadership role in the spiritual evolution of all men. African Americans can build on the foundation provided by the racial character developed by the pressures of captivity. **Blacks**

have been tried in the fire, and have emerged as "pure gold". The view of this author concurs with the theory of the messianic nature of African Americans. This view was held by many early African American religious leaders. They believed that the Creator had commissioned black people to play an intricate part in bringing true salvation to this planet, and all people.

> Yet, "Unless we pass on the strengths of their God-given heritage to the next generation they can never hope to see true, lasting change take place in their community. Our children need both the moral and spiritual foundation with which they can reject the negative values thrust upon them from society. **Blacks have too rich a heritage with too great a God to have the kind of disintegration among our children we are now experiencing. It will take every ounce of energy to reclaim our families"** *Beyond Roots; A Deeper Look At Blacks In The Bible*, William Dwight McKissic, Sr., & Dr. Anthony T. Evans, p. 8-9

The Evolution of God's Man

The reason we must do it is because no one else either can or will. In the larger sphere of human interrelations, God is at work bringing about his plan for the evolution of man. The Creator is indeed, *"The author and finisher"* of the man It has created. **Make no mistake about it though, evolution is a collaborative effort. There is a part we must play.**

> **"Evolution, he maintained, is the unfoldment of God in History"** Georg Wilhelm Hegel, Philosopher (1770-1831)

The truth is that the Creator has "allowed" black people to become oppressed by white people. However it is the motivation of the Creator that must be cleared up. Until now, the prevailing sentiment among Whites, and Blacks for that matter, is that God has been punishing Black people for sins committed by their ancestors.

Blacks have internalized the attitude of their captors. God is not punishing Black people because their ancestors were pagan, heathen or polytheist. This is the classic reversal technique. It was the Europeans that were the heathens and barbarians. It is the European who worshipped idol gods. **Today, the god of the European is money. Blacks too have become idol worshippers by taken on the beliefs and customs of a heathen and backward people. Today many Blacks worship the "Golden Calf" and "Graven Images".**

The records have spoken, however. The Africans had a righteous nation, and the Europeans, according to their own testimonies, were pagans, barbaric, and worshippers of idols.

Many African Americans today, have joined the European in the worship of their idol gods. Historically Blacks did not worship a material or physical god. Nor did they worship numerous gods. **However, perhaps this next scripture can shed some light on what truly caused the fall of the great kingdoms of Africa, the sons of Ham.** This scripture is about the Assyrians; they were descendents of Ham, and a great and mighty people of Egypt.

Truth of Bible has been Compromised

First let us pause to make clear an apparent contradiction. From the perspective of this writing, it would appear that the King James Version of the Bible is not a reliable source for finding the Truth. It is the position of this thesis, that the King James is perhaps the most reliable source available to the laymen. The originals are not available, and they were in Greek and Latin. What must be understood is that these scriptures are not originals, and that even the Greek and Latin versions are copies. In the production of the Greek and Latin versions themselves, there was inserted the doctrines of the men who produced them.

It was at this point that the Truth of Scripture was compromised. Yet, much of the original was apparently retained. Eventually the Europeans or Greeks would alter the essential teachings where it suited their scheme. Most of the history and prophecy are mere rewrites and duplications. The greatest corruption and bastardization occurs in the literal translation of spiritual parables, myths, allegories, and dark sayings, and the practice of following the letter of the scripture, neglecting the Spirit. Today, the King James Version must be rightly divided. This requires knowledge of where the original deviation and compromise was made. Only such a guide is capable of navigating through the confusion.

This next scripture describes a root of the tree of which today's African Americans are the branches; the roots were described as a great and mighty people. If we accept this scripture as true it confirms it was the Creator, who made it so. The heathen Greeks were merely the instrument used by the Creator, to affect It's will and purpose for Blacks. All is unfolding as it should. Everything really is in and has always been in "divine order". The reason for the fall was for Black people to learn the lesson of "humility". Captivity by heathens and barbarians has a way of driving that lesson home. What could be more humbling than the experience of slavery? Listen to this scripture.

45

And it came to pass in the eleventh year, in the third month, in the first day of the month, that the word of the Lord came unto me, saying,
Son of man, speak unto Pharaoh king of Egypt, and to his multitude; Whom art thou like in thy greatness?
Behold, the Assyrian was a cedar in Lebanon with fair branches, and with a shadowing shroud, and of an high stature;
and his top was among the thick boughs.
The waters made him great, the deep set him up on high with her rivers running round about his plants, and sent out her little rivers unto all the trees of the field.
Therefore his height was exalted above all the trees of the field, and his boughs were multiplied, and his branches became long because of the multitude of waters, when he shot forth.
All the fowls of heaven made their nests in his boughs, and under his branches did all the beasts of the field bring forth their young, and under his shadow dwelt all great nations.
Thus was he fair in his greatness, in the length of his branches: for his root was by great waters.
The cedars in the garden of God could not hide him: the fir trees were not like his boughs, and the chestnut trees were not like his branches; nor any tree in the garden of God was like unto him in his beauty.
I have made him fair by the multitude of his branches: so that all the trees of Eden, that were in the garden of God, envied him.
Therefore thus saith the Lord God; Because thou hast lifted up thyself in height, and he hath shot up his top among the thick boughs, and his heart is lifted up in his height;
I have therefore delivered him into the hand of the mighty one of the heathen; he shall surely deal with him:
I have driven him out for his wickedness.
And strangers, the terrible of the nations, have cut him off, and have left him: upon the mountains and in all the valleys his branches are fallen, and his boughs are broken by all the rivers of the land; and all the people of the earth are gone down from his shadow, and have left him.
Upon his ruin shall all the fowls of the heaven remain, and all the beasts of the field shall be upon his branches:
To the end that none of all the trees by the waters exalt themselves for their height, neither shoot up their top among the thick boughs, neither their trees stand up in their height, Ez.31:1-14

Envy, Lust and Pride, a Deadly Combination — *BUY WHAT!*

Whew! The scriptures speak very clear on the subject of pride. Pride indeed comes before a fall. **I include this scripture to help put the fall of the glorious ancient African civilization in perspective and to again warn the reader that the purpose of this writing is not to inflate the ego of the black man.** Yet, the black man needs to know the reason for his fall, and the root cause of the hatred white people have for them. Though what the heathen, who are obviously the Europeans, has done to the African race is horrendous, there is a lesson in it. According to this scripture *"that none of all the trees by the waters exalt themselves for their height".* Unfortunately for the European, pride is his crime also. Perhaps, both the African and European nations are ready to "take heed" of this invaluable lesson.

"If my people who are called by name would humble themselves and turn from their wicked ways…then will I hear from heaven and heal their land."

So, according to the scripture, the pride of the Africans combined with the envy and lust of the Europeans, and set the stage for the fall of the African nations. The Africans pride of course being the major contributor to their own demise. It is not the purpose of this book to make the African look like an innocent victim in this scenario. It is important, that for once, the Truth, the whole Truth and nothing but the Truth is told. Apparently, the African nation needed chastening. Chastening should not be confused with cursing or punishing. Chastening is done by a loving parent, on behalf of its children. It is an act of love.

And ye have forgotten the exhortation
which speaketh unto you as unto children,
My son, despise not thou the chastening of the Lord,
nor faint when thou art rebuked of him:
For whom the Lord loveth he chasteneth,
and scourgeth every son whom he receiveth.
If ye endure chastening, God dealeth with you as with sons;
for what son is he whom the father chasteneth not?
But if ye be without chastisement,
whereof all are partakers, then are ye bastards,
and not sons. Furthermore we have had fathers of our flesh
which corrected us, and we gave them reverence: shall we not much rather be
in subjection unto the Father of spirits, and live?
For they verily for a few days chastened us after their own pleasure; but he for

> *our profit, that we might be partakers of his holiness.*
> *Now no chastening for the present seemeth to be joyous, but grievous:*
> *nevertheless afterward it yieldeth the peaceable fruit of righteousness unto*
> *them which are exercised thereby.* **Hebrews 12:5-11**

African Americans are all children of the Most High God as all other races of people are. The Creator loves all of us. For that reason, African Americans must concentrate on the lessons the Creator would teach, rather than the instrument used. **Captivity was a grievous time, yet, its fruit shall be peace and righteousness. Black people must not waste energy and cause more harm to them selves by hating White people. It is God who chastens the Black man. Many Blacks have Whites in their families or as close friends. The purpose of this Truth-telling, is not to cause dissension and division between family and friends. Most Whites have been duped as well. Both Whites and Blacks are in need of the Truth.**

At this time however, Blacks must face the fact that most Whites, because of the educational system and the socialization process, feel that they are in someway better or somehow superior to Blacks. They still believe that Black people are somehow closer to the heathen and in need of civilizing. They still think they are part of the master race. Western man must learn the lessons the Creator has placed before them in this area. Black people must concentrate on learning their lesson. The lessons must be learned if Blacks are to once again rise to be a great nation of people in the earth.

The primary focus of this writing is the healing, liberation, and elevation of black people. I am not qualified to teach white people how not to hate black people. Charity must begin at home. Blacks must first learn to love themselves again. Then they will have the capacity to teach others how to love. First however, Blacks must learn to love themselves.

Learning about the greatness of their ancestors helps Blacks to appreciate and love their people and therefore themselves. Remember Christian scriptures confirm the greatness of Black people's ancestors. Blacks must not forget however, that all they had was given to them by God, and therefore there was no reason to be proud, only grateful. When Blacks have learned the lesson of humility, there is nothing to prevent the Creator from restoring Blacks to the position of *"the head and not the tail"*. Yet, there is something Black people must do.

A Formidable Foundation to Build the "Black House"

African Americans must embrace the wisdom of their ancestors and learn from their lessons, if Black people are to accomplish the resurrection of the Black man. The knowledge and wisdom of their ancestors combined with the strengths gained during captivity could be combined to create a formidable foundation and stronghold from which to launch the rebirth of a nation.

African Americans must understand that the so-called many gods of the Ancient Africans were merely symbols. The sun was the most perfect symbol for God because it is the sun that gives life to everyone and everything on earth. It was merely a teaching symbol. Blacks do not have to become worshippers of the sun to benefit from the wisdom of this rich symbol and the mental images it produces. **All life is dependent on the Creator for life.** This is the lesson this symbol would teach.

Black people can combine the positive lessons learned from their period of captivity and from the fall of the ancient Africa dynasties with the knowledge left by their esteemed ancestors to aid them in completing their evolutionary journey. **It is time for Black people to leave the land of mental bondage and go to the Promised Land of spiritual freedom. Only they must be willing to make their "Exodus". They must be willing to relinquish the old life. This should not be difficult, in light of the all the pain and suffering the old life represents. Every Black person should all be ready for their "Spiritual Exodus". Yet, some will not leave Pharaoh.**

Shackles Must Be Broken

Blacks can learn from the lessons of the Children of Israel who stumbled needlessly in the wilderness because of the residue left over from their period of captivity. **Blacks must purpose to break the mental shackles that keep them bound to the old life of Spiritual bondage and death.** African Americans can break the economic shackles if they first break the mental ones. Blacks can rise above the oppression, exploitation and degradation. Above all, when they rise again, Blacks must remember to never again *"think more highly of themselves than they ought".* IT IS IMPERATIVE THAT THE BLACK MAN RISES TO TAKE HIS RIGHTFUL PLACE AMONG THE NATIONS OF THE WORLD. FOR IF BLACKS DON'T RISE, HEAVEN HELP US ALL, BECAUSE RIGHT NOW WE ARE UNDER THE DOMINION OF THE HEATHENS…"LORD LIFT US UP WHERE WE BELONG"!

Adisa Franklin

IF THE BLACK MAN RISES NOT

IF THE BLACK MAN RISES NOT,
WE'LL HAVE TO KEEP WHAT WE HAVE,
WE'LL HAVE TO KEEP WHAT WE GOT.
THE DRUGS, THE CRIME, THE DYSFUNCTIONAL ABUSE,
THE POVERTY, THE SHAME, AND CONTINUAL MISUSE.
THE MURDERS AND INJUSTICE
AND THE MISEDUCATION,
THE POLITRICKS AND PROMISES AND FAKE
LEGISLATION.
THEY'VE LIED AND STOLE
AND TAKEN WHOLE CONTINENTS.
AND IMPOSED THEIR CULTURE
WITH ALL ITS DECADENCE.
THEY'RE NOT FIT TO RULE; THEY'RE
COMMITTING GLOBAL SUICIDE.
WHILE EVERYWHERE THEY CONTINUE WITH
THEIR BLACK GENOCIDE.
IF THE BLACK MAN RISES NOT,
WE'LL HAVE TO KEEP WHAT WE HAVE,
WE'LL HAVE TO KEEP WHAT WE GOT!
WHAT WE HAD WAS A TRUE CIVILIZATION,
A PLACE FOR PEACE, A GLORIOUS NATION.
WE KNEW THE POWER OF UNITY AND
HOW TO LOVE ONE ANOTHER.
SISTAS WERE SISTAS AND BROTHAS WERE BROTHAS
CHILDREN HONORED THEIR PARENTS AND
DIDN'T MURDER EACH OTHER.
THERE WAS NO POLICE OR CORRUPT COURTS AND
NO PRISONS OR JAILS,
NO REASON TO MORTGAGE THE HOUSE
TO RAISE THE BAIL.
WE KNEW HOW TO EDUCATE OUR CHILDREN
AND PREPARE THEM FOR LIFE.
THEY LIVED IN PEACE AND HARMONY,
INSTEAD OF THE FEAR AND STRIFE.
AND THIS WE COULD HAVE AGAIN
IF WE WOULD JUST TAKE A STAND
THE WORLD NEEDS THE RULE
OF A RIGHTEOUS BLACK MAN

**BUT IF THE BLACK MAN RISES NOT,
WE'LL HAVE TO KEEP WHAT WE HAVE,
WE'LL HAVE TO KEEP WHAT WE GOT!**

Poem by Adisa

Chapter 3

JUDGING THE TREE BY THE FRUIT

THE DARK SIDE OF EURO-CHRISTIANITY

"There is a way which seems right to a man, but the end thereof are the ways of death". **Proverbs 14:12**

The fact there are multitudes who confess Jesus as their personal Lord and Savior does not lend support to Christianity's validity. Though there are many that "believe" that the doctrines of Christianity are correct that does not make it true. Certainly, to Believers it feels right and seems right, but that still does not make it right. The truth is, Christianity is the way that seems right but the ways thereof is death. Speaking of death, there are more dead who refused to accept Christianity and were put to death by Christians than there are believers today. As we shall see, Christians have killed more people than they have converted. Many Believers do not wish to know this. Some people make the false assumption that if everyone is doing it then it must be alright. This type of behavior is best illustrated in fads. Christianity is the way that leads unto death because it is based on a lie. The tree of Christianity produces corrupt fruit because the tree is corrupt. It is corrupt because it is fraudulent. It is fraudulent because it claims originality and inerrancy both of which are misrepresentations. Both statements are false and deceptive.

"Enter through the narrow gate: for wide is the gate and broad is the way that leads to destruction: and there are many who go in by it. Because narrow is the gate and straight is the path that leads to life, and few that find it."

"Beware of false prophets, who come to you in sheep's clothing, but inwardly

*they are ravenous wolves. You will know them by there fruits. Do men gather
grapes from thornbushes or figs from thistles?
Even so, every good tree bears good fruit, but a bad tree bears bad fruit. A good
tree cannot bear bad fruit, nor can a bad tree bear good fruit.
Every tree that does not bear good fruit is cut down and thrown into the fire.
Therefore by their fruits you shall know them"* **Matthew 7:13-20**

With this scripture in mind let us begin our examination of the fruit of
Christianity. You determine whether it is good or bad. Let's take a look at some of
the more glaring examples of Christianity's fruit. Let us for a moment take a walk
on the dark side; the dark side of Christianity.

Euro-Christianity Lead Man Into the Dark Ages

Euro-Christianity has had nearly two thousand years to produce a higher evolved
and enlightened human being and society. It has failed miserably. The world is
on the brink of global suicide or more precisely, global murder. **Christianity has
failed to demonstrate that the light came into the world with the advent of
Christianity. The truth is that with the advent of Christianity came the "Dark
Ages".** Since the advent of Christianity, its history is replete with destruction and
corruption. From all the religious wars including the present war in Israel, the
corruption and immorality of the priesthood, the infamous witch hunts, African
slave trading, and so on, we see the Church leading man in a downward spiral
instead of lifting humanity up. There are volumes of evidence which suggest that
the spiritual fruit of Euro-Christianity is for the most part either non-existent or
rotten.

Today we see the truth beginning to come out regarding the secret sex life of
many of the Catholic priest. Perhaps the media privately has agreed to not go any
further into their investigative efforts. Certainly we wouldn't want the public to
hear about the many infants buried in the grounds of many Convents the victims of
holy abortions by the Nuns. Nor have they begun to cover the financial and sexual
scandals that are so much a part of religious life today in other Denominations.

Starting with this chapter, we shall focus on the myths and misconceptions
generally accepted as factual regarding Christianity which currently claims more
followers than any other organized religion. It is extremely important for African
Americans to examine the facts because Blacks have embraced Euro-Christianity
with more enthusiasm than those who gave it to them. **Spiritually, for African
Americans, Christianity has had more of a limiting effect. In addition,
because of denominationalism and sectarianism, it has been quite divisive.**

Instead of being a key to the liberation of African minds, it has hindered and limited Black peoples true spiritual understanding and awareness. This is not Church-bashing or Euro-bashing it is simply Truth-telling. Something we've all needed for a long time!

When Men Are Afraid of the Light

It is unfortunate that many African American adults have been afraid of the light of Truth. They would rather not talk about this aspect of Christianity. They would say it doesn't matter or simply try to deny it all together. **When children are afraid of the dark, it is understandable and acceptable, but when adults are afraid of the light, that is a different matter. Then it is pathological and a major hindrance to growth.**

For the lovers and seekers of Truth we shall begin the process of totally dispelling the many myths, misnomers, and outright lies surrounding the origin of Euro-Christianity, its rise to world dominance, the methods it employed, the distortions it has made of the truth, and the end result or the "fruit" of Euro-Christianity. It is time to shine the light into the dark side of Euro-Christianity. **The "tree of Christianity" can only be judged after a fearless and honest appraisal of the "fruit" it has produced. Any judgment that lacks such an appraisal is both dishonest, and inadequate.**

The Greek Connection and Christianity's Early Beginning

Our dialogue begins with the Greek invasion of Egypt or Kemet, since it was the Greeks that are credited with the spawning of Euro-Christianity. **Let us look at how Christianity really claimed its stronghold in determining what men would believe about God, about them-selves and about each other.**

After conquering Africa, the European invaders began to lay claim to the wisdom of Africans. Alexander the conqueror ordered all of Egypt's recorded knowledge confiscated and brought to a central location at the newly established library at Alexandria. He also began to close the various African temples of worship and learning. This was the beginning of the "Dark Ages". Alexander the Great was a Greek barbarian with a lust for power. The power he sought was the power to rule nations of people.

"The Greek invasion of Kemet was primarily responsible for the closing of many temples and consolidation of their curriculums in the newly formed city of Alexandria on the shores of the Mediterranean Sea. **The library**

55

of Alexandria was the nexus of a vast educational complex, which was said to contain more than 700,000 papyrus scrolls. It had a copy of every existing scroll known to library administrators. Many were translated from the Medu Netcher (hieroglyphic) into Greek.

A portion of the library was accidentally destroyed by Julius Caesar during his conquest of Egypt, but it was later rebuilt by his successor Mark Antony around 40 B.C.E. In 391 A.C.E., **The Christian emperor Theodosius decreed that 'all that was ancient was pagan and therefore sinful', and the library were burned to the ground by a mob of Christian fanatics.** As the knowledge of this ancient library faded from the memories of later generations, so, too, did the recollection of the Africans who had founded the earliest civilization in the ancient land that is now called Egypt". *Nile Valley Contributions To Civilization,* Anthony T. Browder, p. 141

"The destruction of the Library and University of Alexandria extinguished the flame of knowledge that had been passed on to the Greeks and Romans by the inhabitants of the Nile Valley. With this glorious light of Egypt extinguished, the nations of Europe would stumble in the darkness for more than a thousand years before knowledge was brought to them during the Moorish conquest". *Nile Valley Contributions To Civilization,* Anthony T. Browder, p. 164

The Western world was consumed with war and weakened by corruption. There was minimum growth in human development, which is the only real progress. Even in possession of all the priceless wisdom of Africa the European nation failed miserably. It would take the rise of the Black man (The Moors) to bring some semblance of humanity and civility to the European society. Without such intervention, the Western world would have perhaps collapsed or destroyed the world long ago. Much of Europe's progress of the Middle Ages can be directly attributed to the contributions of the Black Moors. Any book on the Moors will collaborate with this fact.

The European world was predominantly illiterate until as late as the twelfth century. This would explain the widespread ignorance and superstition, and how idol worship came to be a way of life. This same condition existed with the African captive prior to his introduction to Euro-Christianity. Therefore the same theory would explain the widespread acceptance of Euro-Christianity among African Americans. Until the advent of the Moorish conquest, Europe remained in ignorance, superstition and darkness. In fact it was the Church which led the effort to keep the common people in ignorance. Even the priest was limited in their reading material. This was truly the beginning of a very dark age for man.

"Before 1100 such learning as had existed in Medieval Europe was exclusively for the clergy". Visualized Units in Ancient Medieval History, Russell E. Fraser, William D. Pearson, P. 203

<u>The Deadly Spread of Euro-Christianity</u>

There are numerous dark clouds that overshadow what benefit has been derived from this institution. One very dark cloud is seen in the way the Christian faith was spread. The Christian faith was not spread by devoted and spirit filled Apostles and disciples. Whatever happened on the Day of Pentecost was not responsible for the spread of Christianity. It gained a stronghold in Rome not because of its spiritual efficacy, or the power of the witness of the early Christians, or because of the so called miracles; but because it was institutionalized as the religion of the state. This status made it necessary for Roman citizens to accept Christianity or be in contempt and at odds with the state and the Emperor himself and the Church as well. Christianity was instituted as the religion of Rome primarily because Constantine saw it as a vehicle by which he could conquer and rule.

"Not the least of our debts to Rome is the spread of Christianity throughout the ancient world by means of the Roman Empire". *Visualized Units in Ancient Medieval History,* Russell E. Fraser, William D. Pearson, P.125

In the name of God and Euro-Christianity, Charlemagne waged a relentless war. "One of Charlemagne's aims was to unite the Teutons and Romans of western Europe into one state. **He defeated the barbarian Slavs and Avars** to the east, and carved from their territory the Avaric Mark, a 'buffer' state. **His greatest wars were against the heathen and savage, but Teutonic, Saxons, of North Germany. "Charlemagne enlarged the sphere of civilized life. His conquest and conversion of the Saxons to Christianity gave a firm foundation for the later German nation. By converting the Saxons at the point of the sword, he set an example for later crusades; and he greatly extended the range of Christianity**. By uniting most of West Europe into one state, he advanced the fusion of Romans and Teutons". *Visualized Units in Ancient Medieval History,* Russell E. Fraser, William D. Pearson, P. 143-144

> *"Jesus answered, 'My kingdom is not of this world.*
> *If my kingdom was of this world,*
> *my servants would fight…But my kingdom is not from here"* **John 18:36**

Bloody Christian Wars

Christianity became the dominant religion of the world because of its temporal power (political and economical), and because of raw power and aggression enforced by the sword. Unfortunately, conversion by violence doesn't really count, because it will never produce the inner transformation produced only by a true conversion. It will only produce conformity. Throughout history the European has sought to justify his wars and quest for world conquest, by associating lofty but deceptive goals with it. **The wars were caused because the kingdom in which Christianity sought to establish its dominion was temporal and of the world.** Listed below are thirteen factors listed by a European scholar that describe the reasons for the overwhelming success of Euro-Christianity. (The brackets, represents the author's comments on these factors for the rise of Christendom).

"The Church owed its far reaching influence to a number of factors, some of which were effective only so long as men retained their faith in their teachings.

(1) With the supreme authority centered in the Pope and the councils of important clergymen, the Church was the only centralized force amid the chaos of feudalism. (They were the feudal lords)

(2) **All persons, except Jews, in Western Europe were obliged to accept the authority of the Church or be punished as heretics.** (persons who hold opinions and beliefs contrary to those officially held by the Church-all competition eliminated)

(3) The Church was the recognized interpreter of the Scriptures, and its blessing was essential to salvation. (Total control of doctrines and dogmas)

(4) It was the protector of the defenseless. (Unfortunately there was no one to protect the innocent from the Church)

(5) Its clergy were practically the only educated men in Europe, hence the Church was the source of **what little learning brightened those dark**

days. (Promoted ignorance among the masses, and contributed to the darkness, by not allowing the common man to read)

(6) **Its power of excommunication barred an offender from all religious and social communions and put a curse upon his soul.** (Competition destroyed)

(7) This together with interdict, **the excommunication of groups of people, was a power sufficient to bring the most rebellious princes into line.** (Lust for Political power-temporal power)

(8) **The enormous wealth of the Church included about a third of the tillable land of Europe.** (Materialism and temporal power)

(9) As the chief patron of art and beauty, the Church attracted into its clergy the most intelligent men of the day. (Intelligent but not spiritual)

(10) Through its own system of law and courts it had exclusive jurisdiction (legal authority) in all disputes involving the clergy. (Breeding ground for corruption)

(11) **The Church exercised tax-collecting privileges.** (Materialism and exploitation)

(12) Through legates (papal ambassadors) the Pope dealt directly with kings and princes. (Politics-temporal power)

(14) **Bishops and other important clergy were often feudal suzerains and vassals".** (Clergy-men were the feudal lords) *Visualized Units in Ancient Medieval History*, Russell E. Fraser, William D. Pearson, P. 165

"Next in rank was the Bishop, supervisor of a group of parishes called a diocese. In addition he held church court, officiated in a cathedral **and many times was a feudal landholder**. An Archbishop presided over this division, held court which heard appeals from the court of Bishops **and also was often a feudal landholder**". *Visualized Units in Ancient Medieval History*, Russell E. Fraser & William D. Pearson, P. 166-167

According to these authors, many of the feudal lords were high-ranking clergymen. Here we see the deception of European scholars. They begin by saying that the Church was a "centralized force amid the chaos of feudalism", but ends by saying they were often feudal landholders themselves. So the centralized force was not benevolent as implied. The feudal lords were themselves responsible for the "chaos". They created it by exploiting and oppressing the serfs. The taxes of the "centralized force"-system of feudalism, caused such a burden on the people that all was indeed chaos. The chaos was caused by the oppression and the oppression was caused by a Church seeking material gain.

Corrupt Priesthood

Corruption has been a feature of Christendom since its inception. The priesthood which welded both economic and political power was corrupt and therefore sought only temporal power rather than Spiritual power. The true aim of the church has been temporal and materialistic from its beginning. It is no different today. Today instead of a "tax" the church exacts a "tithe". Although this "tithe" is supposedly voluntary, the leadership goes to great lengths to impress upon the people, that the "tithes and offerings" are for the Lord, and failure to "pay up" amounts to "robbing God". After they get possession of "God's money", the "man of God" then claims it for himself. Such behavior does not uplift humanity instead it tends to lower the level of life. This effect, however, is often denied and overlooked. The entire book of Malachi in the Bible is written to the pastors. Just as today, the pastors were keeping the best of the offerings for themselves. It was the pastors, according to the scriptures, not the people that were robbing God (if God can be robbed).

pastors

"In the West civilization had broken down, but with the aid of the Church was struggling to keep alive, while in Eastern Europe and in Asia the arts of civilization were flourishing. **Strangely enough, however, it was the West which was to dominate the unborn modern world. Explanation of how this came to be involves the story of one of the most contradictory movements in history-the Crusades. Here was a movement which was both barbaric and romantic, a movement of lofty purposes mingled with base and cruel conduct, one which was a conspicuous failure yet of vast significance and which represented an alliance between the two great foes in the West, feudalism and the Church"**. *Visualized Units in Ancient Medieval History,* Russell E. Fraser, William D. Pearson, P.175

"But if thine eye be evil, thy whole body shall be full of darkness.
If therefore the light that is in thee be darkness, how great is that darkness".
Mt. 6:23

A rose by any other name is still a rose; and a cruel barbaric war is still cruel and savage. Though it was coined the "Holy Crusades", it was still a

"unholy war". How can a war be both barbaric and romantic, *"can both sweet water and bitter water come from the same fountain"*? Yet, this was the method often employed by the early church to ensure the dominance of their faith in the world. This infamous legacy is the inheritance of today's Christians. They directly benefit from this corrupt partnership between the early church and the state just as sure as Whites in America still benefit from the slaves labor. As with the crusades the so called "Holy Roman Empire" was holy in name only. The motivation for the Crusades was dark indeed and how great was that darkness.

Truth not Mentioned Among African American Christians

The popularity of Christianity is directly related to the vast numbers of confessing Christians, which was accomplished by obviously wicked means. **The early Church is the shoulders today's African American Christian Churches are unknowingly standing on. The barbarism of the early Church is the legacy of today's Church both Black and White. Of course no mention is made of this "legacy" in Sunday school, where the children and others are led to believe a lie.**

In Sunday school, children are taught that the message of Christianity was spread by the peaceful efforts of the apostles, prophets, evangelist and disciples. According to Christian legend they are supposedly responsible for establishing the Church and spreading the Gospel message. This is obviously a lie and misrepresentation. The people are not told the Truth because the Truth belongs to the "dark side" of Christianity. Tragically, many African American Christian pastors and educators simply do not know the Truth.

"In 1530 the German Protestants drew up a statement of their faith (the Augsburg Confession) and in 1555 **the Peace of Augsburg ended the civil strife for the time being** by again affirming the right of each prince to determine the religion of his own people, a principle which Luther had agreed to. Lutheranism and Catholicism were to be the only faiths tolerated. Thus, the original Protestant demand for freedom of belief for the individual was lost sight of". *Visualized Units in Ancient Medieval History,* Russell E. Fraser, William D. Pearson, P.220

"From 1545 to 1563, therefore, **the Council of Trent**, composed of influential churchmen, met at intervals to discuss reforms. This body reaffirmed papal supremacy and all Church tradition. It made changes in the government of the Church and urged upright conduct upon all clergymen. **To check heresy it prepared an Index of books considered** dangerous for Catholics to read. The Holy Inquisition, a court for the purpose of detecting and punishing heresy, was urged to new vigor in its duties". *Visualized Units in Ancient Medieval History,* Russell E. Fraser, William D. Pearson, P.224

This is dogmatism and hypocrisy at their worse. The Church points a bloody finger at so called heretics and pagans, accuse them of being heathen as they massacre and murder them and label their own acts as "holy". As we have seen in the earlier scripture quoted, Jesus is recorded as saying his Kingdom was not of this world, and therefore "his" servants do not fight. So who ever the early Church was serving with their dark deeds, it was not Jesus. It certainly was not God!

That which is true does not require such a bloody defense or offense. Nor does it have to be forced on people with the threat of a sword or of going to hell. It is a fact that those who championed Christianity were not of those that made peace. It is also true that their method of evangelizing was not peaceful. There is a scriptural reference that explains why this tree (Euro-Christianity) has produced its particular brand of "strange fruit".

"This wisdom descendeth not from above, but is earthly, sensual, devilish.
For where envying and strife is, there is confusion and every evil work.
But the wisdom that is from above is first pure, then peaceable, gentle, and easy
to be entreated, full of mercy and good fruits,
without partiality, and without hypocrisy.
And the fruit of righteousness is sown in peace of them that make peace".
James 3:15-18

Euro-Christianity produces "Strange Fruit"

The reason Euro-Christianity produces strange fruit is because its wisdom is devilish and carnal. It is earthly because it has been derived from information supplied by the senses. It is the "letter" rather than the "Spirit". Therefore, it produces strife and division rather than establishing peace and order. It is full of hypocrisy. Within Christianity are the seeds of confusion, division and destruction that produce "every evil work". Without this seed, it could not produce the strange fruit. Every seed must produce like kind. You cannot get oranges from apple seeds nor can you get evil fruit from holy seed. The corrupted seed is in the false doctrines of the Church manufactured by carnal priest with a lust for temporal power and riches.

A "Holy Crusade" is an oxymoron. It is the height of hypocrisy. The Truth is easily shared and is shared in peace not war. Its very presence destroys lies and falsehoods. It is the possession of righteous men, because its fruit is righteousness. The clergy-men of Christendom have not demonstrated righteousness; instead they have left a trail of death and destruction, with each brief period of peace being just a time of preparation and plotting for the next war.

> "The Peace of Augsburg had been unsatisfactory because it provided toleration for Lutheranism and Catholicism, but not Calvinism. Also many disliked the way in which the Church lands had been divided by this treaty. Protestants were alarmed by the effective work of the Jesuits toward restoring Catholicism in Germany, as well as by the earnest determination of the Hapsburg rulers to stamp out heresy and political disunion within the Empire. Protestants outside of Germany feared that a blow to Lutheranism would weaken Protestantism throughout Europe. *Visualized Units in Ancient Medieval History*, Russell E. Fraser, William D. Pearson, pg. 229

As can be seen it was not the moral influence, or the nobility of the priest, nor was it the purity, simplicity, or power of the Christian teachings as witnessed by the apostles, prophets, teachers and pastors, that caused the success of the spread of Christianity. Contemporary African American Protestants (Baptist, Church of God in Christ, Methodist, African Methodist, etc.) do not care to recognize this dark cloud over the way Christianity was actually spread. It was not by the power of the "gospel" or the power of God but by the power of the "sword". Protestants somehow distance themselves from these earlier acts by disassociating themselves from the Catholic Church and saying they're different. Yet both the fundamental doctrine and the fruit remain the same for Protestants and Catholics alike, it is corrupt. Religious leaders do not wish to acquaint themselves with this dark side of Christianity because such information does not lend support to winning new converts nor does it lend fuel to fire people up for church building fund drives.

Yet, the trail is there, the facts are clear. The methods of the Church were dark because its wisdom was and is dark. It lacks the seed of Spiritual Truth. The Truth has been compromised and corrupted. Euro-Christianity was spawned in the lust for world conquest. Therefore its fruit is death rather than life. The light that is in Euro-Christianity is darkness.

Adisa Franklin

The Trail of Death Left by Euro-Christianity

The fact that Christianity as an institution is responsible for more deaths and has exhibited more corruption than even the institution of government is quite significant as a consideration. The connection of the Catholic Church and Protestant Church to the numerous wars and conflicts throughout history however is undeniable. Even many of today's wars and conflicts are fueled by religious beliefs and differences. Prime examples of this are the wars in Israel and Ireland. The lust for world power and control is often disguised in the evangelizing efforts of Euro-Christianity.

The Church and the State have had the same goal, world domination. For this ungodly reason, many people have been murdered and there has been much destruction.

"From whence come wars and fighting among you? Come they not hence, even of your lust that war in your members: Ye lust, and have not, ye kill, and desire to have, and cannot obtain: Ye fight and war, yet ye have not, because ye ask not, ye ask amiss, that ye may consume it upon your lust". **James 4:1-3**

The record of the wars fought in defense of the Faith is too endless to mention. Each massacre of human life was motivated by defense of the accepted canons of the Church. Witness these next examples of Religious Wars and massacres.

One example on the trail of death left by Euro-Christianity is for the most part, unknown to the majority of Christians. If the truth was known, perhaps, St. Patrick's Day would not inspire the gaiety it does. **"Druid in Old Irish meant 'he who knows'. The Druids were also known to dress in a style similar to the priestly kings of Kemet.** Their heads were often adorned with a ureaus, which was the symbol of the cobra that was worn on the crown of the Pharaoh. **Because of this symbolic imagery, the Druids were often referred to as the 'snake people'. Their presence and ideology were viewed as a direct threat to the development of Christianity in Ireland.** In 432 A.C.E., Pope Celestine I sent a former British slave named Patrick into the region to convert the population."

"In the name of Christianity, Patrick's army slew thousands of Irishmen, and he is said to have founded more than 300 churches

64

and baptized more than 120,000 persons. Patrick also introduced the Roman alphabet and Latin literature into Ireland. He was rewarded by the Vatican with sainthood and today, millions of people throughout the world celebrate Saint Patrick's Day on his feast day, March 17. To the average person, who dresses in green, wears shamrocks and marches in parades this day commemorates the myth of the man who drove the 'snakes' out of Ireland. **What most people fail to realize is that the snakes St. Patrick drove into the sea were not snakes that crawled on the ground, but the 'snake people' who walked on two feet and were known as Druids".** *Nile Valley Contributions To Civilization*, Anthony T. Browder, p. 193-194

"The next ruler was Mary, Catholic half-sister of Edward, daughter of Catherine of Aragon, and wife of Philip II of Spain. During her reign, England, whose people were still largely Catholic at heart, was received once more into the Church. **All anti-Catholic laws were repealed and Protestants were executed in such large numbers that the Queen was nicknamed 'Bloody Mary'.** *Visualized Units in Ancient Medieval History, Russell E. Fraser*, William D. Pearson, P. 222-223

ALL THESE BLOODY MURDERS WERE COMMITTED IN THE NAME OF GOD, AND SUPPOSEDLY IN DEFENSE OF HIS WORD!

"Philip II was a violent enemy of Protestantism. When there were signs of rebellion in Holland, Philip sent the Duke of Alva with an army who instituted a reign of terror. Alva set up a court which earned the name 'Council of Blood', to stamp out rebellion, and the Inquisition was actively searching out heretics and cruelly punishing them". *Visualized Units in Ancient Medieval History,* Russell E. Fraser, William D. Pearson, P. 226

"The Huguenot wars were marked by treachery on both sides. Fearful of the growing influence which the Protestant leader, Admiral Coligny, exerted upon the king, **Catherine brought about a horrible massacre of Protestants (Massacre of St. Bartholomew's Day)".** *Visualized Units in Ancient Medieval History,* Russell E. Fraser, William D. Pearson, P. 228

"The bitterness and destructiveness of the religious wars reached an all-time record in the Thirty Years' War (1618-1648). This horrible struggle, started as a conflict between German Protestants and Catholics, soon expanded into a European war for territory while

the religious question became secondary". *Visualized Units in Ancient Medieval History*, Russell E. Fraser, William D. Pearson, P. 228

"In Germany much property had been destroyed, the population reduced by half and economic activity reduced. It was to take generations for German civilization to recover from the shock of the utter destructiveness of this struggle". *Visualized Units in Ancient Medieval History*, Russell E. Fraser, William D. Pearson, P. 230

AND THEY SAY THAT THE DEVIL IS WANDERING THROUGHOUT THE LAND SEEKING WHO HE WOULD KILL AND DESTROY!

The history of Euro-Christianity is jammed pack with similar facts of wars and strife with religious origins and hidden agendas. **It has been truly a dark time since the coming of Christianity. The death toll is astronomical and the destruction catastrophic!**

"There has not been one year in universal history without wars, violence and destruction. Mankind has not yet reached any appreciable degree of emotional security". *The Essene Book of Creation,* Edmon Bordeaux Szekely, p. 76

This means no matter what we tell our youth about controlling and managing their violence, they see that we are not controlling and managing our violence. The world has been a very violent place since the advent of Christianity.

Christianity and The Quest to Rule the World

The institution of Christendom had a political rather than a spiritual birth. A European Emperor of Rome by the name of Constantine conspired to conquer the world under the banner (the cross) of Christianity. He is reported as claiming to have seen a vision of a cross in the sky and to hearing a voice which said, "Under this sign you shall conquer". As we shall see later in chapter seven, Constantine is credited with the birth of the institution of Euro-Christianity. From its inception, Christianity had a temporal mission it was to become a vehicle to use to dominate and to rule Rome and the world. Emperor Constantine had calculated that it would be the teachings of Christianity that would keep those he would conquer submissive. Every since then the use of the "Bible and the Bullet" has been proven to be quite effective a team.

The war started with a rebellion of the Protestants in Bohemia against the Hapsburgs. When it was suppressed Protestants became alarmed and sought the aid of non-Catholic countries. **One by one England, Denmark, Sweden, Norway and France entered the struggle with mingled hopes of weakening the Empire, gaining land and preserving Protestantism".** *Visualized Units in Ancient Medieval History*, Russell E. Fraser, William D. Pearson, P. 229

"By Philip's defeat with the destruction of the Armada, Spanish imperial power was destroyed and the way was cleared for colonization of the New World by English Protestants". *Visualized Units in Ancient Medieval History, Russell E. Fraser, William D. Pearson*, P. 223

The wars over control and dominance in the world did not end in Europe the New World was colonized by Euro-Christians. As is confessed here, 'the way was cleared for the colonization of the New World by English Protestants'. Meanwhile the rest of the Euro-Christians were fighting to claim the remainder of the world. When Euro-Christians arrived in South America they claimed the land in the name of their God and King. They proclaimed the natives heathens because they weren't Christians and began to rape and pillage the land and the people. This same scenario has been repeated throughout the world by confessing European Christians in the name of God.

Racism, Slavery and Christianity

Racism, considered by many a most insidious cancer on race relations and the source of much confusion, hostility, inequalities, police brutality, hate crimes and other injustices, is based on dogmas and doctrines of men established in Euro-Christianity. It is directly related to the Hamite theory, which was originally promoted by European church leadership. The Hamite theory says that Ham, a son of Noah, was cursed because he saw his father naked and drunk. His curse, was to serve (be a slave) his brothers, who somehow are not black as well. This theory formed the foundation for the justification of slavery. It was fostered by the Church.

Recently, Pope John began to apologize for "some" of the corruption of the early church. Glaringly absent from his apology was any reference to the participation of the Catholic Church in both establishing slavery and profiting from Slave Trafficking?

67

Christendom can legitimately be credited with laying the theoretical foundation for White Supremacy, which is the Mother of Racism. Removing the erroneous "Hamite" theory from the shadows in which it lurks and remains strong will do much to remove any vestiges of its power to infect people's attitudes with the disease of racism.

For the record let us take a moment to get a working definition of racism, because there seems to be some confusion among black people as to exactly what it is. Today the term "reverse racism" has appeared which has caused black people to begin to even call each other "racist". For this work we shall use the following definition of racism:

> **"RACISM is the defense mechanism for fearful and frightened men threatened by low self-esteem based on extreme feelings of inadequacy. The fear is based on the fear of being eliminated by the more dominant seed of the "Melanin Man"-the African.** The inadequacy is based on the innate feelings of lack brought about by the lack of melanin. The coveted color agent of people of color who make up the majority of the people on the planet".

I thank our esteemed Psychologist, Dr. Francis Cress Welsing, for this clear and accurate definition of "racism". It explains the reason why the African was chosen to be the so called servant and have all semblance of his dignity almost destroyed. Africans, historically have out performed Europeans in every area related to the building of a great civilization. Africans have the most of the coveted "melanin". They are therefore the greatest threat. Solution, take their history; take their inheritance; claim that God has cursed them; and then color them depraved, thereby proving that White is greater than Black.

Earl Conrad, author of *The Invention of the Negro*, offers this historical perspective:

> "Fifty years before Columbus sailed westward, **Catholic Spain and Catholic Portugal were engaged in a rivalry to sack Africa, to seize its inhabitants as slaves and to ship them back to Europe and sell them.** Portugal, the first invader, sought and secured the blessings of the Pope and in a series of papal bulls issued from 1443 on, there is the spectacle of the Christian Vatican sanctifying the enslavement of Africans on grounds that they were pagans…"

Haley also described the role that the church played in the institutionalization of slavery:

"One of the most perverse things that I have found in my long research was that the people, in what might be called the hierarchy of slavery, the owners, the agents, the captains of those ships, strove in every possible way to somehow manifest that they were functioning in a Christian context…"

"Most notably, Fredrick Douglas wrote an appendix to his explosive essay, 'Slaveholding Religion and the Christianity of Christ', in which he denounced slaveholding religion with all the rhetorical power he could muster. 'What I have said respecting and against religion of this land, and with no possible reference to Christianity proper; for, between the Christianity of Christ, I recognize the widest possible difference-so wide, that to receive the one as good, pure, and holy, is of necessity to reject the other as bad, corrupt, and wicked. To be the friend of one is of necessity to be the enemy of the other. *Spirituality of African Peoples*, Peter J. Paris, pg. 66

The European---Perpetrators of Righteousness

By depicting himself as the one who civilizes and the African as savage, heathen and cursed by God, the European was able to justify his actions, at least in his own mind. They switched places with the Africans, and now it was the African who somehow needed the wisdom of Europe. **"The Europeans arrogated to themselves the role of civilizing of the African. Set upon in a self-righteous fashion to redeem him from his wicked and primitive ways. This righteous-than-thou attitude has persisted to this day.** The relationship between Europeans and Africans therefore started off on the righteous against the wicked note. The Europeans being the righteous, and the African the wicked"! *No More Lies About Africa*, Chief Musamaali Nangole, pg. 63

"The distorted picture and the lies about the African suited human trade handsomely and justified colonialism magnificently in the eyes of the invading Europeans. The distortion was sinister, as the horrors of captivity and the arrogance of colonialism were later to demonstrate". *No More Lies About Africa*, Chief Musamaali Nangoli, pg. 7

"Colonialism might not have succeeded to the extent that it did in Africa, without missionary work. If there was ever a time when the

African and his culture were parted, (almost for good) it was during the epoch of missionary work in Africa*". No More Lies About Africa*, Chief Musamaali Nangoli, pg. 71

"Having successfully turned him into a Christian the missionary proceeded to preach to the African the ways of Christianity. Love thy neighbor; thou shall not hate; the love for money is the root of all evil. Unknown to the African at that time, the European neither loved his neighbor nor did not hate, nor was himself immune from avarice! When the African found out the truth it was too late, the damage had already been done"! *No More Lies About Africa*, Chief Musamaali Nangoli, pg. 73

Tricked, Hoodwinked, Bamboozled, and Confused

At this point one has to wonder how the European can remain in denial that the Truth has been reversed. His continual denial can only be attributed to his fears of the ever present threat of annihilation by the melanin man. It is still true however it is the savage European who is still in need of civilizing. We have all witnessed in this lifetime the savagery and barbarism by which the European nations continual to conduct their affairs. Witness the way in which the American Government continues to resolve conflicts with other nations. If the average citizen resolved their conflicts the way the government does, we would have a totally chaotic and violent society.

If you are not convinced of this truth, just take another look at the condition of the world today. African Americans are not responsible for the mayhem. Those that run this world are exclusively of the Caucasian/European race of men. It is they only who must take full responsibility for the condition of the world. The Western way is not a very healthy way for Mankind.

Yet, millions of Africans in America and abroad have internalized the attitudes and world view of the Western man thinking them to be correct. Many African Americans and native Africans now believe it was Christianity that brought civilization to Africa and the Africans. In their minds, it is the one thing most needful of Blacks. This is such a tragedy in light of what we should all know by now to be the truth. Indeed too many have been tricked, hoodwinked and bamboozled. It is indeed a sign of confusion when Blacks allow the one race of people who have demonstrated neither, godliness or love toward them, to do their spiritual thinking for them.

So the African captive was taught to "obey their masters", the white man; that it was a sin to steal from the white man; that he should "love his enemy", which happened to be the white man; and to "turn the other cheek" when the white man abused him and his family. Most importantly, he was taught to "suffer patiently" for "Jesus sake", and to wait patiently for his redemption "after death". Black people are not suffering because of Jesus, they suffer because they are black!

Many Blacks have internalized a "White Jesus" as their "personal Savior" and expound the virtues of trusting this Jesus to deliver them. Mostly what they trust him for is "getting to heaven" and a few material blessings. They do not recognize that they are idol worshippers. They do not recognize that they are lost in the confusion of the European scholar and priest that shaped and molded the religion they have embraced with their whole hearts.

Lambs To The Slaughter

Such an extreme display of sheer naiveté, the world has not known. It is with the innocence of little lambs that Black people go into the den of wolves and ask the wolves not to devour them but save them instead. How can a people that have been as brutalized and lied to, for as long as African Americans have, still trust in the fairness of Western man? African Americans are still naïve enough to continue to look to their oppressors (the cause) for a solution to their dilemma which the Western man created for his benefit. They continue to expect that Western man would sincerely address the question of freedom and empowerment for the Black man, or that Western man would willingly tell Blacks the Truth.

Euro-Christianity was given to the captives as an extra measure of protection. It was a chain for their minds, to insure that their captives would remain under control even when the European was not around to control him. Its original purpose has never been abandoned; "Under the cross (and Christianity), you shall conquer". It has always been a tool of the conqueror to insure his safety and his control. It was understood, at least by Europeans, that the purpose of Christianity was not to make the Africans civilized but instead it was to make them docile, passive and "blessed" with an attitude of servility.

As a tool of the conquering Western Man, Christianity had worked in Rome, in Europe and in Africa, why wouldn't it work in the New World. It has! And for much too long! The image of the black man is still affected by it, and it is still used (consciously or unconsciously) to justify acts of inhumanity and injustices perpetuated on African Americans.

"For the sake of big profits Negroes were hunted like beasts on the coast of Africa and shipped to the American colonies. It may be interest to note that the Englishman who originated this body-snatching business, Captain John Hawkins, called the ship in which he transported the victims the Jesus". *Western Civilizations,* Edward McNall Burns, Eighth Edition, Vol. 2, pg. 459

THE BLACK MAN MUST NEVER FORGET THAT IT WAS CHRISTENDOM THAT ESTABLISHED, JUSTIFIED AND PROFITED FROM THE ENSLAVING OF HIS FOREFATHERS.

Biblical Image of Women Negative

Throughout the bible, women are giving a negative spin. From the very first book, probably the most destructive, woman is portrayed as the temptress, the whore and responsible for the downfall of man. In the Proverbs, considerable time is spent warning young men against the wiles of loose women and prostitutes. No time is spent warning young innocent women of the men who would use and abuse them. The woman caught in the act of adultery was about to be stoned, whereas the man, had already been released. When the men of Sodom, demanded the men in the house of Lot for sex, Lot offered his daughters to the men to *"have their way with"*. This was done as if to indicate that women were disposable and less valuable than the men were. The fact that the men were angels does not justify allowing the women to be raped.

Consider these scripture references to woman: *Cursed woman*-2 Ki.9:34*; Wicked woman*-2 Chr.24:7; *Deceived by woman*-Job 31:9; *Evil woman*-Pr.6:24; *Foolish woman*-Pr.9:13; *Brawling woman*-Pr.21:9,19; *Whorish woman*-Ezek.16:30; *Diseased woman*-Mt.9:20; *Jezebel woman*-Rev.2:20; *Contentious woman*-Pr.19:13. On the male end, we find VERY FEW corresponding depictions or references. Instead, there are over thirty references to a *"wise man"*.

A woman supposedly caused the great man of God, David to fall from grace. For lust, he committed adultery and then murdered to cover it up. Later, the downfall of his son, Solomon is attributed to his lust for women. He was supposed to have had as many as *"seven hundred wives, and princesses and three hundred concubines"*. (I Kings 11:3) A woman, Delilah, robbed Samson of his strength. These are only a few of the hundreds of examples of the biblical depreciation and degrading of women.

The Cursing of Womanhood

Certainly there are some positive examples of Womanhood in the Bible. Yet, many scriptures do not flatter womanhood at all. Perhaps the most damning, demeaning and damaging of scriptures to womanhood are these scriptures; *"For the man is not of the woman, but the woman of the man".* **(I Cor.11:8)**; *"For Adam was first formed then Eve. And Adam was not deceived, but the woman being deceived was in transgression".* **(I Timothy 2:13-14)** **Here we find the woman being relegated to an inferior position to the man (second) and being blamed for the fall of man**. **Every man comes from a woman.**

"To the woman He said: I will greatly multiply your sorrow and your conception;
In pain shall you bring forth children; Your desire shall be for your husband,
And he shall rule over you" **Genesis 3:16**

So the woman being subject to her man is the curse of God! If this is the case why would today's Church place this "curse" upon the "redeemed" women of the Church who supposedly are no longer under the curse? Again, why would a New Testament writer namely Paul act as if the curse was still operational under the Dispensation (Age) of Grace. Why aren't women asking these questions? Women are told by the same writer to be silent in the church and learn at home. Being cursed of God would of course make her unworthy of sharing the throne with man.

Perhaps this is the reason that the woman had to be removed from the Holy Trinity and replaced by a Ghost. In the original African Trinity, there was the Father, the Mother and the son (Osiris, Isis and Horus). Certainly, there are some positive examples of women in the Bible, however the balance is toward the negative rather than the positive.

One has to really search in the New Testament to find a female minister. Perhaps God overlooked them when he was pouring out his Spirit. At least for male church leadership, this must have been the case. This contempt for womanhood began in Greece where the woman was always of the lower class, and carried to Rome. It was sustained by the priest and scholars of Euro-Christianity.

Because of the disdain for women in the hearts of white Christian men, the early Church initiated a sick, cruel witch-hunt that subjected women to various sordid interrogation tactics and some creatively barbaric methods of dying.

"The earliest persecutions for witchcraft were those resulting from the crusades launched against heretics by the Papal Inquisition in the thirteenth century. A second campaign against witches was initiated by Pope Innocent VIII in 1484, who instructed his inquisitors to use torture in procuring convictions. But, as we have seen, it was not until after the beginning of the Protestant Revolution that witchcraft persecution became a mad hysteria. Luther himself provided some of the impetus by recommending that witches should be put to death with fewer considerations of mercy shown to ordinary criminals. Other Reformers quickly followed Luther's example. Under Calvin's administration in Geneva thirty-four women were burned or quartered for the alleged crime in 1545. From this time on the persecutions spread like a pestilence.

Women, young girls, and even mere children were tortured by driving needles under their nails, roasting their feet in the fire, or crushing their legs under heavy weights until the marrow spurted from their bones, in order to force them to confess filthy orgies with demons. To what extent the persecutions were due to sheer sadism or to the greed of the magistrate, who were sometimes permitted to confiscate the property of those convicted, is impossible to say. As late as the eighteenth century John Wesley declared that to give up the belief in witchcraft was to give up the Bible". *Western Civilizations,* Edward McNall Burns, pg. 463

Only a sick, cruel mind, the mind of a man with complete disdain for womanhood could practice such sinister and crude methods of torture. Pope Innocent VIII really wasn't very innocent. This disdain originated among the early Greeks, who are given the most credit for the creation of Euro-Christianity. The "Fathers" of Christianity, were all sexist, they had no love for the female component of humanity. As we have seen, every great European Christian male leader from Calvin and Wesley to Luther, all shared the same contempt for womanhood. Consequently, today not only within the Church, but in the general society, women are considered of somewhat lesser value.

Sexism and Euro-Christianity

The white Christian men who built the institutions of this potentially great country shared this sexist view. Sexism permeates this society because Euro-

Christian values are woven into the infrastructure and very fabric of European society. The position of women in this society has been severely limited and handicapped because of the fallacies promoted by white male church leadership. Because of attitudes fostered by the church, women are paid less for working the same job as a man. They will likely pay more for repairs on their car and home. If Feminist were aware that the root cause of the problem of second-class citizenship for women was in the teachings of the Christian Church, they could be much more effective in impacting this socially dysfunctional and destructive attitude.

Unfortunately, even a woman's ministry gifts are subject to be overlooked and disregarded in church. Doctrines of Men inserted into the scripture, instruct women to be submissive to men and to be silent in the church. Such doctrines rooted in the teachings of the church are the root causes of "Sexism" in society. Because of such "doctrines of men" inserted in the scriptures, women ministers are often forced to split off and start their own church in order to find access to a pulpit for their ministry.

In the bible, the apostle Paul is credited with saying, *"Let the women learn in silence with all subjection"*, and *"I suffer not a woman to teach, nor usurp the authority over a man"*. (I Timothy 2:11-12) In the mainstream Black Churches, this scripture is often overlooked because women are needed for Sunday school class as teachers. Some of the denominations allow women to assume the role of an evangelist or missionary, granting limited access to the fiercely guarded male dominated pulpit.

Few denominations permit the women to as they would say usurp authority over the man and become overseers, pastors and bishops. This occurs even though the scriptures their male counterparts preach from says, *"I will pour out my Spirit upon all flesh, and your sons and daughters shall prophecy"*; and *"God is no respecter of persons"*. Such behavior by African American pastors and clergymen is called "cognizant dissonance" in the world of the Psychologist. It means the attempt to hold two contradictory ideas as true at the same time. It is a form of neurosis.

Within the Holiness churches, women are forced to dress plain, with no make-up, and no jewelry because of one scripture: *"In like manner also, that women adorn themselves in modest apparel, with shamefacedness and sobriety, not with braided hair or gold, or pearls, or costly array"*. (I Timothy 2:9) This scripture has resulted in a most controlling and oppressive environment for women within this denomination. Once again we find the Black Church following the pattern of the White Church. By this I mean, they are seen here preaching a dogma based on the letter of the Scripture. The spirit of the passage is "Remember, the clothes does not make the woman of God therefore do not neglect the "inner woman" make sure she is beautiful and adorned in the spirit. Make her your priority.

In spite of these historical facts and in the midst of this blatant sexist attitude, Black women are traditionally and presently the strongest supporters of organized Christianity. There are Black women who leave very meager dwellings to drive to elaborate churches were the Pastor lives the lifestyle of the rich and famous, and contribute out of their meager funds. Socially this is explained by the presence of high numbers of homes and families with little or no constructive male input. Some women admit to living vicariously through the Pastor and his wife or simply fantasizing about the preacher. Many preachers, whether consciously or unconsciously cater to this tendency while continuing to maintain a chauvinistic attitude toward the same women. This results in creating a crutch rather than a real remedy. This binds the women to the pastor rather than to God and makes her dependent emotionally.

The World is Still in Darkness

By all standards, the world we live in is ethically, morally and spiritually in the dark. There are no standards today. **We live in a dark world. It is full of neurotics, psychotics, perverts, confused and violent people. This darkness is a continuation of the original "Dark Ages" began in the first century of this Christian era. As Christianity grew in dominance, the world grew darker.** During the "Middle Ages" an attempt was made by Europeans to rectify the darkness they had created. It was called the Reformation and it failed miserably. This is made obvious by the fruit it produced. The Truth is once again confessed and confirmed by the perpetuator, Euro-Christianity.

> **"...the dolorous fact remains that for large numbers of men ethics had lost their true meaning. The cardinal aims were now gratification of self and victory in the struggle to make the whole world conform to one's own set of dogmas".** *Western Civilizations,* Edward McNall, pg. 463

> **"So doubtful was the quality of moral standards among the Catholic clergy that the Reformers of that faith found it necessary to introduce the closed confessional box for the protection of female penitents.** Formerly women as well as men had been required to knell at the knees of the priest while confessing their sins". *Western Civilizations*, Edward McNall, pg. 459

Christianity's Worldly Kingdom

The church and the state historically has either worked together or fought each other in their grasping for material wealth and power. During most of its history, the Church has either worked together with the state in grasping for temporal power or fought against the state for the same reason:

"The pope, moreover, found a natural ally in Pippin against a hostile Lombard King of Italy. Pippin (King of the Franks) reduced Lombardy to a tributary state, and bestowed upon the pope a large district of Italy, extending across the peninsula from North to South, and including Rome and Ravenna. **This donation was the beginning of temporal (political) power of the papacy, which was to expand into one of the most tremendous forces of Western history.** It also gave the occasion for the bitter strife between the popes and later German monarchs over the exact terms on which the donation was made". *Visualized Units in Ancient Medieval History*, Russell E. Fraser, William D. Pearson, pg.142-143

This fulfilled the original aim of Euro-Christianity; the goal of a temporal kingdom based on material wealth and power. It never has mattered how; "By any means necessary" has always been the creed and motto of Euro-Christianity. It would be interesting to tally the value of the wealth of the Church and particularly the Black Church. As in days of old, the Church continues to drain the wealth of the people to build its own little worldly kingdom.

"The growing spirit of nationalism caused kings and peoples to object to the interference in temporal affairs which the Popes had practiced from time to time. Money was constantly draining to Rome from all parts of Europe. **The wealth of some churchmen aroused the ire of many Europeans who were living in poverty. Clergymen were not all sincere and devout men and they shocked the people with the ungodly lives they led".** *Visualized Units in Ancient Medieval History*, Russell E. Fraser, William D. Pearson, pg. 216-217

"The immediate effect of the Reformation in improving conditions of morality appears to have been almost negligible. Perhaps this is explainable in part by the return to the legalism of the Old Testament. But probably the chief cause was the fierce antagonism between the sects. A condition of war is never favorable to the growth of a high morality. Whatever the reasons, the licentiousness and brutality continued unchecked. Even some of the clergy who were closely identified with the work of religious reform could scarcely be said to have been armored with the breastplate of righteousness". *Western Civilization,* Edward McNall Burns, pg.459

Not much different from today wouldn't you say? The Church today is still impotent when it comes to impacting the conditions of the society. In our example such lack of righteousness produced some peculiarly sordid behavior instead; consider this observation. **"In view of the fact that insanity was regarded as a form of demonic possession, it is not strange that the sufferers from this disease should have been cruelly treated. They were generally confined in filthy barracks and flogged unmercifully to drive the demons out of their bodies. A favorite diversion of some of our ancestors was to organize parties to visit the madhouses and tease the insane".** *Western Civilization,* Edward McNall Burns, Eighth Edition, Vol. 2, pg. 459 When these authors refer to "our ancestors", it is to be taken literally. Be assured, the "our" makes reference to Europeans.

HOW MUCH LOWER CAN HUMANITY SINK!

"The effects of the Reformation upon the virtues of truthfulness and tolerance were woeful indeed. Catholic and Protestant Reformers alike were so obsessed with the righteousness of their own particular cause that they did not hesitate to make almost any extreme of falsehood, slander, or repression that seem to guarantee victory for their side. For example, Luther expressly justified lying in the interest of religion, and the Jesuits achieved a reputation for tortuous reasoning and devious plotting for the advantage of the Church. No one seemed to have the slightest doubt that in the sphere of religion the end justified the means". *Western Civilizations* Edward McNall, pg.460

"The Eastern Empire, with its capital and its cultural and commercial center in **Constantinople was not subject to the barbarism which existed in the West".** Visualized Units in Ancient Medieval History, Russell E. Fraser, William D. Pearson, pg. 176

"The artists and writers of the Intellectual Revolution strove to imitate classical models. They chose classical titles and themes for many of their works and embellished them wherever possible with allusions to antique mythology. **Deploring the destruction of ancient civilization by 'Christian barbarians', they were unable to see much value in the** cultural achievements of later centuries. In particular, they despised the Middle Ages as a long night of barbaric darkness". *Western Civilization*, Edward McNall Burns, pg. 513

"Judged by the immediate purpose of taking the Holy Land from the Seljuks, the Crusades were a conspicuous failure. Judged by their effects upon the Western World, they represent one of the great chapters of history". *Visualized Units in Ancient Medieval History*, Russell E. Fraser, William D. Pearson, pg. 181

The Carnal Crusades

It seems Euro-Christianity and Western man were determined to prove that no matter how low man sunk, he could sink even lower. The so called Holy Crusades took man into the bowels of barbarism, and called it the work of the Lord. Western scholars continue to attempt to misrepresent history even as they make confessions. Somehow this savage and barbaric attempt to force a religion on people became a "Great chapter of history". Yet, the confessions are there to set the record straight. The European Christians that would go on to rule the world have barbarians for ancestors. The crusades failed because of its carnal mission and its savage methods. This explains its strange fruit of corruption, death, and destruction.

A testimony was given revealing that even Martin Luther, the Father of the Protestant branch of Christianity, was a "sexist" and a "liar". We must remember that Protestants are a branch of Christianity and that the tree is Euro-Christianity itself. Christianity has not worked for Western man, and it has not and will not work for African Americans. The Black Church still does not reflect anywhere near the greatness of its glorious past (original African worship of the Creator) because they are lost in the darkness of Christian theories and dogmas. Because of wickedness in high places, Blacks and Whites alike live in darkness.

"This raises other questions of great urgency: Are we really civilized today? Have we not substituted the trappings of civilization-our triumphs in science, technology, and the computer 'revolution'-for civilization itself"? *The Destruction of Black Civilization*, Chancellor Williams, pg. 94

Slipping Into Darkness

We are told, by the media and the government, how, we as Americans are progressing. Progress is a word invented by European scholars. It is intimately connected to technological advances and the economic mega-boom of big business. Much to the dismay of the average citizen, the price to humanity for progress is way of the scale in terms of the human suffering caused by the so-called progress. **We are progressing further into darkness.** The damage to the ecological system (Mother earth) and to the real quality of life cannot be measured. Cancer, the nation's number one deadliest disease, is directly related to progress; the chemical pollution and food additives. The oceans and seas are being contaminated with oil, plastic and other chemical pollutants. The local rivers and streams are becoming unfit for humans. Many are already at dangerously toxic levels. The vital rain forests are being destroyed for lumber.

The growth hormones given to livestock have been identified as a factor in the cause of more than 60% of Americans being obese. **Immorality is being openly promoted by the media networks.** The food chain is being tampered with without the public's knowledge. Scientist, with questionable morals and ethics are probing the genetic code of human life. **The United States has the largest prison population in the world, yet crime is rampant throughout the states.** Healthy families have all but become extinct. The dreaded sexually transmitted disease "Aids" has reached epidemic levels in some communities. **Abortion in America has killed over 40 million babies. Life for the average citizen is stressed, alienated, meaningless, confused, depressed, violent and fearful. Yet our government and media continue to report that we are progressing. Progressing toward what is the question. Destruction is the answer.**

The majority of African American families are single parent. With most African Americans, finances are a problem. Our children are totally out of control. Dissension and division plague the black family. Yes, we have progressed, we're in the midst of a "great technological revolution", but the effect it has had on the quality of life is very unsettling. **These are dark times and America needs the Church to be the light it talks about!**

The State of the Church

There is a stark contrast between the priest and clergymen of Euro-Christianity and the early African/Egyptian priesthood. The church and state had to be separated in Western societies, not because the two should not work together, but because of the corruption of the Church which was in reality competing with various States for worldly power. Wherever and whenever the Church has welded power, the people were always oppressed and exploited.

Consequently, neither Black nor White Churches have been a factor in providing light for the dark world in which we live today. Today the clergy have reversed things from the way it was in ancient Africa among the priesthood. Today, the Clergy expect the congregation to bless them. Instead of blessing the people, **today's class of clergymen, take the money coming into the church and build their own personal little kingdoms full of the little material trinkets that they lust and crave after. Instead of teaching the people all knowledge pertaining to life, they grow fat in their gluttony for the riches of this world, and for glory they have not earned!**

Not since the days of the ancient African/Egyptian priest have this profession been free of corruption. This fact is quite significant and worthy of note by those clergy in positions of leadership today, and their followers.

The Black Church has White Roots

The Black Church continues to grasps for the riches and power of this world. There has not been a change in how the medieval church operated and the Church of today, even in the black community. The **Church leaders continue to amass fortunes while too many believers live at or below the poverty level. The effect of the Black Church on the morals and ethics of the lives of the people is negligible.** In addition, the inter-rivalries make unity in the community nearly impossible. We need an alternative.

The roots of the Black Church are unmistakably white. African Americans did not come to America Christians nor is Christianity the original religion of Blacks. It was spoon fed to early slaves by White evangelist from both the North and South. There is not one Black Denomination that did not get its original pattern from a White Denomination. In fact each original Black Church sought legitimacy from its White counterpart. The Black Baptist sought the approval of the White Baptist to organize a separate church. Even the African Methodist went to the White Methodist to ask permission to organize the African Methodist Church.

It is interesting to note that in spite of these facts, out of ignorance and a seeming lack of choices, African Americans continue to delight in calling themselves Christians and Catholics. This is equivalent to Jewish people embracing the world outlook of Nazism and joining Nazi organizations. We must take our proverbial "heads out the sand" quit being "Ostrich Christians" and acknowledge the truth about Christianity so that we can reach a conclusion based on knowledge rather than instinct, emotions and blind faith.

listen!

Black Preachers, hopefully, will one day no longer tell Black congregations about how a White man is going to "one day" save them from their hellish condition, and began to tell them of the need to save them selves. They will no longer direct Blacks to look outside of themselves for salvation; for salvation lies within the Kingdom which is within each man and woman. We all must "save' ourselves if we would be saved. The truth is that we all must resurrect our spirit man, the hidden man of the heart. This man must be set free and only the Truth will affect his release. That would be good fruit. **The strange fruit must be replaced with "good fruit". For that we need a new tree, a "good tree".**

Chapter 4

WHAT EURO-CHRISTIANITY STOLE

THIEVES IN THE TEMPLE

George James in *"Stolen Legacy"* documented the fact that what had been presented to the world as Greek Mythology was really stolen African Mythology and Cosmology. This chapter takes that case a step further and asserts that Euro-Christianity is stolen African Mythology and Cosmology as well. Many scholars have already documented the fact that the symbols, myths, language, rituals, holy-days, and moral teachings of Euro-Christianity were all plagiarized from the teachings of the Mystery Schools of Ancient Egypt/Africa. **Euro-Christianity is a fraud because it misrepresents itself as original when actually it took African myths and teachings revamped them and gave them back to the world as something they had received directly from god. There is no denying it, the truth is written on stone on the walls of the temples of Africa and on recently discovered documents. What they have, they stole. The focus of this chapter is the specifics of what was stolen.**

Stolen Concepts and Symbols

- THE MYTH OF A SAVIOR GOD
- THE 4 NATIVITY SCENES (WRITTEN IN STONE ON THE TEMPLE WALLS)
- THE TRINITY
- THE IMMACULATE CONCEPTION
- THE SYMBOL FOR LIFE CALLED THE ANKH (ORIGIN OF THE CROSS)

- THE CREATION STORY
- THE TEN COMMANDMENTS
- AFRICAN HOLY-DAYS NOW CALLED HOLIDAYS (CHRISTMAS AND EASTER)
- AFRICAN GODS AND OUR DEITIES
- THE RESURRECTION
- ETERNAL LIFE
- AFRICAN SACRED AND HOLY SCRIPTURES
- JUDGMENT DAY
- CONCEPT OF ONE GOD

The Tricksters called the "Jacobites"

In addition, and perhaps most critical, Euro-Christianity stole the inheritance of African Americans and other Africans in the Diaspora. They can be rightly labeled the "Jacobites of Antiquity". As Jacob tricked Esau out of his "rightful inheritance", so has the European tricked the African out of his inheritance? He took the wisdom of Africa, changed some names and Europeanized it, and gave it back to the African as a "new and improved" word from god, His final word; His only legitimate word.

Grand Theft

Theft and fraud on such a grand scale has never been duplicated. And certainly no other theft was to have such great and grave ramifications. This crime has affected the fate of all humanity. Speaking of duplicating; that is exactly what the Europeans did. They made a copy! The extent of the duplications is proof beyond any reasonable doubt that the teachings of Euro-Christianity were plagiarized. Let us review the testimonies and confessions that solve the mystery of this "the most disastrous crime in history". We will begin with the biblical story of Jacob, Esau and Esau's birthright. Its relevance will soon be made clear. It highlights a "key piece" to the puzzle.

"But Jacob said, 'Sell me your birthright as of this day'. And Esau said, 'Look I am about to die; so what is this birthright to me"? Then Jacob said, 'Swear to me as of this day'. So he swore to him, and sold his birthright to Jacob. And Jacob gave Esau bread and stew of lentils; then he ate and drank, and went his way. Thus Esau despised his birthright". **Genesis 25:31-34**

"Now Rebekah was listening when Isaac spoke to Esau his son. And Esau went to the field to hunt game and to bring it. So Rebekah spoke to Jacob her

son, saying, 'Indeed I heard your father speak to Esau your brother, saying', bring me game and make me savory food for me, that I may eat it and bless you in the presence of the Lord before my death'. Now therefore, my son, obey my voice according to what I command you. 'Go now to the flock and bring me from there two choice kids of the goats, and I will make savory food from them for your father, such as he loves" **Genesis 27:5-10 NKJV**

"So he went to his father and said, 'My father'. And he said, 'Here I am. Who are you, my son'? Jacob said to his father, 'I am Esau your firstborn; I have done just as you told me; please arise, sit and eat of my game, that your soul may bless me'. Then Isaac said to Jacob, 'Please come near, that I may feel you, my son, whether you are really my son Esau or not'. So Jacob went near to Isaac his father, and he felt him and said, 'The voice is Jacob's but the hands are the hands of Esau'. And he did not recognize him, because his hands were hairy like his brother Esau's hands; so he blessed him. Then he said, 'Are you really my son Esau'? He said, 'I am'. He said 'bring it near me, and I will eat of my son's game, so that my soul may bless you'. So he brought it near him, and he ate; and he brought wine, and he drank. Then his father Isaac said to him, 'Come near now and kiss me, my son'. And he came near and kissed him; and he smelled the smell of his clothing, and blessed him and said:

...therefore may God give you
...of the dew of heaven,
...of the fatness of the earth
...and plenty of grain and wine.
<u>*...Let peoples serve you*</u>
<u>*...and nations bow down to you.*</u>
<u>*...Be master over your brethren,*</u>
<u>*...and let your mother's son's bow down*</u>
<u>*to you*</u>... **Genesis 27:19-29**

"But He said, 'Your brother came with deceit and has taken away your blessing'. And Esau said, 'is he not rightly named Jacob? For he has supplanted me these two times. He took away my birthright, and now look, he has taken away by blessing'! **Genesis 27:35-36**

According to this scripture, Esau despised his birthright, and made light of it. He took his birthright for granted. Jacob on the other hand placed great value on Esau's birthright, he wanted to be first. He lusted for Esau's

85

possession. **To him it was priceless. He treasured the blessing of his "father". The problem is that he stooped to cunning and deceit to secure his coveted prize.** So Jacob stole Esau's birthright and his blessing. In the same way, Western man envied the Africans place in society. Africans were esteemed a great people by their neighbors. Western man decided to steal the Africans birthright and the blessing that rightfully belonged to the African. Through trickery and deceit Western man took what belong to his brother. Yet, a corrupt beginning can only result in establishing a house built on corruption. Though in the context of this passage, it appears that God blesses this mess, in reality the universe does not like to be fooled. In fact, it cannot.

The Motivation for the Crime-The Key

At one time, the black man had established a great inheritance for his seed. Today, that birthright is despised by black people. It is taken for granted and is not considered valuable at all. African Americans as Esau, think little of their inheritance of wisdom, the wisdom that would be the source of great blessing. African Americans are too concerned with survival and chasing the American Dream to be concerned with their inheritance. In contrast, Western man saw the value of the wisdom of Africa. It caused him to lust for the African's position. He wanted to be esteemed above other races of men like the African. He wanted others to serve him.

Western man began to plot and scheme. He came up with a plan. He would steal the Africans birthright and tell the African that he never had one. Western man began to claim Africa's history and accomplishments as their own. Next they claimed the African's wisdom and knowledge as their own. Plagiarism is intellectual theft. Euro-Christianity is built on lies, corruption and falsehoods with a thread of Truth. **For this reason, scripture has to be rightly divided, and opened up, because until now, the Truth has had a veil placed over it.** Let us examine the evidence and watch this crime of mega proportions unfold.

> Throughout the ages the losers in any conflict have been forced to give up their wealth, their women and their knowledge. "Egypt was systematically raped and pillaged for more than a century before academicians developed an archaeological methodology for excavations. By then, countless monuments had been destroyed, thousands of papyri and mummies were burned and some of the finest statuary in the world had been spirited away in private collections". *Nile Valley Contributions To Civilization,* Anthony T. Browder, pg.189

The First Sacred Scriptures

The "Holy men of old", who were inspired of God to write the original "Holy Scripture", resided in the original "Holy Land", in North Africa. All other sacred "text" can be traced back to this original "Word of God".

"The so-called 'Book of the Dead' was a compilation of the prayers that were inscribed on the walls of the tombs or written on papyrus scrolls, which were buried with the dead. These sacred pronouncements were discovered by the grave robbers who violated these tombs in search of fame and glory, and regarded these writings as 'the books of the dead'. According to Wallace Budge, celebrated translator of the Book of the Dead, **"these texts were...known to have existed in revised editions and to have been used among the Egyptians from B.C. 4500 to the early centuries of the Christian era".** Budge admits that the correct name for the 'Book of the Dead' is derived from the words (pert em hru), which has been translated as 'coming forth by day', a reference to the rebirth or resurrection of the soul of the deceased, a concept that first existed in the Nile Valley". *Nile Valley Contributions To Civilization,* Anthony T. Browder, pg. 87

"There are a number of significant religious references which emerged from the 'Book of the Coming Forth by Day', they include:

The conception of heaven
The soul of man going to heaven
The soul of man sitting on a throne by the side of God
God molding man from clay
God breathing the breath of life into man's nostrils
The concept of creation through the spoken word
Moral concepts of good and evil
Traditions of hell and hell fire. *Nile Valley Contributions To Civilization,* Anthony T. Browder, pg. 88

All these concepts were stolen from Africa's storehouse of wisdom. Most of the concepts were miss-understood by the European founders of Christianity. Absolutely no credit is given to the Africans as the originators of the concepts. This is done by whitewashing the Egyptians who developed the wisdom and changing their racial make-up. Most of these concepts, because of Western mans lack of understanding, have been presented to the world in a corrupt and perverted form, that form however, has been presented to the world as the unadulterated <u>"Word of God"</u>.

First Nativity Scene

The evidence for this aspect of the crime cannot be hidden or denied. It is written on stone on one of the Holy Temple walls in Africa. It must be entered in as evidence and proof that the "Holy child", the child of prophecy, was born in Africa.

Carved on the walls of the Temple of Luxor (circa 1380 B.C.E.) are scenes which depict the following:

1. The Annunciation-The Netcher Djhuiti is shown announcing to the virgin the coming birth of their son, Heru.
2. The Immaculate Conception-The Netcher Kneph, who represents the Holy Ghost, and the Netcher Het-Heru (Hathor) are shown symbolically impregnating Aset by holding ankhs (symbols of life) to the nostrils of the virgin mother-to-be.
3. The Virgin Birth-Aset Is shown sitting on the birthing stool and the newborn child is attended by midwives.
4. The Adoration-The newborn Heru is portrayed receiving gifts from three kings, or Magi while being adored by a host of gods and men. *Nile Valley Contributions To Civilization,* Anthony T. Browder, pg. 95

"In the appendix to *Ancient Egypt*, Massey listed more than 200 direct parallels between the Jesus legend and the Osiris-Horus cycle. The earthly Jesus is equivalent to Horus; Jesus the Christ corresponds to Osiris, the resurrected God". *Nile Valley Contributions To Civilization*, Anthony T. Browder, pg. 60

Gerald Massey *(Ancient Egypt)* says, "The Black Jesus is a well known form of child Christ worshipped on the continent of Europe". *Nile Valley Contributions To Civilization*, Anthony T. Browder, pg. 67

First Trinity

That the concept of the "Trinity" was given "birth" in Africa, where the first trinity of the Father, and the Mother and Son is found, is a no-brainer:

"The story of Ausar, Aset and Heru is the first story in the recorded history of man of a holy royal family (the Trinity), immaculate conception, virgin birth and resurrection. Evidence of this Trinity is known to have existed in ancient Nubia as late as 3300 B.C.E.

Larousse Universal Dictionary, in referring to Isis says: "One of the most ancient of the divinities of Egypt, she formed with Osiris, at the same time for son and husband, a mythical trinity in which is to be found the Holy Trinity of the Christian religion". *Sex and Race*, J.A. Rogers, pg. 75

First to use the Concept of the Immaculate Conception

The "Immaculate Conception", another concept, essential to Euro-Christianity, is a stolen African concept. In the eyes of the African priest and nation all of creation was immaculately created by the one Creator who needed no consort to birth anything. There is a picture drawn in stone depicting the scene of the "Immaculate Conception" of Heru.

"Aset was without child before the murder of Ausar, but by means of certain powerful words given to her by the Netcher Djhuiti (Thoth), who represents divine articulation of speech, Aset resurrected her slain husband. **Shortly thereafter, Aset conceived a Child upon being immaculately impregnated by the spirit of her husband and gave birth to a son, Heru (Horus),** who avenged the death of his father by slaying his uncle Set. He (Ausar) was commonly referred to as the 'good shepherd' and is the personification of the cycles of death and rebirth, and of spiritual salvation". *Nile Valley Contributions To Civilization,* Anthony T. Browder, pg. 89

"...if the parallels between the mythological history of Isis and Horus and the history of the Mary and the Child be considered, it is difficult to see how (Europeans) could possibly avoid perceiving in the teaching of Christianity reflections of the best and most spiritual doctrines of the Egyptian religion". *The Gods of Egypt*, Sir E.A. Wallis Budge, pg. 189

"In fact, the earliest statues of the Virgin Mary and Christ in Europe as far north as Russia were Black. And even today, evidence can be found of this. In Poland, she is called the Black Madonna of Czestochowa. In Spain, there is a Black Madonna from Nuria called the 'Queen of the

Pyrenees'. In Russia, Notre Dame of Kazar is a Black Virgin. One can find a Black Christ: In France, the Cathedral of Milan. In Germany, the Cathedral of Augsburg. In Italy, the Church of San Francisco (at Pisa)". *Sex and Race,* Vol. I, J.A. Rogers

The Ankh and the Origin of the Cross

The "cross" is also a very obvious mutation and perversion of an original African symbol. Today the cross of Euro-Christianity symbolizes the death of God's son, whereas the Ankh represented his resurrection. This resurrection is depicted in stone within an African temple as well. In the scene which depicts the restoration of life to Horus, the Ankh is placed to his nostrils and he is given life.

"**The ankh was the ancient Kemetic symbol for life. It represented the unification of the feminine and masculine forces in the universe and the creation of new life. It portrayed both the physical and spiritual aspects of life. Symbolically, the oval represents the womb, the vertical shaft depicts the phallus and the horizontal bar expresses the coming of new life, resulting from the union of man and woman.** The cross is a symbol common to Christianity. During the Middle Ages, the cross was a symbol of the Christian belief in the resurrection of Jesus the Christ. **Much later, Christians began to emphasize the death and suffering of Jesus and portrayed his image on crucifixes. A crucifix is a cross with the image of the dying Jesus**". *Nile Valley Contributions To Civilization,* Anthony T. Browder, pg. 67

The First Creation Story

The "creation story" is a definite duplication. It first appeared in a Memphite, Egyptian cosmology. It was also written in stone centuries before the fraudulent appearance of the creation story of Euro-Christianity:

"Ancients believed that creation came into existence through various methods. One method was creating through utterance (command), such as we find in the biblical narrative. **The creative 'word' idea also appears in a Memphite Egyptian cosmogony. Ptah, the most high god of Memphis, created everything by his word (heart and tongue).** Though this extant account is dated 700 B.C.E., it derives from an original text dating from two thousand years earlier. The 'work' was the activation power of Ptah's thoughts. His 'heart' (mind) represented thought, and his 'tongue' (word) was the symbol of command, or power". *The Mysteries of Creation,* Rocco A Errico, pg. 91-92

"Light is usually the first creative act described in early Mesopotamian cosmologies. For instance, in the Egyptian cosmogony of Hermopolis, light appears immediately after chaos. **The biblical creation account also follows this order making light primary. However, there is a major difference between these accounts. Light is divine in the Egyptian epic.** In Genesis 1, light is not divinity. It is simply a creation of God". *The Mysteries of Creation,* Rocco A Errico, pg. 96

"One of the greatest African Ethiopian temples was located at Abu Simbel, or Isambul, in Nubia. **When an English traveler named Wilson visited this temple, he saw sculptured on its walls the story of the Fall of Man as told in Genesis. Adam and Eve were shown in the Garden of Eden as well as the tempting serpent and the fatal tree".** Commenting on this fact, Godfrey Higgins asked: **"How is the fact of the mythos of the second book of Genesis being found in Nubia, probably a thousand miles above Heliopolia, to be accounted for"?** Anacalypsis, Vol. I, pg. 403

Such facts cannot be denied or explained away. You cannot claim that what you have is an original if I have the same thing which was produced prior to yours. My version would have to be the original. Your claim would be rejected and dismissed as an obvious fraud in any just court of law. **The realm of religion appears to be exempt from this fact, but it is not. You cannot steal another people's religion, symbols, myths, sacred days, and deities, and pretend to be their author.** Though the state and government may give the church this license to commit this major crime, there is a higher court. Its judgment is both righteous and true and certain.

> **"The world's first religious principle was substantiated. It was verified when a slab of basalt was unearthed in Egypt bearing an inscription with Cushitic script relating to a treatise on the moral concept of Right and Wrong by King Ori in the year 3758 B.C.E. King Ori declared that they are 'Moral forces of God".** *Nile Valley and His Family,* Prof. Yosef Ben-Jochannan

They Even Stole The 10 Commandments

I believe the eighth commandment, forbids man to steal. Yet, this commandment is blatantly violated in the theft of the "Ten Commandments" by Euro-Christianity. This is no surprised since Euro-Christians have almost never adhered to the teachings they have forced on others.

"The 10 Commandments originally came from the 42 negative confessions of the Black Egyptians (4100 BC) from the Book of the Dead and Papyrus of Ani:

NEGATIVE CONFESSIONS (4100 BC)

1. I have not committed theft
2. I have not slain man or woman
3. I have not uttered falsehood
4. I have not defiled the wife of a man

TEN COMMANDMENTS (700 BC)

1. Thou shalt not steal
2. Thou shalt not kill
3. Thou shalt not bear false witness against thy neighbor
4. Thou shalt not commit adultery

SOURCE: *Tutankhamen's African Roots*, Haley

Stolen African Holy-Days

Nothing was too sacred to be stolen. Even the origin of the two key holidays of Euro-Christianity was celebrated in Africa, long before the advent of Christianity. The decision to keep the African holidays was a compromise calculated to make the new religion acceptable to the Africans. Even the Jewish "Passover" is taken from African mythology and originated among the Africans.

> **"She (the Church) utilized the gods by making their (Egyptians) festivals the days of commemoration of the Christian saints or even took them over bodily and adopted them so that Isis and Horus became the Virgin Mother and her son..."** *Biblical Anthropology*, H.J D. Astley, pg. 74

The Liberation of the African Mind

"In the Story of Civilization, Vol. IV, Will Durant writes: 'Statues of Isis and Horus were renamed Mary and Jesus; the Roman Lupercalia **and the Feast of the Purification of Isis became the Feast of the Nativity; the Saturnalia were replaced by the Christmas celebration".** *Biblical Anthropology*, H.J D. Astley, pg. 74

Aside from Professor ben-Jochannan's work on the subject of Black Hebrews, others have expressed similar opinions, J.A. Rogers writes: **"The Falashas, or Black Jews of Ethiopia are probably very ancient. They claim lineal descent from Abraham, Isaac and Jacob,** call themselves Beta-Israel (The Chosen People) and **observe the Passover".** *What They Never Told You In History Class*, Indus Khamit Kush, pg. 208

Stolen Deities

Many of the African "Deities" or symbolic gods, were simply renamed and made white, but kept some of their original African meanings. One deity, namely Heru or Horus, Egypt's "son of God" became an idol God in Christendom under a different name. The parallels are too pronounced and too numerous to overlook or deny.

"In both the Nile Valley account and the Christian account, God is self-created, creates heaven and earth, divides the waters, creates the light and separates it from the darkness and creates man. **The parallels between these two religious systems are numerous and striking,** but because much of the early research on Kemet was conducted by Christians, historical information was doctored to suit their particular religious beliefs". *Nile Valley Contributions To Civilization,* Anthony T. Browder, pg. 86

J.A. Rogers boldly proclaims: **"the earliest Gods and Messiahs on all the continents were black".** *What They Never Told You,* Indus Khamit Kush, pg. 45

"One of the elements most often duplicated in Europe was that of the African concept of God. The Netcher of the Nile Valley evolved to become the gods of the Greeks and Romans. The names of the African Holy Royal Family of Ausar, Aset and Heru were changed by the Greeks to Osiris, Isis and Horus. They were later referred to as the "Father, Son and Holy Ghost in early Christendom". *Nile Valley Contributions To Civilization*, Anthony T. Browder, pg. 189

93

"Very few people realize that on Easter Sunday as the Pope stands on his balcony overlooking the multitudes and delivers his sermon praising the resurrection of the son of God, Jesus the Christ, he faces a 6,000 year old symbol that represents the resurrection of the Nile Valley Netcher Ausar". *Nile Valley Contributions To Civilization,* Anthony T. Browder, pg. 191

Everlasting Life is an African Concept

A pivotal concept of Euro-Christianity is the concept of everlasting life. This concept is again obviously Egyptian/African. Some of the pyramids were built as tombs to house eternally, the physical bodies of the kings who had gone on to the other life.

"The people of the Nile Valley were the first human beings to express a profound belief in a doctrine of everlasting life. They preserved the bodies of their dead by a yet undiscovered process of embalming, and entombed these bodies in elaborately inscribed funerary monuments. Prayers and litanies played a major role in preparing the soul of the recently departed for its journey through the underworld and guaranteed its safe passage to God in the next world". *Nile Valley Contributions To Civilization*, Anthony T. Browder, pg. 87

Stolen Scripture and Sacred Text

It has been documented that the first sacred scriptures were produced and published by Africans and that the majority of European religious text is merely copies and paraphrases of these earlier text.

COMPARISON BETWEEN AKHENATON'S HYMM TO THE ATON AND PSALM 104

Akhenaton's Hymn (1353 B.C.)
The world is in darkness like the dead.
Every lion cometh forth from its den:
all serpents sting. Darkness reigns.
When Thou risest in the horizon…the
darkness is banished. Then in all the
world they do their work.

All the trees and plants flourish, the birds
flutter in their marshes…all sheep
dance upon their feet.

The ships sail up stream and down stream
alike… The fish in the river leap up
before thee; and thy rays are in the
Midst of the great sea.

How manifold are all Thy works!…Thou
didst create the earth according to
Thy desire, men all cattle…all that
Are upon the earth.

Psalm 104 (1000 B.C.)

Thou makest the darkness and it is night,
wherein all the beasts of the forest do creep forth
The young lions roar after their prey

The sun riseth…Man goeth forth unto his
work and to his labour until evening.

The trees of the Lord are full of sap…wherein the birds make their nests…
The high hills are a refuge for the wild goats.

So is this great and wide sea, wherein are things creeping innumerable,
both small and great and beasts…There go the ships.

O Lord how manifold are thy works! In wisdom Thou made them all…The
earth is full of thy creatures.
Nile Valley Contributions To Civilization, Anthony T. Browder, P. 94

If that does not convince you that the books of the Bible are duplicates and copies, what will it take???

Egypt, an exquisitely illustrated art book, by Ceres Wissa Wassef, contains a similar connection: "The Book of Proverbs has much in common with Egyptian collections of wise sayings; it contains in particular several profound ideas adapted from the teachings of Amenemhet (first millennium BC*)*". *What They Never Told You*, Indus Khamit Kush, pg. 207

"The earliest examples of Egyptian ethical philosophy were maxims of sage advice similar to those of the Book of Proverbs and the Book of Ecclesiastes in the Old Testament". *World Civilizations, 5ᵗʰ Ed.* W.W. Norton, N.Y., pg. 37

The Proverbs of Solomon came from the Wisdom of a Black Egyptian named Amen-En-Eope:

SOLOMON'S PROVERBS
---Beware of robbing the poor
---And of oppressing the afflicted
---Consider these thirty chapters
---They delight, they instruct
---Knowledge how to answer him that speaketh

AMEN-EN-EOPE'S WISDOM
---Rob not the poor for he is poor
---Neither oppress the lowly gate
---Have I not written for thee thirty sayings
---Of counsels and knowledge
---That thou mayest make known truth to him that speaketh
Black Man of the Nile and His Family, Yusef A. ben-Jochannan

Stolen Wisdom

After the conquerors have stolen the women and the wealth, sooner or later They get around to stealing the wisdom. That is if the wisdom of the conquered exceeds that of the conquerors. Plato, Aristotle, Pythagoras, and numerous other Greeks took part in this phase of the crime. Incidentally, both Plato and Aristotle are given credit for having considerable input in the shaping of Euro-Christian philosophy and doctrine.

"The creation of this new center of learning was due in part to Alexander's conquering of Egypt and the closing of the numerous temples and universities that were situated along the Nile River. **Hundreds of thousands of papyrus scrolls were taken to Alexandria, where they were translated, catalogued into ten subject areas, arranged alphabetically by author and stored in the ten research halls designated for specific fields of study.** The library also contained an observatory, dissecting rooms, botanical gardens, a zoo and lecture halls. The library was also a center of religious research. **It was where the Hellenized Jewish** scholars produced the first Greek translation of the Old Testament, the Septuagint". *Nile Valley Contributions To Civilization,* Anthony T. Browder, Pg. 162-163

"The whole Christian Bible was derived from the sacred books of Egypt, such as: The Book of the Dead, The Pyramid Texts and the Books of Thoth". *What They Never Told You,* Indus Khamit Kush, pg. 63

Stolen Images

The amount of stolen images is phenomenal even the United States government got in on the Grand Theft. In front of the White House, stands a replica of what has been renamed: obelisks. The American Dollar has the Egyptian pyramid with the "Eye of Heru" as its capstone.

"There are host of images from Kemet which have also made their way into religious iconography. **The paintings and carvings of the winged Netcher Maat served as the protype for the Christian concept of the angel.** Maat represented the principles of truth, righteousness and reciprocity and her symbol of the 'scale of justice' was used to weigh the souls on **their day of judgment.** In some religious paintings of the Middle Ages, images of the angel of God can be seen holding the scale of Maat". *Nile Valley Contributions To Civilization*, Anthony T. Browder, pg. 191

"These ram-headed edifices represented the Netcher 'Amen' who was also referred to as 'Amun' and 'Amon'. This name means 'hidden' and refers to the hidden or unseen presence of God. **This word is still used today at the conclusion of many prayers, and is a lasting reminder of the powerful influence of ancient Kemetic Religion".** *Nile Valley Contributions To Civilization*, Anthony T. Browder, pg. 118

Stolen History

The history of the "Chosen People" in the bible is the history of the African people, manipulated to appear as if it was all about the nations of Europeans. This theft enabled the European to steal our birthright and our blessings. It is blessed to observe the trend in the Black Church toward recognizing and accepting its own culture. Many are taking African names and wearing traditional African garments to church. **We must go further however, than merely "blackenizing" Euro-Christianity. This has been the trend all along in the Black Church. We must take back all that Western Man has taken.**

"In the words of a distinguished American disciple of Gerald Massey, Dr. Alvin Boyd Kuhn: **"The entire Christian creation legend descent into and exodus from Egypt, ark and flood allegory, Israelite history, Hebrew prophecy and poetry, Gospel, Epistles and Revelation imagery, all are now proven to have been the transmission of ancient Egypt's scrolls and papyri into the hands of later generations which knew neither their true origin nor their fathomless meaning".** *What They Never Told You In History Class,* **Indus Khamit Kush, pg. 64**

Stolen Prophets

Recently, it has been established that most of the prophets were in fact black. Someone expended a lot of effort toward keeping the racial identity of key biblical characters known to be African a secret. Lately, there has been a move within the Black Church to recognize and honor these prophets as Blacks. The prophet Zephaniah is documented in scripture as being of "Hamitic" blood. **"Luke is perhaps the only author in the Bible who would be classified as a son of Japheth (European). Luke was a Greek"** *(Beyond Roots: In Search of Blacks in the Bible,* William D. Mckissic, pg. *49).* **Recognizing that Adam, David, Solomon, Joshua, Jesus and other key figures of the scripture were black is undoubtedly a positive step, yet the full significance of these facts has not been discerned.**

Africans even Practiced Circumcism First

"Circumcism", a religious ritual practiced by Jews and the American Medical Association, originated in Africa:

> "There can be no doubt that the Colchians are an Egyptian race…My own conjectures were founded first in the fact they are BLACK-SKINNED and have WOOLLY HAIR, which certainly amounts to little since several other nations are so too, but further and more especially on the circumstance that the Colchians, the Egyptians and the Ethiopians are the only nations who have practiced circumcision from the earliest of time". *Herodotus Histories, Book III*, pg. 104

The Ark of the Covenant and The Holy of Holies

The "Ark of the Covenant", a key piece in the history and development of Euro-Christianity, comes from Africa. The "Holy of Holies" is also African. The temples of worship in Africa were constructed according to the pattern, described in the first five books of the Old Testament.

> "The Ark of the Covenant, built and set up by Moses in the wilderness, according to the Sacred volume-and which has not been seen-is precisely similar in all measurements to the 'Stone Chest' still to be seen in the King's Chamber of the Great Pyramid and which is undoubtedly the original, although the contents are gone. According to the ritual, it should have contained the 'Coffined One', and we know that miniatures of this used to be carried around the Egyptian temples at Memphis on state occasions during religious rites". *Black Man of the Nile and His Family*, Prof. Yusef A. Ben-Jochannan

THIEVES IN THE TEMPLE

From the evidence presented, there can be no doubt that "thieves" had gotten in the "temple" and stolen all of the material for what was is now called Christianity and the Bible. Sacred scripture was reworked and returned to the Africans and the world in a "new and improved" version. Only the original was accurate however, undoubtedly the new version lacks any real improvements. Wake up Black America!

> **"In a different work I suggested that a major reason why so many later Christian missionaries failed in Africa was because they were bringing refurbished religious doctrines that came from Africa in the first place.** The religious belief in sacrifice for the remission of sins was an African belief and practiced at least 2,000 years before Abraham". *The Destruction of Black Civilization,* Chancellor Williams, pg. 69.

> **"While the people and history of Africa were being appropriated, their religion, philosophy, science, and symbols were stripped of all traces of their Africanness, modified to suit a new cultural orientation and then reintroduced into society as 'original creations'.** When Kemet was conquered by foreigners, it was not uncommon to find the images of African personalities modified to reflect the appearance of the new rulers of the nation." *Nile Valley Contributions To Civilization,* Anthony T. Browder, pg. 227

"A small statue of a Sphinx on display in the British Museum actually states that the 'face of the statue was reworked' during the Roman occupation of Egypt. A visit to the catacombs of Alexandria, Egypt, reveals numerous images of African Netcher with European faces. **The constant manipulation of African images reflect a psychological need that the foreigners had to project themselves into a history and culture that was not their own".** *Nile Valley Contributions To Civilization,* Anthony T. Browder, pg. 227

Stolen Religion

Euro-Christianity is emphatically stolen African cosmology and philosophy. Every essential concept, symbol, myth and history is African. This immolation of African culture should be taken as the highest form of flattery by African Americans.

"According to Dr. Martin Bernal of Cornell University, the Greeks and Romans believed that their religion came from Egypt up until about 100 A.D. Furthermore, Egyptian religion survives in Christianity itself. It is more accurately to view Christianity as a Judaeo-Egypto religion, rather than a Judaeo-Greek religion, though the New Testament was written in Greek and was influenced by Greek culture". *African Civilizations as Cornerstones for the Oikoumene,* Lawrence E. Carter

It was an African who first declared to the world, there is but one God. His name was Akhnaton. This is monotheism not polytheism. This concept was widely accepted among Africans and was the foundation of their society and civilization. It is time to face-up and fess-up.

That, which the Western man has presented to the world as Christianity, was stolen from Africa and the holy people of that ancient land. They stole it and we have to take it back. They have taken that which was sacred and profaned it. The very act of theft was profane. They took something, which was pure and corrupted and contaminated it because of their vile affections and lust for worldly power and riches.

truly vile and evil

100

AND NOW FOR OUR FINAL WITNESS!

> **"Professor Churchward in his work Origin and Evolution of Religion holds that the African Pygmies and the Negroes were the real originators of Christian religion".** *Sex and Race, Vol. I,* J.A. Rogers

THE VERDICT IS IN…GUILTY!

Chapter 5

WHAT EURO-CHRISTIANITY ADDED

<u>THE DOCTRINES AND COMMANDMENTS OF MEN</u>

"Hypocrites! Well did Isaiah prophesy about you, saying: These people draw near Me with their mouths, and honor Me with their lips, but their heart is far from Me. And in vain they worship Me. Teaching as doctrine the commandments of men". **Matthew 15:7-9**

It is a sad fact, but it is true; much of what is taught from the pulpit today has come down to us not from God, but from men. There are four major factors that contributed to the development of "Doctrines and Commandments of men": (1) The desire of the framers of Christian doctrine to control the thoughts and actions of men, (2) The inability of the Church fathers especially the Greek fathers to comprehend the mysteries hidden in the scriptures, (3) The racist and sexist attitudes of the early Church priest and clergymen, (4) The lust for power and material wealth.

<u>The Word Within the Word</u>

Here the process of rightly dividing what is true from what is false in Christian doctrine and dogma intensifies. This chapter reflects a very important process in the effort to de-mystify and add clarity to the interpretation of scriptures. **As seen in the above scripture, some of the doctrines that were preached during the time of the formation of Christianity were not inspired by God. What is of importance is that the doctrines of men produce a form of worship that** is hypocritical. **They do not produce godliness among believers. Its fruit is merely a form of godliness.**

Today we see the truth of this statement as the sins of the Church are exposed daily in the news. It is even more important at this time to expose the inadequate attempts by Western scholars and clergy to interpret what they stole from Africa's holy men. There is "a word within the Word" which must be rightly divided from what has been added and corrupted. In order to do so we must have knowledge of the original design. This chapter challenges the fundamental doctrines of Christianity.

> **"Unfortunately the magnificent original intuitions of the great masters very often lose their vitality as they pass down the generations. They often are modified, distorted and turned into dogmas, and all too frequently their values become petrified in institutions and organized hierarchies. The pure intuitions are choked by the sands of time, and eventually have to be dug out by seekers of Truth able to penetrate into their essence".** *The Essene Book of Creation,* Edmond Bordeaux Sxekely, pg. 8

Doctrines of Men are Doctrines of Control

It is said in order to understand a thing find first its reason for being created. To understand Christianity we must first determine who created it and why. Christianity as we know it today officially began at a meeting in Nicaea. This was called the Nicene Council. For it was in Nicaea that the fundamental belief of Christianity was laid. The fundamental belief in Christianity is that Jesus was God in the flesh. In this chapter we will begin to take a look at this fundamental belief and how it came to be the basic tenet of Christianity. The idea of Jesus as God will be discussed in depth in Volume II. One thing which should become apparent to the reader is that the acceptance of this belief which many today accept on an emotional whim took great pains to get established within the first Christian church.

Another apparent fact is that the methods used to establish this belief were not Christian in substance or appearance. The foundation was laid but the building material used were fear, intimidation, hypocrisy, arrogance, ignorance, manipulation, violence and very little if any demonstration of righteous or holy character.

In addition, the bishops who participated in the Nicene Council did so under the ever present threat of excommunication from the Church. This of course tainted the vote which would take place later. We will begin by looking into the character and actions of Emperor Constantine, the Greek emperor who is given credit by Christendom for its beginning. Emperor Constantine as we shall see is called the "Father" of Christianity because he was the central character in its formation. As we discovered in Chapter 3, "we are indebted to the power of Rome for the spread of Christianity throughout the world". (*Visualized Units Ancient Medieval History*)

Emperor Constantine saw in Christianity a means of control. Whether he understood how his tool would work is a mute point. He obviously understood the power of the appearance of God's sanctioning of his actions. He understood that backing his authority up with the authority of God would make him a very powerful man. In his eyes, his authority would go unchallenged if it could be made to appear that, his authority was given to him by God. It worked! The first Article of Faith was a Commandment of Men, the man who commanded that it be obeyed was the then all powerful emperor of Rome, Constantine. As confessing Christians, it is his commandment in which you have believed and accepted as Truth.

Though given credit for being the "Father of Christianity" there is very little discussion about this man in Christian circles. In addition, in some text he is grossly misrepresented making it necessary to shed some light on Constantine. As "the Founder" of Euro-Christianity, it is important that Christians and others be familiar with this man's character and deeds. Consider this testimony given by some contemporary historians:

> "Constantine the Great, the first Christian emperor of the Roman World, ...conceived and executed the design of summoning the Council of Nice; in which Synod he might exert all of his influence to effect a reconciliation among the contentious prelates and churches, as well as conciliate their favor, and unite all in support of his character and dominion." *History Of The First Council Of Nice*, Dean Dudley, pg. 24

The Encyclopedia Americana agrees with this assessment of Constantine's motivation:

> "But his zeal for Christianity was excited not less by the knowledge, that the religion, which was embraced by a majority of the Roman empire must prevail, and the strength of the government must be increased by

protecting it, than by a wish to apply its consoling powers of relief of a heavy conscience." *History Of The First Council Of Nice*, Dean Dudley, pg. 95

Two vital facts are established here: (1) That the religion of Christianity was established for temporal (worldly) power rather than spiritual edification. (2) That the originator of Christianity was Greek not African! These facts should cause those African Americans who have denied that it had European origins and those who say that its origins don't matter to seriously reconsider their position.

"The principal faults of this founder of the Christian power in Rome were, according to Mosheim, Gibbon and other historians, very similar to those of our English sovereign Henry VIII., founder of the Protestant ascendancy in Great Britain. He was willful, voluptuous, and self-conceited. His heart was capable of extreme cruelty, as shown by his acts toward several of his near relatives. Even his son, named Crispus, fell victim to his jealous resentment. He assumed that he was born to reign, and held his commission from God". *History Of The First Council Of Nice*, Dean Dudley, pg. 18

Gibbon says: "that, after Constantine had put his wife's father to death, in Gaul, he gained a victory over the Franks and Allemanni, and gave their chiefs to be devoured by wild beast in the public ampitheatre in Treves. Another historian says, a great number of French youth were also exposed to the same cruel and ignominious death. "Yet," says Gibbon, "his reign in Gaul, excepting his destruction of Maximian, seems to have been the most innocent and virtuous period of his life. *History Of The First Council Of Nice*, Dean Dudley, pg.18

Gibbon continues:

"In Constantine we may contemplate a hero, who so long inspired his subjects with love, and his enemies with terror, degenerating into a cruel and dissolute monarch, corrupted by his fortune, or rose by conquest, above the necessity of dissimulation. His old age was disgraced by the vices of rapaciousness and prodigality, and he lost the esteem of his subjects".

Mosheim says:

> "Constantine's life was not such as the precepts of Christianity required". He put to death his own son, and his wife Fausta, on a groundless suspicion, and cut off his brother-in-law Licinius and the unoffending son of Licinius, contrary to his plighted word. Nevertheless, the Greek Church has canonized him, and adores the memory of Constantine.-J.R. Schlegel

> "According to his (Constantine) plan, sovereigns were instruments to carry on the affairs of the world, so they might imitate the Heavenly King, and make laws for nations, slay their subjects at pleasure, as the laws of nature do, and wield the sword and fire, and every kind of vengeance, against their foes, without overstepping the bounds of their proper sphere; and whatever God allowed to be successful, bore the stamp of his approval, inasmuch as it would not have been permitted unless it were right. He was taught by the bishops that God sent his only Son to be crucified for the benefit of mankind; therefore a sovereign might order his son to sacrifice for the good and peace of society. Under the influence of such fanaticism, he perhaps committed all his bloody crimes without feeling their real enormity. But his character and influence cast a dark shade over the Christianity which he established. *History of the First Council of Nice,* Dean Dudley, pg. 21-22

> "It is one of the most tragical facts of all history", says John Stuart Mill, "that Constantine, rather than Marcus Aurelius, was the first Christian Emperor. It is a bitter thought how different the Christianity of the world might have been, had it been adopted as the religion of the empire under the auspices of Marcus Aurelius, instead of Constantine". ---*Essay on Liberty*, pg. 58

Prodigal Religious Leadership

Tragic indeed! What is most tragic is that so little is known about this dark beginning of Christianity and by too few that consider themselves religiously educated and knowledgeable. What is even more tragic is the group of African Americans who don't wish to know this type of information. By the way when Gibbon describes Constantine with the words prodigality, rapaciousness and dissolute for the sake of clarity I give you their meanings; (1) Prodigal Son (2) Lustful predator (3) Unrestrained immorality. Constantine could be characterized as a false prophet or even more accurately…fake prophet.

It is indeed a dark cloud that hangs over Christianity! As we have seen, in Chapter three, because of the reason for Christianity's conception it had a very bloody beginning and an even bloodier history. These are facts! Christianity's founder we know to have had a very questionable character and equally questionable motives. These facts are a key to understanding the conditions that laid the foundation for the development of "doctrines of men" inserted in scripture. Constantine indeed "cast a dark shade over the Christianity which he established." It is the dark shade that has kept the world in darkness unable to see the light of Truth. Now let's look at where the lie got inserted. We will witness now where the "Great deception that would deceive nearly the entire world", began.

"BEWARE THOSE, WHOSE LIGHT IS DARKNESS!"

"Now the works of the flesh are manifest, which are these; Adultery, fornication, uncleanness, lasciviousness, idolatry, witchcraft, hatred, variance, emulations, wrath, strife, seditions, heresies, envyings, murders, revellings, and such like: of the which I tell you before, as I have also told you in the past, that they which do such things shall not inherit the Kingdom of God." **Galatians 5:19-20**

For this purpose we will return to the scene of the crime, the Great Holy Synod, the Council of Nice! Here we will view the methods used by Constantine to execute his plan to fortify his power over the priest of Africa and ultimately the African people. We will also take a look at the character and composition of his partners in crime, the bishops that attended this history changing event. We will ask the question did these "Fathers" of the Church have the fruit of the Spirit or did they portray the works of the flesh? In Chapter seven we will look in depth at these holy fathers of Christian Doctrine and Dogma and ask ourselves the question, 'Should we trust and rely on these men today to lead us to God or tell us what we must do to please Him?'

The Men of The Nice Council

Later we find Constantine claming that the vote of those who attended the Council was unanimous. Did these men really vote their conscience? Where they holy men? Where they men of honesty and integrity? Let us see if these men were really on one accord and men that were being led by the Spirit of God. Was a victory for Constantine and the Council a victory for God?

"The great and holy Council of Nice having been convened by the grace of God, and by the appointment of the most religious emperor, Constantine." *History of the First Council of Nice,* Dean Dudley, pg. 94

I hope all of our readers caught this deception crouched in eloquent and great swelling words. As one can glean from this quote from this Western man; he cannot be trusted to tell the truth. It is impossible for the narrator to be referring to Constantine for Constantine was not even a religious man. At the time he had only dabbled in Platonism. Constantine was not religious he was superstitious at best. The so called Holy Council of Nice definitely was not holy! Strife is a sure sign that the flesh is operational rather than the Spirit. Outright lies, bearing false witness, are a sure sign that the flesh is dominant.

"This is unmerited adulation. Constantine, although he exhibited much zeal for all the concerns of the Church, had never, as yet, received baptism, and continued to remain without the pale of the community of believers, being only a catechumen." Neander says, "It is most probable that, carrying his heathen superstition into Christianity, he looked upon baptism as a sort of rite for the magical removal of sin, and so delayed it, in the confidence that although he had not lived an exemplary life, he might yet, in the end, be enabled to enter into bliss, purified from all his sins." *History of the First Council of Nice,* Dean Dudley, pg. 94

Constantine the Heathen

By heathen the writer is referring to Constantine's attachment to Apollo, the Greek sun god. "Constantine claimed Apollo, one of the gods of Greece, as his patron, and even after becoming a Christian he stamped Apollo's image on one side of his coin, and the initials of Christ on the other." *History of the First Council of Nice,* Dean Dudley, pg. 15 (The truth is Constantine did not confess Christianity until his death bed his claim to be a believer was a sham. Could Constantine have believed Apollo was the Christ?)

Let's take a look at the other men; the bishops of the Nicene Council:

"One reports that St. Nicholas, the red-faced bishop of Myra, whom we sometimes call 'Santa Claus,' got so enraged at Arius, that he slapped him on the jaw." *History of the First Council of Nice,* Dean Dudley, pg. 60

Athanasius, the Great. This last named intrepid supporter of the Nicene Creed was born at Alexandria, A.D. 296...He ever took the lead in the

Arian controversy, sometimes triumphing, and at others suffering from the accusations of his opponents. At the Council of Tyre, A.D. 325, he answered to the charges of murder, unchastity, necromancy, encouraging sedition, oppressive exactions of money, and misuse of church property. His works are chiefly controversial. In those directed against Arius and Arianism." *History of the First Council of Nice,* Dean Dudley, pg. 74

"Apollinaris…was one of the many Christian fathers, who, in that age, were very much attached to Platonism." *History of the First Council of Nice,* Dean Dudley, pg. 103

"Macedonius, bishop of Constantinople, a great Semi-Arian teacher, founded the sect of Pneumatomachi, who held that the Holy Spirit is a divine energy diffused throughout the universe, and not a person distinct from the Father and the Son." *History of the First Council of Nice,* Dean Dudley, pg. 103

"He (Constantine) said the crimes of the priests ought not to be made known to the multitude, lest they should become an occasion of offence or of sin." *History of the First Council of Nice,* Dean Dudley, pg. 99

Perhaps it was Constantine who established this sordid practice that we are witnessing today as an age old practice of the Catholic Church. The practice of hiding the sins of Pedophile Priest has caused much irreparable harm for thousands. Let's look for a moment at one of the good guys, one of the Heretics.

"The followers of Eusebius, who were led by evil doctrines, then assembled for deliberation, and came to the following conclusion: We are also of God. 'There is but one God of whom are all things…They also dwelt particularly upon the following doctrine, contained in the Book of the Pastor: 'Believe above all that there is one God, who created and restored all things, calling them from nothing into being." *History of the First Council of Nice,* Dean Dudley, pg. 76

"It was remarked, that the Eusebians signified to each other by signs, that these declarations were equally applicable to us for it is said that we are the image and the glory of the glory of God." *History of the First Council of Nice,* Dean Dudley, pg. 76-77

From these quotations from Western mans own account of the men of the Council we see that they were not on one accord. Members of this council had been accused of being unchaste, of murder, necromancy, sedition, taking money by force and fraud. Constantine even believed such crimes should be kept hidden. Many of us are thankful that this attitude at last is beginning to give way to an attitude of honesty and integrity. Maybe now we can begin to make the Church a safe place for our children. One bishop was accused of being attached to Platonism. And there were many others present who held views that were contrary to the view issued by the Council after a deceptive unanimous vote. It is interesting to note that the view that they were seeking to eradicate from the Church was that what applied to the Christ equally applied to the rest of the Sons of God having been made in the image and glory of God as well. Fortunately this view has resurfaced within the Church and is gaining in momentum.

Why Christianity Got Created

What did Constantine see in the new religion? He saw primarily a vehicle by which to rule; later in life he had hoped that it would help him escape hell at death. This aspect of his beliefs seems to reflect the mood of today's Christian. Many in the church are there because like Constantine they hope their being baptized and confessing with their mouths that Jesus is Lord will permit them to escape hell when they die. Unfortunately as with Constantine too often this is the major reason too many African Americans go to church. Too many are merely seeking some release from the burden of everyday life and some magical way to get God to release some material blessing; **all are hoping their faith will get them into paradise.** Yet true joy and peace continue to elude them. Let us continue.

To better understand what happened at the Council we need to understand the situation surrounding this illustrious gathering. Although Christendom gives us the impression that its religion was handed down from on high to holy men of old who were inspired and led by God to gather the books of the Bible together and spread the religion of love over the entire earth, let us see what really happened, and determine if indeed it is possible that the Truth was corrupted by the Fathers of Christianity. Again, let us see if these men are worthy of our continued "faith" in the doctrines they have passed on to us.

The reason the Council was convened was because there was a great schism among the ranks of the bishops concerning mainly the true nature of the Christ and secondarily the time of Easter celebration. Apparently there were a large number of bishops that did not subscribe to the dominant view.

"Great dissensions had arisen in the church of Egypt about the nature of Christ, and the time to celebrate Easter, by which Constantine was much troubled. He therefore ordered a convention to be held at Nicea in Bithnia..., *History of the First Council of Nice,* Dean Dudley, pg. 14

How the Controversy Got Started

Western man attempts to present the controversy as originating from one statement made by Arius called today the 'Strong statement of Arius'. However, it is obvious that one statement could not constitute a "great dissension". Once again Western man is presenting the picture in the light that best suits his purposes. Let's look at what Christendom said caused Constantine to call the Council together and look at what really happened as well. Reportedly, after the installment in the Episcopal office at Alexandria of a new Presbyter, a conflict arose between the bishop and Arius:

"After Peter of Alexandria had suffered martyrdom, Achillas was installed in the Episcopal office, whom Alexander succeeded. The latter bishop, in the fearless exercise of his functions for the instruction and government of the Church, attempted one day, in the presence of the presbytery and the rest of his clergy, to explain, with perhaps too philosophical minuteness, that great theological mystery,---the Unity of the Holy Trinity. A certain one of the presbyters under his jurisdiction, whose name was Arius, possessed of no inconsiderable logical acumen, imagining that the bishop entertained the same view of this subject as Sabellius the Libyan {African, who taught, in the third century, that there was but one person in the divine essence}, controverted his statement with excessive pertinacity; advancing another error, which was directly opposed indeed, to that which he supposed himself called upon to refute. 'If said he, 'the Father begat the Son, he that was begotten had a beginning of existence; and, from this, it is evident that there was a time when the Son was not in being. It, therefore, necessarily follows he had his existence from nothing.' Having drawn this inference from his novel train of reasoning, he excited many to a consideration of the question; and thus, from a little spark, a large fire was kindled." *History of the First Council of Nice,* Dean Dudley, pg. 28

As we shall see Africans were teaching that there was one person in the "divine essence". Ironically the African race has been accused of worshiping many gods but we find here the Africans standing firm on monotheism and Western man advancing the three gods in one theory which is essentially polytheistic. We will provide a more detailed look at the background around this clash in opinions in chapter seven. For now suffice it to say that Arius was a member of what was called the Exterior Coptic priest. A group of priest dedicated to the ancient way and the ancient African world view.

Understanding this fact and its significance will go far in shedding light on why there was a controversy in the first place. The way it is presented here is as though it was a new view and perhaps an isolated view being voiced by an ignorant African bishop. As we shall see this was not the case. The doctrine expounded by Arius was closer to what the Africans had taught in the Egyptian temples for centuries. More later on the Exterior Coptic Connection.

The Response of The Council

In response to the deep divisions that had existed since the Greeks had conquered Egypt and not the so called "Strong Statement of Arius," Emperor Constantine called for the Council of Nice meeting to be arranged. The purpose of the Council called by this pagan and heathen emperor, was ultimately to crush any further resistance by the African priest whose view still held power even though they were a people who had been defeated militarily.

Arius the African

At the Council meeting the deck was stacked against Arius from the beginning. For one thing he was not present to defend his view. He was mysteriously absent. Ultimately the emperor welded all the power because any disagreement with him could be deadly or certainly extremely detrimental to ones reputation, material wealth and position in the Church. History tells us the major faction of opposition to the obviously new view was an African bishop by the name of Arius. Arius believed that the new position was incorrect and deviated from the truth as the ancient holy men of his country had taught. Let's pause for a moment and take a look at this man whose character has had a shroud of defamation placed over it. Let's look at Arius the Heretic.

Before going further into the meeting lets look closer at Arius through the eyes of his contemporaries.

"Arius son of Ammonius, the celebrated originator of the Arian doctrines, was a presbyter of the Alexandrian Church, and presided over an independent parish of that city, by the name of Baucalis, where he had been placed a short time before Alexander became bishop. He was rigid ascetic, and acquired great respect from all. Arius died suddenly at Constantinople, perhaps by the poison of his enemies, A.D. 336, and his opponents rejoiced at his death---See Dr. Murdock's note to Mosheim's Institutes, vol. I. p. 297. N.Y. edition, 1852, pg. 28

"Arius, described by some writers as distinguished for beauty, grace, learning, and eloquence, and by others as very ugly, though by no means ignorant and immoral, had, perhaps imbibed his idea of the nature of Christ from Lucian of Antioch, who suffered martyrdom in 312. after the Council of Nice, discontent with its decisions began soon to appear and spread even back to Alexandria, in spite Constantine's earnest efforts to check it." *History of the First Council of Nice,* Dean Dudley, pg. 102

Arius speaks for himself:

LETTER OF ARIUS TO HIS FRIEND, EUSEBIUS OF NICOMEDIA, DESCRIBING HIS DOCTRINES, WHICH OCCASION THE OPPOSITION AND SEVERITIES OF ALEXANDER;

"Arius, unjustly persecuted by the Pope of Alexander, on account of that all-conquering truth, which you also uphold, sendeth greeting in the Lord to his very dear lord, the man of God, the faithful and orthodox Eusebius. Ammonius, my father, being about to depart for Nicomedia, I consider myself bound to salute you by him, and withal address myself to that natural affection which you bear towards the brethren, for the sake of God and of Christ; apprising you that the bishop oppresses and persecutes us most severely, and that he causes us much suffering. He has driven us out of the city as atheists, because we do not concur in what he publicly preaches; namely, that the Father has always been, and that the Son has always been, and that the Son is unbegotten as the Father; that he is always being begotten, without having been begotten; that neither by thought, nor by any interval, does God precede the Son, God and the Son having always been; and that the Son proceeds from God." *History of the First Council of Nice,* Dean Dudley, pg. 38

"We are persecuted because we say that the Son had a beginning, but that God was without beginning. This is really the cause of our persecution. *History of the First Council of Nice,* Dean Dudley, pg. 39

<u>Those in the Flesh will always Persecute Those who are of The Spirit</u>

At the Council meeting Arius's position was deemed heretical and several hundred bishops who were mostly Greek agreed to excommunicate Arius. Though many of the bishops disagreed with Arius there were many in the African churches that agreed with him. Soon after this Synod was held another Council meeting was convened by two hundred and fifty bishops that were sympathetic to Arius's views. But, because Constantine suggested it would be best for unity or better yet uniformity among the bishops; the Greek bishops proclaimed Arius a heretic and condemned him.

> "Most of the bishops were Greeks." *History of the First Council of Nice,* Dean Dudley, pg. 49

Most importantly the emperor was a Greek barbarian who was an enemy of Truth. It was he who decided for the bishops then asked them to agree. Of course we know that emperors and kings do not ask but command their subjects. Listen to reports of the atmosphere at the Council meeting. This is very important because in this meeting the vote was taken that decided the "theory" which today's Christian would place his faith in. If nothing else we know from the reports that Arius was a man with principles, he was a man that took a stand for Truth.

"But as then he that is born of the flesh persecuted him that was born after the Spirit, even so is it now." Galatians 4:29

> "The Arians, fearing lest they should be ejected from the church by so numerous a Council of bishops, proceeded at once to condemn the doctrines objected to, and unanimously signed the confession of faith. They contrived, however, to retain their principal dignities, although they ought rather to have experienced humiliation. Sometimes secretly, and sometimes openly, they continued to vindicate the condemned doctrines, and brought forth various arguments in proof of them. Wholly bent upon establishing these false opinions, they shrank from the scrutiny of learned men." *History of the First Council of Nice,* Dean Dudley, pg. 74

And again:

> Concerning the Article of Faith maintained by the Council, Socrates said, "When these articles of faith were proposed, they were received without opposition; nay, our most pious emperor himself was the first to give them their assent, and subscribe to these very articles. It was suggested,

however, that the word homoousios (consubstantial) should be introduced, an expression which the emperor himself explained…And the bishops, on account of the word Homoosius, drew up the formula of faith which was finally adopted." *History of the First Council of Nice,* Dean Dudley, pg. 69

One has to wonder what would have happened if Arius had been present along with all the bishops that agreed with him and they all stood firm for the Truth, what Christianity might be like today. Instead of standing however, their fear of Constantine caused them to vote against their conscience. This vote taken by the framers of the Christian faith was fixed. Was this God at work or the enemies of God? I do not believe God was the author of this confusion.

Where Truth got Compromised

"It was suggested (by Constantine), that the word Homoosius or Consubstantial should be introduced (added), an expression that the emperor explained." (brackets and emphasis mine) Here we see where the lie got inserted by Constantine. This lie would serve as a foundation for other lies which could now be inserted. This is the "great" lie that would deceive the world almost 2000 years! The response of Arius addresses a central issue in this new word that it could not be found in scripture was obviously the most learned position. Arius spoke in vain however for the Emperors ears were deaf having already set his agenda. Though perhaps the least capable of running this meeting or at least giving spiritual direction to it, Constantine was the one who supposedly explained what this new word meant.

"The complaint of the Arians, that these precise words are not to be found in the Scripture is a vain argument." *History of the First Council of Nice,* Dean Dudley, pg.77

Why that would be a vain argument I'm not sure, it sounds quite valid a complaint. It meant that this "one" addition was unscriptural and should be protested! As we have seen instead of protesting fear and intimidation reigned at this Holy Synod. **The emperor disguised his "ultimatum" in an eloquent "offer" to the bishops to sign the document called "The Article of Faith."** This was the ultimate usurping of religious power. Here is where the seed of Japheth (Western man) the Jacobite "man" by clever deceit steals the inheritance and hence the blessings of the African. From here it would not take long to take this race of people who where the crown of civilization and make them the tail.

With this move, power was to forever be lost to the Egyptian/African priest that had developed the blueprint for this "new religion."

As we said earlier Christianity conquered Africa. Though Alexander conquered Egypt/Africa nearly seven hundred years earlier with this move Constantine must be given credit for the Spiritual defeat of Africa. He conquered the mind of Africa.

The Council at Nice Created A Doctrine of Darkness

The first Article of Faith was a Commandment of Men, the man who commanded that it be obeyed was the then all powerful Emperor of Rome, Constantine. As confessing Christians, it is his commandment in which you have believed. This new doctrine was for sure a Dark Doctrine.

Though Constantine was the main character he was supported by the greater number of Greek bishops present. **The second factor in the development of the commandments of men is the spiritual ignorance of the Greek priest.** The African involvement and influence was severely limited and only those African contributions that conformed to the more dominant European perspective were accepted. **It is ironic because they were trying to formulate an understanding of what, was fundamentally African teachings**. A more in depth view of the quality of the intellectual and religious input of Europeans will be shared in chapter seven, *Upon Whose Authority*.

The Greeks were not the authors of the scriptures they found themselves in possession of. They therefore lacked the understanding of the dark sayings, metaphors, symbols and myths. This led them to rely on a surface understanding of what is now known to have been the teachings of the Egyptian Mystery Schools. The meaning was a mystery to them. The teachings of the Mystery Schools were mainly metaphysical or relating to the world beyond the physical senses.

The church Fathers admittedly attempted to use the senses of the carnal or natural man to interpret these dark sayings and continually failed to receive any revelation on the subject. In frustration they declared it a mystery beyond comprehension. They were telling the truth; it was beyond "their" comprehension and ability to explain. The result of this lack of understanding was a "corruption" of that which had hidden meaning. This became *"the corruption that is in the world"* that we must be saved from according to the Bible. The carnal mind can never understand spiritual matters. It is carnal

117

knowledge that creates doctrines and commandments of men. Note: 325 A.D. was the date of the Council of Nice meeting.

> "The Church doctrine of the trinity was not fully formulated or established until 325 A.D. When the Genesis creation account appeared, monotheism was at its peak. Thus the Semitic writer would never portray, or hint that God was a trinity of persons. Neither would he suggest a triune nature" *The Mysteries of Creation*, Rocco A Errico, pg. 117.

The Making of an Idol God

The Trinity is a doctrine that no one in Christendom has ever been able to explain. Because the Europeans lacked understanding of this symbol, they established the forever nebulous concept of the Three-in-one God. This was done primarily to place the man Jesus in the godhead. The doctrine of the Trinity was conceived in darkness. They claimed it was a "Mystery of God"; it was more likely a mystery to God who claimed in the Christian Bible that He would share his throne with no one.

> *"Thou shall have no other gods before me."*
> *"Thou shall not make unto thee any graven image, or any likeness of anything that is in heaven above, or that is in the earth beneath, or that is in the water under the earth."*
> *"Thou shall not bow down thyself to them, nor serve them: for I am the Lord thy God am a jealous God...*
> *"And the Lord said unto Moses, Thus thou shall say unto the children of Israel, ye have seen that I have talked with from heaven."*
> *"Ye shall not make with me gods of silver, neither shall ye make unto you gods of gold."* **Exodus 20:3-4-5-22-23**

Maybe these Old Testament warnings do not apply to these New Testament Saints. Perhaps because they were under Grace they no longer needed the Ten Commandments. They had a new covenant with God, they cut a new deal, now they could worship idols, and could put other gods before the Most High God, Creator of the heavens and the earth. Because of the vote of the Council of Nice, today Christians wear crosses of gold and silver around their necks, saying this is my God, he hung on a cross one day so I wear it to remember he suffered for me. Sounds good but do you not know my dear Christian brothers and sisters that any image that can be made with hands is an idol, even the golden image of a man that was supposed to be born of a virgin. Your gold cross with the figure of a man on it represents a god of gold and a graven image because it is the image of something that is in the earth, namely a man. Remember, ***"God is not a man that he should lie,"*** **whether the image is a bird, bull or man it is an idol if you say it is an image of God.** We will share more on this critically important subject later in Vol. II.

> "According to some historians, the idea of the Triad and Trinity originated with Plato, and was discussed by the Platonists.---See Gibbon's Decline and Fall of Rome, chap. 21. source: *History of the First Council of Nice,* Dean Dudley, pg. 28

What Euro-Christianity Added Was a Lie

After the Council meeting and vote the emperor claimed overwhelming victory. In his opinion the Council was a success. The reason for his excitement now he could appropriate for himself the divine authority of God to back his decisions and actions no matter how deprived and sadistic they might be. For to him it was power and control by any means necessary. He reported that what had occurred was pleasing to God and conducive to unity. However as we shall see unity among the bishops was not restored and neither was God pleased. What he did achieve however was conformity

> "Every doubtful point obtained a careful investigation, until doctrines pleasing to God and conductive to unity were fully established, so that no room remained for division or controversy concerning the faith." *History of the First Council of Nice,* Dean Dudley, pg. 97

> Arius response to the persecution: "Arius, upon his excommunication at Alexandria in 321, retired to Palestine, and wrote various letters to men of distinction, in which he labored to demonstrate the truth of his doctrines, thereby drawing over immense numbers to his side, and particularly Eusebius, Bishop of Nicomedia, a man of vast influence. These bishops held a council in Bithynia, probably at Nicomedia, in which two hundred and fifty bishops are reported to have been present. All we know of their acts and decisions is that they sent letters to all the bishops of Christendom, entreating them not to exclude the friends of Arius from their communion, and requesting them to intercede with Alexander that he would not do so. This first Arian Council has often been overlooked by the modern writers." *History of the First Council of Nice,* Dean Dudley, pg. 101-102

It would take centuries for the Powers of Rome to vanquish the Arian opposition. There was more written documents to burn, many people to run out of town and silenced and unfortunately much blood to be shed. Eventually as we know Christianity would win and nearly all dissenting opinion and views silenced by Western man and his religion.

> "These objects were all attained by means of the Council, except the principle one. Arianism, though checked for a short time, again burst forth with tenfold energy, and long agitated the religious world. However, it finally was completely vanquished and eradicated from the high places of Christendom." *History of the First Council of Nice,* Dean Dudley, pg. 24

> 'Dean Stanley says, "The Creed of the Council of Nice is the only one accepted throughout the Universal Church, and the Council alone, of all ever held, still retains a hold on the mass of Christendom." *History of the First Council of Nice,* Dean Dudley, pg. 69

With the New Faith Came a New God

The new faith was based on faith in a new god, a physical god. The God which it is said that no man has seen now is able to be seen. **People no longer worship the unseen, invisible God of the universe. Instead they worship a form of a man who they call "God in the flesh".** The focus of a materialized god is things that are of the material world, the temporal world. Thus, credibility is given to materialism.

This attitude of materialism is reflected in the petitions of today's African American Christians. Instead of asking for and seeking wisdom as Solomon in the bible, they seek the blessing of material wealth and prosperity. They seek the blessing of physical health and well being. They ask God for things to consume on their lust. But they do not ask God how they may worship their Creator in spirit and in truth. Oh no, that would mean giving up the things. The scripture says that we should seek first the kingdom of God and his righteousness.

> *"For the time will come when they will not endured sound doctrine,*
> *but after their own lust shall heap to themselves teachers*
> *having itching ears; and they shall*
> *be turned to fables".* **2 Tim. 4:3**

THAT TIME HAS COME AND IS NOW HERE!

We are the "they" spoken of in this scripture. We have accepted for the Word of God the fables and commandments of men, invented and inserted by an unrighteous emperor and some weak priest from the first millennium. We have heaped to ourselves, teachers that tickle our imagination with what we think we want to hear, and nothing changes. We are a lustful generation. We lust for the things of this world with such intensity that most of our activity is centered on acquiring wealth in order to purchase more things.

Materialism is the god of those who lust after the riches and comforts of this world. It is the god of gold. Because of it, the Truth is neglected. *"No man can serve two masters: for either he will hate the one, and love the other; or else he will hold to the one, and despise the other. You cannot serve both God and mammon"* **(Matthew 6:24).** Mammon is another word for materialism. As is seen in the history of the Church and the present day actions of the Church, their god is money. This is the naked Truth. Examine any local assembly and the facts will be evident for you to witness. The primary focus and the one in which the greatest amount of energy is expended in the Church today is fundraising. They fish more for dollars than "sinners".

The "doctrines of the commandments of men" have hidden the Truth and therefore the Truth must be revealed. We have believed interpretations of scripture that has placed blinders over our eyes. The commandments of men are the source of much religious confusion and division. Most important, are the limiting affect these doctrines have on the spiritual development of the believers. We must discover the "word within the word" and renew our minds as we have been instructed. Then real change will occur. Until then, I suppose we'll have to keep what we got.

In the next chapter we will continue to address vital and relevant questions as we look further into other areas of religious misrepresentation by Western man hidden in the doctrines of Christianity.

A good example of the literalization method of the Euro-Christians is the teaching of the Orthodox Church on the resurrection of the body. In literalizing, the spiritual aspect of the metaphor is entirely lost. Listen to this commentary by the legendary and widely quoted bible commentator, Matthew Henry:

> "The bodies of the saints, when they shall rise again, will be greatly changed from what they are now, and much for the better. They are now corruptible; they will be then incorruptible, glorious, and spiritual bodies, fitted to the celestial world, where they are ever afterwards to have their

eternal inheritance. The apostle here makes known a truth unknown before, which is that the saints living at our lords second coming will not die, but be changed, that this change will be made in a moment, in a twinkling of an eye, and at the sound of the last trump. At this summons the graves will open, the dead saints shall rise incorruptible, and the living saints be changed to the same incorruptible state. The reason for the change. This corruptible body must be made incorruptible; this mortal body must be changed into immortal. There is a day coming when the grave shall open, the dead saints revive, and become immortal, and put out the reach of death for ever. When they rise glorious from the grave, they will boldly triumph over death. It is altogether owing to the grace of God in Christ that sin is pardoned and death disarmed". *Matthew Henry Commentary in One Volume,* pg. 1825

During my time in the preaching ministry, I too relied on old Matthew to shed light on the scripture I was seeking to understand. Then, a passage such as this would have been real impressive. That was before I came to myself and reclaimed my mind. Now the childishness of such language is obvious. **Mr. Henry and Christendom have taken the phrase, "the resurrection of the dead", literally and then attempted to fit the understanding to the letter. There is no apparent recognition that the resurrection of the dead refers to the spiritually dead, just as the death resulting from the forbidden fruit resulted in the spiritual death of Adam and Eve.** The physical body of man will return to the earth as other scripture clearly indicated in the statement, "dust to dust and ashes to ashes" pronounced over the dead body of one who has transitioned.

The Spirit and the flesh belong to two different dimensions. In reality, the Spirit cannot be made flesh nor can the flesh be made Spirit. There, will never come a day when the bodies of dead men will come out of the graves. At one time, Christians circulated a poster depicting this scene which is called, "the Rapture". It showed a picture of a European Jesus in the clouds looking on as people floated out of cars and houses, while graves burst open and the dead floated up to Jesus as well. Most of the bodies in graves have already experienced the only change they will ever make; they have decomposed and returned to the earth.

The literal interpretation method leads us to these infantile "revelations" and "visions" and labels them orthodox, thereafter, no one is supposed to question or challenge the nonsense. Nonsense!

<u>Christianity Based on the Letter of Scripture</u>

Euro-Christianity is based on the "letter" of the scripture; that is a literal interpretation. For this reason the understanding remains hidden and locked away through ignorance. Christendom based its doctrine of belief in God's plan of salvation on what is termed the "exoteric" or outer version. The wisdom that is concealed is called the "esoteric" aspect. Christendom has made this word taboo by associating it with the occult. Even the word occult merely means that which is hidden. Which explains the European distaste for the word; it was hidden from them. **Therefore the second key is to understand that the Europeans did not understand.**

Further evidence of the darkness of Euro-Christianity is seen in the practice of judgment. Supposedly, Christendom is established on the premise that Jesus the Christ gave his life for the Church. Actually, Jesus, according to scripture was judged and condemned by the church, which demanded of the state that he be put to death. Since then, the Church has practiced condemnation and punishment of anyone that disagrees with what Jesus was supposed to have taught. Such irony is unreal. The Church continues in its hypocrisy even today.

The darkest of dark doctrines is the doctrine of "original sin". Such beliefs did not exist among Africans. Nor has any other religious group adopted this premise of man's beginning. The doctrine of original sin says that each man, because of the sin of Adam, is born in sin and shaped in iniquity. Every other religious discipline starts with the premise, "God doesn't make junk". **To people of other creeds, man is simply born with the potential to actualize the attributes of his Creator on earth. This is his destiny and responsibility.** The African Mystery schools were founded on this premise. The purpose of the instruction was to assist the student or disciple in accomplishing this task. Today's Christian begins with the deceptive assumption that he was shaped in iniquity and can only hope for redemption by acceptance of the correct faith formula, by faith. This redemption is not supposed to become a reality though until after one dies, that is unless Jesus returns before he dies. This misunderstanding is illustrated in the earlier excerpt by Matthew Henry.

Perhaps the most blinding and most damaging doctrine of Euro-Christianity is the doctrine of "original sin". This doctrine is the most fundamental doctrine of Christendom. It is the doctrine that the value of all other Christian doctrine is founded on. Without the original sin theory, none of the other doctrines would make sense. The theory of original sin is based on a literal interpretation of the Genesis Creation Story and the writings of St. Augustine, an African bishop in the Roman Empire. Augustine said that he arrived at his conclusions from information derived from his physical eyes, by observing the actions of men. Yet, we are told in scripture, that flesh and blood (five physical senses) cannot reveal the kingdom to man. The Truth is a spiritual matter which must be discerned with the heart (spirit).

What Should We Do Now That We Know

If you are a confessing Christian unfortunately Constantine is the man you must thank for giving you something to believe in and the words to say in your confession. The problem with this scenario is that you have placed your trust in a man who history describes as a being a "Prodigal Son," extremely immoral, excessively cruel and savage, a pagan and heathen, hungry for power and a lustful predator. The light attributed to this man by some Western scholars in an attempt to deceive us was surely dark. In addition his cohorts in crime the bishops which attended the Council at Nice weren't much better guides. These were hypocrites who honor God with their lips only. Fear and intimidation, immoral behavior, questionable ethics combined with ignorance and lust for power to disqualify them as being relevant to the outcome of the Council meeting.

The one person with integrity was the person who was condemned and ran out of town by the Council. It was he that was described as a man of wisdom and a righteous man who was greatly respected and well liked by many.

It should be apparent that the authority of the Council of Nice to establish the fundamental doctrine of Christendom was questionable for an overwhelming number of bishops were sympathetic to the opposing view. It should also be apparent that the conclusion reached at this infamous council meeting is equally questionable. Something got added and it was a little lie, but as scripture reports, *"A little lie will leaven the whole lump."* In the next chapter we will answer some vital and relevant questions as we look further into the numerous religious misrepresentations by Western man hidden in the doctrines of Christianity. When one accepts this deception as true it leads to mental and spiritual bondage; the condition of many Religious Blacks in America. If you would be free, falsehood must be rejected and the Truth embraced. This means that the Doctrines and Commandments of men that have been added to sacred scripture must be discerned and rejected.

Chapter 6

WHAT EURO-CHRISTIANITY MISREPRESENTS

MAKE SURE GOD SAID IT BEFORE YOU BELIEVE IT

The coming of the lawless one is according to the workings of Satan,
With all power, signs, and lying wonders, and with all
Unrighteous deception among those that perish,
because they did not receive the love of Truth,
that they might be saved. And for this reason God will send
them a strong delusion, that they should believe a lie"
II Thessalonians 2:7

Below is a partial listing of things that have been misrepresented by Euro-Christianity:

What Euro-Christianity Misrepresents

- ITS TRUE ORIGIN
- ITS FOUNDING FATHERS
- ITS SORDID HISTORY
- THE BIBLE AS THE UNADULTERATED AND INERRANT WORD OF GOD
- ITSELF AS AN ORIGINAL RELIGION INSPIRED BY GOD
- THE NATURE OF GOD
- THE NATURE OF MAN

- GOD'S JUDGMENT
- JESUS AS THE ONLY BEGOTTEN SON OF GOD/GOD IN THE FLESH
- THE DEVIL
- HELL AS A LITERAL AND PHYSICAL PLACE
- THE PLAN OF SALVATION
- THE MEANING OF THE FALL
- THE ORIGIN AND MEANING OF THE TRINITY
- THE RESURRECTION OF THE DEAD

To Misrepresent is to be Fraudulent

Christianity misrepresents itself as an original religion when in fact it is a copy and collection of parts of other religions in existence during that period with as we have seen a few major additions. This is a crime punishable by law in every other arena except religion. In religion there has been little accountability required of the messages preached from the pulpit. It is not the premise of the author that the state should correct this flaw. Any change must be instituted by the people who adhere to the faith. I firmly believe, that, "if the followers would lead the leaders would follow". I ask, "Where are the prophets of God of today"? Where are the Isaiah's, Jeremiah's and Hosea's of today who would set God's church in order?

There is a saying among Christians that goes, "If God said it, I believe it". This of course is in reference to the "Word of God" which is supposed to be errorless. This sentiment among Blacks is expressed by a Black author quoted in this work. He is well acquainted with the history of Africa. He is the son of a pastor, and a retired University of Arkansas school teacher. He is also a graduate of Quachita Baptist University with a B.A. degree in Religion. He had these words to share about the Bible: "I believe in the inerrancy of the Scriptures in their original languages. **I believe the King James Version of Scripture is authoritative...as the yardstick and rulers that we purchase are sufficient and reliable for us to use as an authoritative measuring device, the King James Version of the Bible is a reliable, trustworthy document to give us guidance and direction in the Christian life".** *Beyond Roots,* Rev. William McKissic, Sr., pg. 49

If an educated man such as this can come to a such a faulty conclusion, what can be expected of the average black Christian who has only attended a few Bible studies and heard sermons from the pulpit "about" the Bible. We will not attempt to deal with such a weighty question in this chapter. We will devote the entire next chapter on the Bible and the Euro-centric view that the Bible is the flawless word of God. In that chapter, we will examine exactly what it means to take such a position, as well as critically examine the Euro-Christian view.

Actually, this is a very good stance to take. If God said it, that should settle it. However, there is a key word here; it is the word "if". The "if God said it" portion must first be settled. The fervor with which African Americans approach this noble position of "if God said it, I believe it", is reminiscent of the way in which our ancestors approached the subject. To their religion they gave their all, and to this extent the enthusiasm exhibited by African Americans who have embraced Christianity is commendable. However, we must settle the question of whether or not God actually "said it". This should be a prerequisite to taking such a firm stance. That **is we should make sure God said it, "before" we believe it. The scriptures put it this way,** *"Beloved believe not every spirit, but try the spirits whether they be of God"* (I John 4:1)

Spirit of Christianity has Never been Tested to see if it is of God

Much of what we believe today, we believe because someone we trusted told us it was true. It is a matter of custom especially among African Americans to accept what is acceptable to ones family. **It is customary for African Americans to believe there is a God and that you should worship Him the way your parents and grandparents have. The truth is, the spirit of the tree of Euro-Christianity has never been tested by African Americans to see if it be of God. As a result, much of what we believe is the doctrines and commandments of men. These doctrines are a misrepresentation of the Truth. These misrepresentations are therefore lies, deceptions and falsehoods, and they are perpetuated by Western man.**

"Failure to see and interpret Truth results in falsehood and misrepresentation. In itself, wrong is simply lack of Truth, a negative condition".

In this chapter we will highlight the numerous areas that Euro-Christianity has misrepresented itself. Most of the topics are covered in depth in other chapters. However, **we will focus on three important misrepresentations in this chapter; (1) the Church doctrine of supernatural phenomenon and miracles, (2) the Europeans masquerade as the master-race by divine selection, and (3) the question of Euro-centrism Vs. Afro-centrism.**

African American Christians are taught by way of *"eloquent"* **sermons full of** *"great swelling words"* **from their pastors, that God did miraculous things during the time of the early Christians.** We are told that he opened up the Red Sea in order to allow the "Children of Israel" to escape from the pursuit of the army of the Pharaoh of Egypt. We are told that God used a donkey to talk to one prophet; we are told that a widow's oil was supernaturally replenished because she fed the prophet of God first. We are told that Noah and a few others gathered two or seven of every animal on the planet including polar bears and other animals afar off. Supposedly, they lived together in a small ark and the predators did not devour their natural prey. One prophet was supposed to have made the sun stand still for a day. Peter's shadow was supposed to have healed some people. Jesus was supposed to have walked on the water and fed over five thousand people with two loaves of bread and five fish. These and other incredulous feats are tucked away in the minds of many intelligent African American Christians as too taboo to touch. Their only response is, "one has to believe something", why not believe God"? The answer is, make sure God said it first!

"When I was a child, I spoke as a child, I understood as a child, I thought as a child; but when I became a man, I put away childish things."
I Corinthians 13:11

Doctrine of Dispensationalism Describes a God that Changed

Again, the childlike faith of African Americans in Europeans is astounding. Christendom attempted to answer this mystery as to the change in God's methods of operation with a new concept called "dispensationalism". Hidden in this concept is the lie that somehow, God did change. Of course for those who had raised the question concerning the change, this was a very unsatisfactory answer.

Some Christian clergymen began to fabricate stories about supernatural occurrences in their church services. The motivation for this was greed and power. These fabrications seemed to give validity to the belief that God yet worked miracles "through" his "men of God". Fortunately, many of these con men have been exposed and their trickery uncovered. A Peter Popoff was busted getting his messages from God from his wife in the audience. She was wired with a mike connected to an earphone hidden behind Mr. Popoff's ear. Benny Hinn, a very successful charismatic preacher has also been exposed.

And They shall Follow Signs and Lying Wonders

Such signs and wonders, according to the scriptures, were supposed to be a sign for unbelievers. **Supposedly, according to Black theology, the miracles of God were a sign that God used to convince unbelievers that He was real** thereby making them believers. It appears that today, the Christians believe that the signs are for them. Many follow televised reports of such miracles as fervently as the star of "X" Files searches for the truth that is out there somewhere.

Many said believers follow the signs for a confirmation that God is still alive and still working miracles. They see people on TV getting out of wheel chairs and tossing canes into the audience, and are convinced of His reality. **These events are for the most part, massive fund raising events, based on trickery. They are an overwhelming success, because many believers need the signs to believe.** A major reason there is such a tremendous response is because there are so many Christians that are physically ill and materially lacking. The predominant reason however is that many have not personally experienced communion with God and therefore need assurance that he is yet real and still cares. They are saying *"Lord I believe, but help me with my unbelief."*

The signs and wonders we follow are not from God and are not true, they are lying wonders. The so-called healing holy water, the strips of cloth that have been anointed with a special anointing, are all lying wonders designed to free dollars from the pockets of those who "believe". **That is not to say that I do not believe in the miraculous. I have experienced numerous miracles in my life. I have seen the miraculous intervention of an all powerful Creator God in many personal situations.** Yet, Euro-Christianity is replete with fake healers and prophets that only con the people out of their money for a carrot stick of a promise. Of course those who do not receive their healing are at fault not the fake healer.

The Euro-Christian view of how God interacts with His Creation is that occasionally, God suspends the natural laws and operates supernaturally. Naturally, according to this view, God's act would be supernatural because he is not like natural man. Although this may seem feasible it is a lie and a misrepresentation.

God is the Creator of Natural Laws

Our Creator has established natural laws that govern its creation. The Creator does not violate those laws to prove to unbelievers or believers that God is real. These laws govern the entire universe and all its phases of expression. They govern mental and emotional activity just as sure as they govern the physical law of gravity. There are laws of creation on every level of creation, both in the physical and the meta-physical realms.

Some of the operations of these natural laws seem miraculous, but that is because so few are able to consciously work with the laws. There are Spiritual laws that seem to the unlearned, miraculous in their operation and manifestation. The understanding of these laws are distorted and mystified, rather than clarified, by Euro-Christianity.

"Every good gift and every perfect gift is from above, and comes down from the Father of lights, with whom there is no variation or shadow of turning." James 1:17

Some people are taught that the mystery as to why God operated in such an unnatural way before and doesn't now, can never be understood therefore one has to just believe. Non-sense, no one "has" to "just" believe anything. There is always a choice. There is always an alternative. In this case it would only seem natural that at some point, African Americans would begin to search out these alternatives. Until now, this has not been the case.

We have received the teachings of Euro-Christianity as based on the inerrant, irrefutable, and infallible, "Word of God". And on that we have taken our stand of faith, to be tried, but never to waver from what we have been taught. Why should we challenge the authority of Euro-Christianity? After all, did it not come from reliable sources? Unfortunately, until now most African American Christians didn't know the origin of the form of faith they have embraced. Even more tragic is that too many do not care to know the door to their spiritual awareness has been effectively closed by their false beliefs.

Now we have received, not the spirit of the world, but the spirit which is of God; that we might know the things that are freely given to us of God. Which things also we speak, not in the words which man's wisdom teacheth, but which the Holy Ghost teacheth; comparing spiritual things with spiritual. But the natural man receiveth not the things of the Spirit of God: for they are foolishness unto him: neither can he know them, because they are spiritually discerned. But he that is spiritual judgeth all things, yet he himself is judged of no man. I Cor.2:12-15

The Fathers of Christianity Were Not Spiritaul

The foolishness spoken of here is the foolishness of not recognizing the laws of the Spirit. It is foolish to believe fables and old wives tales. Man's wisdom cannot teach us about such Spiritual matters. Nor can the man who is not spiritual discern them. Those that are spiritual will judge these matters properly. They will understand that by the Spirit of God we can understand anything. Euro-Christianity must be judge by those who are "truly" spiritual.

The "Fathers" of Christianity were not spiritual men. By now this should be quite obvious. How could you not believe the confessions of the men themselves? Yet many remain deceived, this is the great falling away from the Truth.

"Let no one deceive you by any means; for that day will not come unless the man of sin is revealed, the son of perdition, who opposes and exalts himself above all that is called God or that is worshipped, so that he sits as God in the temple of God, showing himself that he is God" **II Thessalonians 2:3,4 NKJV**

Today Western man uses his religion to exalt himself above all other races. He pretends that only he understands what's best for all men. I believe it was the Last Poets who said, "The White man has a god complex." He has falsely misrepresented himself as an exclusive member of the race in which God Himself belongs to. He has caused men to worship the white race through the subliminal message imbedded in the false image of a white Jesus, as God in the flesh. This message supports the misrepresentation of Western man as a righteous and godly people and members of the master race. We know however they could not be a godly people because we have judged righteously their historical actions and their fruit. Besides, in order to be a master race you must first master yourself not others. To master self is truly to be godlike.

Today, instead of mastering himself, the son of perdition is truly revealing himself to the world through his acts of cruelty and apparent disregard for human life. **The falling away was the result of the teachings of the man of perdition being overlaid on the teachings of the Ancient African Priest. Euro-Christianity is a strong delusion that has led us to believe a lie.**

"For the mystery of lawlessness is already at work; only He who is restrains will do so until He is taken out of the way. And then the lawless one will be revealed, whom the Lord will consume with the brightness of His coming. The coming of the lawless one is according to the workings of Satan, With all power, signs, and lying wonders, and with all

Unrighteous deception among those that perish,
because they did not receive the love of Truth,
that they might be saved. And for this reason God will send
them a strong delusion, that they should believe a lie" **II Thessalonians 2:7**

Have you received their baptism of lies, *"since you believed"?* Are you trusting in a lie? Have you received *"the mark of the beast"* in your *"forehead"?* That is to ask, "Does the Beast (unregenerate man) control your thoughts, and have you believed what he believes???" Have you received his lie and misrepresentation as the Truth? He has demonstrated that he is *"a liar"* and that *"the Truth is not in him"*. **Why would you trust in a known "liar".** He has lied about history. Historically, he has demonstrated only Beast-like behavior. He has been at war every since he began to rule the world. He has carried death and destruction wherever he has taking his culture and religion.

African Americans have a choice. A choice as to what they will believe. The choice is between Westerns mans world view and the African world view. These are two very distinct world views. In is interesting that Europeans have been able to challenge Afro-centrism (in school curriculums) with help from blacks. We will discuss Afro-centrism in depth in the next chapter, "Upon Whose Authority; A Call for an African Spiritual Frame of Reference. For now, let us take an introductory look at Euro-Centrism.

Euro-centrism is Foundation for White Supremacy

Euro-centrism is the incumbent and therefore it is difficult to unseat. It is taken for granted, even by blacks, that this view is the correct view. **Go ahead, be honest with yourself. You have never really questioned or challenged the belief system and philosophy of Euro-Christianity. You have never stopped to seriously question whether what you have chosen to believe is of the Truth or not.** If you did, you never actively sought the answers. **Euro-centrism is by nature a racist view.** It is formulated by Europeans, who have both admitted and demonstrated their racism. **Euro-centrism is based on the false assumption that the white race is a superior race. It can only flourish in an environment of deceit, lies and falsehoods.**

The Euro-centric view will always have a limiting rather than a liberating affect on African minds. In the next chapter we will probe more thoroughly this very important area in order for you to make an informed decision. It is important because this is the viewpoint of two of our most critical institutions, the church and school.

Foundation for Euro-centrism is Deception

Western man uses Euro-centrism to justify his claim to being the master race, the superior race. The race that is divinely suited to rule. The purpose of the misrepresentations is to make this illusion appear real. If you have not purged your consciousness of this viewpoint, chances are you are a black person with a white mind. That is an oxymoron. The Euro-centric viewpoint makes you view yourself as inferior. Whether you are conscious of it or not, if you have not renewed your mind, you are thinking white.

The power of the Beast can only be destroyed by the brightness of the coming of God or Truth. Do not be deceived by his signs and lying wonders, he has shown himself to be the lawless one. **His teachings will condemn you to spiritual death. Come out of condemnation. Leave the teachings of the Beast with the Beast. He is unrighteous therefore you can never learn righteousness from him.** Stop following signs and believing in lying wonders.

We have judged the fruit of the teachings of the unrighteous one and have found them wanting, we have found him to be a thief and a fraud, we have found that he has taught for truth the doctrines and commandments of men, and have grossly misrepresented God and his master plan for the evolution of man. He has, in the name of God, spread pestilence and death the world over. He has almost destroyed entire nations of people, and is now busy destroying the earth itself.

Euro-centrism A Racist View of the World and its People

Many of the misrepresentations of Euro-Christianity can be explained by the Western man's failure or inability to see and interpret the truths hidden in the teachings of the African Mystery schools. The other explanation is founded on the Euro-Christians desire to establish themselves as the master-race in the eyes of those whom they would conquer.

It is time to wake up and try the spirits, and see if they be of God. We have a choice. Chose Truth and chose life or keep the lie and accept death. It is my desire for you that you chose to free your African mind. The choice for African Americans in the 21st century is to be African or not to be. It is the choice to be free of dominion by Western mans corrupt belief system. Such values and attitudes are hazardous to the health of African minds.

"The development of Afrocentrism and multiculturalism was a natural response to a Eurocentric system which has defended and protected its involvement in the history of 'slavery, colonialism, segregation, apartheid, racism and neoracism'. There is no way a people can justify the enslavement and the enactment of genocidal policies against another human without the creation of religious and educational systems to legitimize their actions. It would stand to reason that as the oppressed people of the world begin to assume positions of leadership, and define themselves and their history for themselves, their former oppressors would decry such acts as ludicrous". *Nile Valley Contributions To Civilization*, Anthony T. Browder, pg. 247

In summary, we must never forget to be vigilant to try the spirit to see if it be of God and to make sure that God actually said it before we decide to place our faith in it!

Chapter 7

UPON WHOSE AUTHORITY

A CALL TO AN AFRICAN SPIRITUAL FRAME OF REFERENCE

"Authority: the right to command and to enforce obedience, superiority derived from a status that carries with it the right to give orders and to expect obedience, the power to require and receive submission." *The Book Your Church Doesn't Want You To Read*, Tim C. Leedom, Editor, pg. 403

"It is better to hear the rebuke of the wise, than for a man
to hear the song of fools"
Ecclesiastes 7:5

It is not easy to receive rebuke. Therefore I am most grateful to those of my readers who are still with us. Your attentiveness to the material being presented here indicates that you are a lover and seeker of Truth. Know that it is a deep love that leads me to do what I am doing. It is a love not only for my people but for all of God's creatures. Dear beloved Christians, clergy and lay persons, until now I have spoken very candid and straight forward and I know to some it may have appeared that I am perhaps a little hard on the European. Please, understand it is not my desire to stir up hatred and division between the races. I personally have European friends and supporters who I know love me and I love them. They have shown me that God is yet working among all the races to move the evolution of His man forward.

The truth is there are major religious movements among Whites that are expounding the African world view of oneness, of the unity of the universe. These movements are founded on books such as *The Course in Miracles, Quantum Physics* and *Conversations With God*. The Black community has yet to duplicate such movements. These movements are termed New Age when in reality they are ancient African Truth resurrected.

However, the world is in the condition it is in because a few Europeans desire to continue their rule over the masses of people. It is their desire and to their advantage that the races remain divided and ignorant. It is my desire that all men be united. **Before African Americans can unite with others in a healthy manner they have to first learn to love themselves again. Their sense of self worth must be restored otherwise in their attempt to show love to others it will be a dysfunctional type of love. Not loving themselves Blacks will continue to immolate Whites because they will deem Whites most worthy of their adoration. At the same time, Europeans must learn a new respect and appreciation for African Americans so glaringly absent at this time.**

self love

For these reasons the truth must be told. And for these reasons I must he honest and straightforward and present what I have learned for your consideration. **For me the rebuke is a labor of love from the heart to each heart and mind that will receive it.** I hope it is received as such because someone has to do the job. The task at hand involves the tearing down and destroying of a belief system that is based on a lie.

The Voice of One Crying In The Wilderness

The only way to destroy a lie is to bring it into the light. As long as the truth is allowed to be tucked away in a dark corner it is ineffectual. Nevertheless the lie must be shown to be a lie before the truth can be received. The invisible chains that have kept Blacks at the bottom rung of the ladder of social progress must be made manifest before they can be broken. Indeed, the liberation of the African mind is the key to Black Salvation. By that I mean we must put the light on the truth about African Americans past as well. I am the voice of one crying in the wilderness of Western civilization to the people I believe will and must right that which is wrong.

"The voice of one crying in the wilderness: Prepare the way of the Lord; Make His paths straight. Every valley shall be filled and every mountain brought low; the crooked places shall be made straight and the rough ways smooth; and all flesh shall see the salvation of the Lord." **Luke 3:4-6**

It is the opinion of the author that African Americans are the valley which needs to be filled. And of course it is Western man who needs to be brought low. The crooked places Western man has established must be made straight and where he has made it rough for people of color it must be made smooth. **The recent barrage of religious, political and financial scandals should serve as a wake up call that something is seriously wrong and needs to be corrected immediately.** My people do not be lulled to sleep at this time rouse yourselves for the task at hand. God needs some Jeremiahs to get His house in order. No serious applications will be turned down. If you will work for the Lord there is a place for you.

"The harvest is plentiful, but the laborers are few. Therefore pray that the Lord of the harvest to send out laborers into His harvest."

Having said that let us resume our task of *"rooting out, pulling down, destroying and tearing down"* that unholy thing that has exalted itself in the very temple of the Lord. Let us *"prepare the way of the Lord and make straight His paths"* in order that we may *"build and plant"* a new way of life. **Do you not agree that it is time?**

In order for African Americans to accomplish the task at hand it is important for them to first recognize that Western man has yet to produce the fruit of a spiritually enlighten race of people. They have not shown themselves worthy of controlling the destiny of humanity. African Americans must begin to think for themselves. For this reason I admonished African Americans to not mistrust and be critical of your own scholars unless you are willing to be equally critical and questioning of the dogmas of other people? The question that needs to be asked is based on the definition of authority; "Should Blacks continue to submit to the authority of Western man"?

"The problem is essentially the same in our African homeland. There, too, 'white' is still the standard of excellence, of what is right, wise and best." *The Destruction of Black Civilization*, Chancellor Williams, pg. 206

Christianity Created by Europeans

As we have seen it is without question that Western man is responsible for the Doctrines of the Christian Church whatever branch or denomination you belong to. **European men without question are the authors of Christian doctrine, dogma and theory. Because they are the authors they have been the authority as well. It is they who have determined what is Orthodox or acceptable.** This information is readily available and actually quite obvious. One merely need reflect on the race of the one that Christianity is based on. Since the fourth century Jesus has been depicted as European, although all scripture that describe Jesus and his physical attributes describe him as Black. This was done by Europeans at the Nicene Council. This was done because this new image reflected the image of the race which had created the new religion. The language of Christendom is Greek. The original New Testament was written in Greek **While, it is true that Africans have a presence in the bible, the presence of Africans in the selecting of the canon of scripture and the defining of doctrinal positions as we have seen was minimum or non-existent.**

The one prominent exception to this fact is Augustine. Augustine was an African. His contribution to Christendom is singular yet quite significant. Unfortunately, it was Augustine who contributed the concept of the "Original Sin". However, it was the Greeks who decided to include his observation as their doctrine. It is important to note as we shall see later, that Augustine admits to relying on the observations of his natural man. He admits his conclusions lack spiritual insight and revelation by admitting his conclusion was based on what he saw with his natural eyes. Any Catholic encyclopedia will provide the reader with this information. Now that this issue is settled once and for all let us continue. A more in depth look will be provided on this false doctrine in Vol. II of this work.

There is one outstanding characteristic of the men that created Christianity; they didn't know what they were talking about. Even though it was reported that Constantine explained the "new" theory, we find in Constantine's own testimony that this could not have occurred.

Let me explain. The material being discussed at the Council of Nice was essentially African theology. Constantine was not the first emperor to attempt to get Whites included in the African Godhead. When Alexander conquered Egypt this necessity was immediately realized. The European emperor that would replace Alexander was named Soter. He was Egypt's second European ruler. Ptolemy I Soter changed his name to Serapis which means "savior" and tried to get his image associated with the Egyptian image of the Son of God Heru or Horus.

For over seven hundred years Whites had been attempting to preempt Egypt's gods as their own. Constantine succeeded he won the war of the minds. He was a very shrewd emperor. Not only did he have the backing of the Greek bishops he had bought the allegiance of some prominent African bishops as well. The key African bishop was Sylvester I a member of the African Melchite Coptic community of priest. Let us look at this development from its inception.

"After the Melchite Coptic Egyptian priests and priestesses in the temple of Memphis, Egypt fulfilled Ptolemy I's request and provided him an image of himself made into a god, man-made religion (not universal spiritual consciousness as practiced by the Ancient Egyptians) came into existence for the first time in human history. Ptolemy I, attempted to put this man-made icon/image of himself into all the sacred temples throughout Egypt alongside the Ancient Egyptian god, Osiris." *The Historical Origin of Christianity*, Walter Williams, pg. 5

"However this devious scheme of Ptolemy's was rejected by the entire sacred priest society throughout Egypt (except in Memphis, Egypt). Angered by this rejection, Ptolemy I, Soter, proceeded to close all sacred Ancient Egyptian Temples or buildings for the purpose of spiritual fellowship. The closing down of our ancestors' sacred temples during the reign of Ptolemy I, Soter, completely eliminated the last of the pharonic sacred institutions of ancient Egypt. This was the beginning of the erosion of the spiritual unity that the Ancient Egyptian priesthood had tried to keep in place throughout Egypt during this time." *The Historical Origin of Christianity*, Walter Williams, pg. 5

Rejecting False Gods

So we see that Constantine was not the first to make the attempt to create a false god. This was the first religious persecution and it was not of Christians as Western Christian scholars like to report. A latter generation of Melchite Coptic priest followed the example of the Memphis Coptic priest and in exchange for favors i.e. the right to hold religious services in their homes, and some monetary gains, continued to compromise with the new rulers. This is the real source and origin of the great schism that troubled Constantine. It became a great schism when the numbers of Coptic Exterior priest grew. By the time of Constantine the succession of periods of persecution and gifts of favor had worn down the resistance of the priesthood. Yet some continued to reject this new image and doctrine being created by the new rulers. The leader of this group of priest as we have seen was Arius.

At the time of Emperor Constantine the African community of priest were once again oppressed and grievously persecuted. Constantine further divided the community by offering Sylvester I a most unique gift. In exchange for his allegiance Sylvester would be made the first Vicar or Pope of his religious community and all persecution would cease. Suffice it to say Sylvester sold out for a life of ease and a position of authority. Let's look closer into this development. Let's look at this first Judas of history.

> "It began with a quarrel over the reconciliation of the traitors, clerics and bishops who were responsible in handing over their sacred writings to the Imperial Roman Emperor, Diocletian, during the Diocletian persecution of 303 A.D. Questions were raised regarding the validity of the ordination conferred by bishops who had conformed to the imperial demands."

> "They reasoned that the part played by the minister in the administration of the holy baptism for sanctity was substantial and not merely instrumental. Therefore, they maintained that a minister without grace could not confer the holy sacrament of baptism. Since they held that all persons outside of the Coptic Religious Community lacked grace and holiness which was required in the ministry, sanctity could not be obtained outside the Exterior Coptic Religious Community. For them their religious community was an exclusive caste that should not be contaminated by contact with known sinners, least of all, with the infamous traitors who had handed over the sacred writings to be burned by the persecutors and who refused martyrdom…The holy Coptic Exterior Religious Community contained no known sinners for it was absolutely separated from the world of sinners."
> *The Historical Origin of Christianity*, Walter Williams, pg. 18-19

It is interesting to note here who the real righteous men were in this scenario. The Coptic Exterior Religious Community is the community that the heathen emperor Constantine is at odds with. We have seen the character of Constantine and his crew at the Nicene Council. Now we see that the men that were excommunicated and proclaimed heretics were those seeking to maintain the Truth as seen through the eyes of the true Holy Men of Old. Within the African/Egyptian priesthood there were no known sinners. This should be a significant factor in judging the outcome of the Nicene Council "vote". It would seem prudent to at least make an inquiry into the nature and content of the view that was rejected. As we have seen holiness was a requirement within the first African church. Would not it be a wonderful thing if we returned to that standard? Remember, Arius the Heretic, was a member of this true Holy and Sanctified Community of Priest.

Unfortunately for confessing Christians today, the same thing cannot be said of the creators of their faith. **Before Christianity the knowledge taught by the Egyptians produced righteousness proving that the tree was good. After Christianity the knowledge taught by the Christians produced a very different**

fruit. What does that prove about the little lie introduced by Constantine? What now can we say of the tree of Christianity?

The stone that was rejected was the true "cornerstone" of the true Church. It had spiritual power. The teachings of Ancient Africa/Egypt had the power to regenerate the falling nature of man and produce men that manifested the fullness of the stature of Christ. The holiness exhibited by the Exterior Coptic Priest community demonstrated this fact.

Euro-Christianity Lacks Spiritual Power

Though the majority of African American Christians believe they are going to heaven when they die, the teachings of Christendom have done little to elevate the spiritual condition of the lives of Black people on earth. The excuse given is these are the "Last Days and it's supposed to be like this. This view and the attitude it produces breeds apathy as Christians become so other worldly they just accept things as they are. Let me make something very clear at this junction by Spirituality I do not mean morality. There is a vast difference in these two terms although they are related. **True morality is to Spirituality as the fruit is to the tree. Morality is the outgrowth of Spirituality.** To be truly moral one must as Scripture suggest *"walk in the Spirit".*

Walking in the Spirit requires the recognition that you are more than flesh and blood waiting to be redeemed at death. **A person that "acts" moral yet lacks love and has a mind full of false judgments is not a Spiritual person.** As African American Christians we are quite moral, at least on the surface, but overall our spiritual development has been severely limited by our enthusiastic acceptance of Euro-Christian philosophy, doctrines and creeds as a guide. **If we, and we must, are to heal, elevate, empower, and liberate ourselves beyond the year 2004, we will have to embrace whole-heartedly our African spirituality. It is time that we reclaim the African mind (wisdom) for African people.**

Christian Dogma and Doctrine lack Clarity

Finally, let us look at the new theology given to the world by Emperor Constantine. If Constantine was the one who led in the dialogue concerning the new doctrine then the priest that voted in his favor surely did so under duress or in extreme ignorance. Listen to Constantine explain his new concept in a letter to Arius and Alexander.

LETTER OF CONSTANTINE TO ALEXANDER AND ARIUS

"When you, Alexander, inquired of your presbyters what were the sentiments of each on **a certain inexplicable passage of the written Word**, thereby mooring a subject improper for discussion, you, Arius, rashly gave expression to a view of the matter, such as ought, either never to have been conceived, or if, indeed, it had been suggested to your mind, it became you to bury in silence. **For indeed, how few are capable either of adequately expounding, or even accurately understanding the import of matters so vast and profound! Who can grapple with subtilties of such investigations, without danger of lapsing into excessive error**?" *History of The First Council of Nice,* Dean Dudley, pg. 43

Here we find Emperor Constantine telling Alexander and Arius that the doctrine he would later introduce and explain was inexplicable. Bishops from the Council meeting also would write letters later saying that they had indeed thoroughly examined this new doctrine introduced and explained by Constantine and found that it was acceptable to them as sound doctrine. Are we to believe that sometime between the writing of this letter by Constantine where he says that the passage is inexplicable and anyone attempting to explain it would lapse into excessive error and the Council of Nice meeting where he was reportedly the one who explained this same passage to the bishops, that somehow he got a new revelation. **Without a new revelation Constantine could not have explained the new unexplainable doctrine.** Let's look at what they finally voted on as gospel truth and see if indeed they clearly understood what they were creating. Let's continue with Constantine's letter.

"They revile like the Jews, conspired against Christ, they deny his divinity, and declare him (Jesus) to be on the level of other men. They collect all these passages which allude to the incarnation of our Savior…and bring them forward as corroborative of their own impious assertion; while they evade those who which declare his divinity, and the glory which he possesses with the Father. They conceal their pernicious doctrines by means of their plausible and persuasive mode of conversation; they think thus to deceive the unwary….**'We are able,' say these evil-minded individuals 'to become like him, the sons of God.'**

"The Father is the Father because he has a Son, hence it is that he is called Father. He did not beget his Son in time. Is it not impiety to say that the wisdom of God was at one period not in existence? For it is written, 'I was with Him, being joined to Him, I was his delight..' **The Sonship of our Savior has nothing in common with the sonship of men. And it is, on**

<u>**this account, that our Lord, being, by nature, the Son of the Father, is worshipped by all**</u>." *History of The First Council of Nice,* Dean Dudley, pg. 35

"John the pious apostle, perceiving the greatness of the Word of God above all created beings, could find no terms adequate to convey this truth, neither did he presume to apply the same epithet to that Maker as to the creature. <u>**The Son of God is inexplicable, and beyond the comprehension of the evangelist, and perhaps the angels.**</u> Therefore, I think that those should not be considered pious who presume to investigate this subject in disobedience to the injunction, 'Seek not what is too difficult for thee, neither inquire into what is too high for thee.' The knowledge of many things incomparably inferior is beyond the capacity of the human mind, and cannot be attained." *History of The First Council of Nice,* Dean Dudley, pg. 34

"We believe, as is taught by the apostolical church, in the only unbegotten Father, who is the author of his own existence. <u>**The mind of man could not possibly invent a term expressive of what is meant by being unbegotten. To say that the Son was, that he has always been, and that he existed before all ages, is not to say that he is unbegotten. We believe that he is the only begotten Son of God, as was taught by the holy men who vainly endeavored to clear up the mystery, but failed, and confessed that it was beyond their powers.**</u> Besides this pious opinion of the Father and the Son, we confess the existence of the Holy Ghost, which truth has been upheld by the saints of the Old Testament, and by the learned divines of the New. We believe in one catholic and apostolical church, which cannot be destroyed, and which never fails to defeat all the impious designs of heretics. Besides this we receive the doctrine of the resurrection from the dead, of which Jesus Christ, our Lord, became the first fruits. He possessed a true, not a suppositious body, and he derived it from Mary, the mother of God." *History of The First Council of Nice,* Dean Dudley, pg. 35-36

<u>Constantine Defends his Error</u>

Here we have the Father of Christianity vainly attempting to defend his faith. It is obvious that Constantine did not have the spiritual insight to present a view that he admits no one even the pious John could explain. He remarks that the so-called enemies of the Church who deny that Jesus was God in the flesh, have collected numerous scripture that support their view and are presenting a plausible and persuasive argument. They say, he comments, that we are able to become as Jesus Sons of God. I am so grateful that this view was not entirely crushed by this tyrant because it is resurfacing even as I write. Recently Pastor Creflo Dollar and other ministers within his circle have begun to preach this powerful message and it is being received by the Church as valid and the truth. The reason; unlike Constantine's new additional word, the statement of Arius could be found in numerous scripture. Jesus is recorded as saying in John 10:34-35; *"Is it not recorded in your law, I said, "You are gods"? If he called them gods, to whom the word of God came and the scripture cannot be broken."*

Contrarily Constantine comments that the Sonship of Jesus has nothing in common with the sonship of man. For this reason, he continues, Jesus is worship by all. This part, at least we know is true. Because of Constantine, Jesus is worshipped by all as a deified man; God in the flesh. Constantine then reveals the reason for inserting this man in the godhead; that Jesus might share the Glory of the Father. Before Jesus Western man had no one of their race to glory in except their so-called "great" conquerors. They were by no means associated with anything divine or sacred, this was their chance, and they took it. **The false worship of Jesus must cease for it is idol worship of the worst kind for African Americans. It causes them to worship another race and to believe that they have the blueprint established by God for their salvation. Rather than a religion of liberation Christianity is a religion of control.** Therefore in order for African Americans to take back that control, they must first take back their wisdom.

> "They make matters worse from the viewpoint of the blacks...the whites where systematically preempting the whole of Egypt, even as adopting as their own black institutions they could not easily destroy. And they were wise enough to see that to control Africans they would have to control the African religion." *The Destruction of Black Civilization*, Chancellor Williams, pg. 54

How The Books of The Bible Became "The Word of God"

Many African American Christians are unaware of how the books of the bible got selected. They "assume" that God somehow made sure that "His Word" was preserved and was not allowed to be corrupted by man. This we should know by now is not so. But for the sake of certainty let us look at how the books of the bible really became the "Word of God".

> "When the Church mythologists established their system, they collected all the writings they could find and manage them as they pleased. It is

a matter altogether of uncertainty to us whether such of the writings as now appear under the name of the Old and New Testaments are in the same state in which those collectors say they found them, or whether they added, altered, abridged or dressed them up.'

"Be this as it may, they decided by vote which of the books out of the collection they had made should be the Word of God, and which should not. They rejected several; they voted others to be doubtful, such as the books called the Apocrypha; and those books which had a majority of votes were voted to be the Word of God. Had they voted otherwise, all the people, since calling themselves Christians, had believed otherwise---for the belief of one comes from the vote of the other. Who the people were that did this, we know nothing of; they call themselves by the general name of the Church, and this is all we know of the matter." *The Book Your Church Doesn't Want You To Read*, Tim C. Leedom, Editor, pg. 86

God Did Not Inspire the Selection of The Books of The Bible

So we see that the Bible became the "Word of God" the same way that Jesus became God in the flesh; it was by popular vote. We have seen what the "Fathers" of Christianity were like. They were men who had questionable motives and ethics as well as men who lacked the understanding of the nature of the subject they were voting on. In addition there was politics involved. Could there have been political reasons for the selection of the books of the bible as well? Of course it could have. There is obvious reason to doubt that the books that ended up in the bible were actually books that spoke for God. It is more likely that they were selected for there ability to speak for the men who selected them. Could they have erred? Let's see.

"The church's claim to special inspiration in forming the canon is obviously endangered if it erred in even one instance. If it made as many mistakes as scholarship indicates, then its claim to inspired prudence in selecting the books of the canon is thoroughly shattered. And what becomes of the 'old orthodoxy' or any form of Christianity without an infallible canon and without an infallible church which determined the canon in the first place." *The Book Your Church Doesn't Want You To Read,* Tim C. Leedom, Editor, pg. 124

Bible Is Not Infallible or Inerrant

Originally this same infallibility was claimed by the popes of Rome. The image of the infallibility of the Roman Church leaders has been forever shattered by recent revelations and admissions by the pope himself. The Catholic Church has had to publicly apologize for its errors and omissions. It is time for the issue of the infallibility of the "Word of God" to be resolved as well. **It is impossible for the bible to be infallible unless the men that selected its books were infallible. This we know was not the case.**

Perhaps one day in the near future we will hear public apologies from Christendom regarding the issue of the infallible and inerrancy of the bible as well. **Not only is the selection of canon a major cause to view the bible with some degree of skepticism but the numerous revisions are reason enough to sound the alarm. Without question the bible has been tampered with.** This implies the need to seek in other sources reliable information to be used for our spiritual edification. The King James Version in which most Christians rely on was supposed to be translated from the original tongue. However, we find this to be false information.

> "In 1611 the new version was published. Although the title page describes it as 'newly translated out of the original tongues', the statement is not entirely in accord with the facts. The work was actually a revision of the Bishops' Bible on the basis of the Hebrew and Greek. It did not win immediate universal acceptance, taking almost fifty years to displace the Geneva Bible in popular favor. In other words, the KJV was a revision of the Bible based on the Bishops' Bible which was a revision of the Great Bible, the Great Bible being based on the Matthew, Coverdale and Tyndale Bibles.

To revise according to Webster's New World Dictionary is: To read over carefully and correct, improve, or update where necessary; to change or amend something. **According to this definition, the Bible has been corrected, improved and changed. This would imply that its original form was not correct and therefore needed to be changed. There has been revision upon revision of the Bible which means that it has lost some of it original meaning.** The "Word of God" has been changed (revised) so many times that without knowledge of its original content it would be impossible to determine what errors were made in its many revisions. Without such knowledge it is quite difficult to rightly divide the "Bible". We now know that the Bible has historical as well as experiential errors. In addition as was stated in the above quotation we find that the very first page of the KJV is deceptive because it is misrepresented as being a revision of the original tongue.

African Wisdom Worked

As we saw in chapter one, what the Ancient African cultures had worked. We have also seen that Western man's knowledge base has not worked. Why wouldn't African Americans seek to make the wisdom of Africa work for them today? Truth is universal and timeless. If it worked then, it will work now. It is a fact that because of the wisdom of our ancestors, people traveled to Egypt in Africa, called the holy land to be instructed in the way. **African temples and mystery schools were devoted to the development of the highest virtues in man.** To the priest the pillars of civilization, the goal of life was to manifest our divinity or god-hood (the Christ). In fact they were dedicated to that which the Scriptures instruct believers to devote themselves. In Romans the eight chapter, the bible says that *"the whole creation groans and travails, waiting for the manifestation of the Sons of God"*. The temples in Egypt, Africa were designed to teach man how to manifest his divinity, symbolized in the African concept of the Son of God.

African society promoted above all else the divinity of man and the means for its attainment. It used as a basis for this accomplishment the system of thought called Maat. The Spiritual principles inherent in Maat formed the basis for a righteous and civilized nation.

"Maat is associated with the seven cardinal virtues, the keys to human perfectibility: truth, justice, propriety, harmony, balance, reciprocity, and order." *Nile Valley Contributions To Civilization,* Anthony T. Browder, pg. 82

Let's continue to look into that which Constantine and the Western world was looking to destroy and the body of knowledge they usurped and corrupted with the vote of the Nicene Council.

Count C. F. Volney in his book Ruins of Empires wrote, "All religions originated in Africa." Professor Breasted, famous Egyptologist, also maintains that "the Ethiopians were the first to give religious thought and aspiration to the world." *What They Never Told You In History Class,* Indus Khamit-Kush, pg. 48

"About 3000 B.C. the Pyramid Texts were already speaking with authority of the constitution of man, his survival after death, and his relation to the life of the cosmos." *What They Never Told You In History Class,* Indus Khamit-Kush, pg. 49

In the Journal of African Civilizations, Charles S. Finch M.D. in summation of the books written by Gerald Massey says the following: "In the works of Gerald Massey, *Book of Beginnings, Natural Genesis, and Ancient Egypt,* written in six volumes...If there is a unifying theme that runs though these six volumes it is this; that Africa was the source of the world's people, language, religions, myths, and symbols and Egypt Africa's mouthpiece. In Massey's view, Egypt brought the African genius to its highest expression and then proceeded to instruct the world in Africa's wisdom. Inner Africa was the mother, the great Nile the father, and Egypt the brilliant son and fulfiller." *The Works of Gerald Massey, Studies in Kamite Origins, -What They Never Told You In History Class,* Indus Khamit-Kush, pg. 157

"The universe was viewed as the omnipotent expression of one great Supreme Being, which manifested itself within all of the functions and principles that govern the universe and maintain balance and harmony." *Nile Valley Contributions To Civilization,* Anthony T. Browder, pg. 83

"From the beginning of time Africans have always had a belief in one god, self-created and all powerful. Upon observing the wonders of the universe, man began to see the many manifestations of the one Creator reflected in all that existed and identified them as aspects of the One." *Nile Valley Contributions To Civilization,* Anthony T. Browder, pg. 86

Lawrence W. Levine (*Black Culture and Black Consciousness*) concludes: "For the most part when they looked upon the cosmos they saw Man, Nature and God as a unity; distinct but inseparable aspects of a sacred whole." *The Spirituality of African Peoples,* Peter J. Paris, pg. 32

"So great was the achievement of the Africans in the Nile Valley that all the great men of Ancient Europe journeyed there." Herbert Wendt, *In Search of Man, - What They Never Told You In History Class,* Indus Khamit-Kush, pg. 244

The scholar Amelineau expresses a similar view, "I see no reason why ancient Greece would keep the honor of ideas that she borrowed from

Egypt." *What They Never Told You In History Class,* Indus Khamit-Kush, pg. 247

"Religion was (and remains) a vital part of the lives of most Africans. For some it encompassed their entire existence. It substantiated and explained their place in the universe; their culture, and their relationship to nature and humankind; it also dictated their roles in the community and society at large. Religion among most African ethnic groups was not simply a faith or worship system; it was a way of life, a system of social control, a provider of medicine, and an organizing mechanism." *Africanisms in American Culture,* Joseph e. Holloway, -*The Spirituality of African Peoples,* Peter J. Paris, pg. 37

African Wisdom Good Enough For Blacks and Whites

The body of African knowledge worked for the Africans and would have worked for the Europeans if they had been seeking how to become virtuous men; men in harmony with the will of the Creator. It could have perhaps helped Western man create a social structure that was sound and civilized. Note: Western man stole and plagiarized the Africa's knowledge it was not borrowed.

The family structure in Africa was designed to pass on this wisdom from generation to generation. The stories that the Griot shared and the songs that the children were taught accomplished this in a very natural and stress free manner. The relationship between husband and wife, parent and child, young and old, individual and community, and the individual and his God were well defined. **The ancestors of African Americans gave to the world the foundation for every scientific development and the knowledge base for every intellectual achievement. Their spiritual teachings and sacred scripture form the knowledge base for every other people's religious teaching. Is not their wisdom good enough for us?**

Where would the world be today without the wisdom given to the world by the Egyptians, a dark skinned people from the land of Kush? Where would America be without the contribution of African Americans? What if African people had not charted the stars and the heavens, would N.A.S.A. have a space program? What if George Washington Carver had not taught the southern white farmers how to rotate their crops, would they have survived? What if the ebony architects of the pyramids had not shared their knowledge of geometry with the world, would we have the tall skyscrapers? Black people built the first boats, the first roads, did the first crop irrigating, the first metal refining, and it goes on and on. **How is it**

we have been taught to disrespect and reject our own wisdom? Why is it we would rather rely on others to define and interpret spiritual wisdom and our very existence for us?

European Scientific, Philosophical and Religious Backwardness

The European scientist still thought the world was flat and that the sun revolved around the Earth as late as the 1400's. This is only one area that they are late in discovering something that Africans understood thousands of years ago. The ancient Africans understood the Creator long before the advent of the time of Jesus and the founding of the Roman Empire. All essential aspects of Euro-Christianity have their origin in the sacred teachings of Ancient Africans. **Western man has not demonstrated that they have even understood their own copycat religion. Yet, these are the minds that Blacks rely on to lead them back to their Creator and to lead them to life.**

Our scholar George James documented the fact that so-called Greek philosophy was really stolen African wisdom. **The proof is there also, and in fact, the confessions are there, that indict Western mans theft of Africa's sacred teachings to use in the creation of their counterfeit and fraudulent religion called Christianity.**

European Spiritual Authority Unreliable

Western man is not a reliable interpreter of Africa's sacred spiritual symbols and mythical method of teaching higher truths. It is incumbent on Blacks to do their own interpreting of this sacred scripture. Blacks must seek a new perspective of this long neglected body of knowledge. Webster defines Protestant as, a member of any of Christian churches that are not Roman Catholic or Eastern Orthodox. Those that are Protestant and you should know that if you are Baptist, Methodist, Church of God and Church of God in Christ, you are Protestant, should rejoice that Martin Luther established the truth that scripture is subject to private interpretation. The methods of interpretation of sacred scriptures remain as much a mystery to the average European religious scholar as the method of the construction of the pyramids remains hidden from the European physical scientist.

As one can easily discern, once informed, and having faced the truth, that the mind of the early Western scholar, philosopher, and priest (clergy) lacked spiritual clarity and would go so far as to even reject spiritual wisdom, knowledge and understanding. This is because the Western mind in general relies on things that can be discerned and therefore affirmed by the physical senses and subject to the domain of the rational mind.

The mind of Western man has given us Catholicism, Protestantism Romanticism, Feudalism, Pragmatism, Materialism, Existentialism, Idealism, Marxism, Fascism, Imperialism, Feminism, Utilitarianism, Humanism, Socialism, Communism, Capitalism and a sundry of other "isms", all of which do not work. What is critical for African American Christians to understand is that the European "creation", called Christianity will not work for them either.

Spiritual Awareness Lacking

In each of the above list of disciplines and systems of thought, spiritual awareness is glaringly absent. As valiant an effort to interpret the Mystery teachings they had plagiarized from the Africans their authentic originators, the result has always been limited by the mind of Western man. His propensity for relying on sense (carnal) data to form his opinion of Truth is the reason for the limitation. For some reason, Western man tends to fall in the category of those who "having ears, hear not, and eyes but see not". **Apparently, it is difficult for the European psyche to accept the reality of knowledge derived other than by the five senses.**

The Spiritual aspect of the matter is almost wholly misunderstood, ignored or rejected. This is true in the realm of Psychology, Science and Religion. Today, admittedly, there are exceptions to this rule. And fortunately, they are not being rejected, excommunicated, declared heretics and ran out of the country. It is ironic that much of what some European religious communities are teaching is an understanding of that which was established as valid by ancient Africans millenniums past. Because of this fact both Whites and Blacks are finding a new connection with their source of life the Creator of all life and for this reason they are learning the sacredness of all aspects of God's creation. It most be noted that the Orthodox Churches have deemed these Religious communities as cults of "New Age Thinking". It is true there is "nothing new under the sun". These aren't new teachings they are old African teachings resurfacing in the time of need.

The tragic aspect to this development is that many African Americans are too limited in their scope of awareness to recognize the truth of their ancestors reflected in the teachings and even more tragic is the absence of similar pioneering efforts among African Americans Religious Leaders.

It is interesting that many African American Christians try to avoid the fact that the authority that they have based their faith in is European. This may be especially true of the clergy. They are in denial. **This must cease!** We all must look this reality squarely in the face. When we do, we see not only the problem but also the solution to the dilemma.

It is critical that the practice of relying on the spiritual authority of Western scholars of Religion by African American clergy is discontinued. If we have judge the tree by its fruit, it is not difficult to make this decision. The survival of African Americans depends on their willingness and ability to arrive at their own conclusions of the master plan of life as taught by the Jesus of Scripture. African American clergy must truly study to show themselves approved in order to rightly divide the truth from the error and falsehood that has been inserted in scripture through the selection and rejection process and in the many revisions of the bible. For this, they must go back to the source.

Be Still and Listen to God

It is often quoted in church services and meetings that *"if Gods people that are called by His name would humble themselves and repent that God would hear us from heaven"*. Apparently African Americans have not humbled themselves and repented, for we still need to hear from heaven. **It is time for Blacks to "stop, be still, and listen to the voice of their spirits, where the Creator speaks to us all. We do not need an intermediary; did you not hear that the veil of the temple has been rent asunder? We can all go boldly and directly to the throne of God and seek His face, and seek his wisdom, knowledge and understanding. We have not knocked so the door has not opened, we have not sought so we have not found. Instead of relying on someone else, it is time to rely on self or more specifically our god-self; the God within".**

The present discussion is limited to a focus on our institutions and the need for new institutions that will create a new standard of life for a new man. In a subsequent work we will focus on what we must do as individuals to accomplish this mighty task. However the most important thing is learning to listen to God within for it is He that is our true guide and He that will lead us to victory. Amen!

Black Church Different in Form Only

I humbly charge the African American clergy to be humble enough to admit that they have accepted another's view of the world, themselves and their God. There is no way to deny that in its present state, the Black church is

different from its White counterpart in form only. Certainly the Black Church is somewhat independent in their day to day operations. Yet they have too long been dependent on others for doctrinal understanding and religious study methods for preparation for the ministry.

The religious or more specifically, the spiritual wisdom of the ancient Africans must be vindicated within the sanctuary of the African American Church. Proper credit and recognition must be afforded it in the Black Church if nowhere else. **The African American Clergy must recommit to study the origin and development of Euro-Christianity and the African mythology and cosmology that predate it and from which it sprang and form its own spiritual knowledge base and world view.** Such a change in perspective will result in a change in results. When we know better we will do better. African American Clergymen must begin to teach the truth about Christianity's origin from the pulpit.

In the words of a distinguished American disciple of Gerald Massey, Dr. Alvin Boyd Kuhn: **"The entire Christian creation legend descent into and exodus from Egypt, ark and flood allegory, Israelite history, Hebrew prophecy and poetry, Gospel, Epistles and Revelation imagery, all are now proven to have been the transmission of ancient Egypt's scrolls and papyri into the hands of later generations which knew neither their true origin nor their fathomless meaning."** *What They Never Told You In History Class,* Indus Khamit-Kush, pg. 64

Blacks Must Accept Four Facts

There are four facts African American must come to grips with immediately: (1) Blacks are not spiritually, economically, or legally (politically) free. (2) The average European feels superior to blacks, is not interested in Black Salvation, and would prefer not to integrate with blacks. (3) It is critical that African Americans understand that Western man is not competent to rule this world. (4) And perhaps of even more importance Blacks must realize that as a people Blacks will not be economically or politically empowered until they are spiritually liberated from the darkness of Western religion for it is a crutch and not a vessel of deliverance. It was a "Trojan Horse" a gift that Blacks should have refused.

"Re-emancipation has not entirely removed the scars of captivity in their minds, (sons and daughters of former captives) any more than it has removed the attitude of superiority in the minds of sons and daughters of former captive owners". *No More Lies About Africa,* Chief Musamaali Nangoli, pg. 5

If those of us who suffer the most from the corruption that is in this world do not take a stand; if we do not overcome our apathy, fear, ignorance, dependence, and disunity and take responsibility for providing a real solution to the dilemma in the lives of African Americans, life in the Black community will continue its downward spiral which means we are all doomed.

"No longer must our race look to whites for guidance and leadership... A race without authority and power is a race without respect." Marcus Garvey, *No More Lies About Africa,* Chief Musamaali Nangoli, pg. 109

Power comes from defining your own existence. When the Black man displays the capacity to think for himself again, his accent to power and authority is guaranteed. No one will respect the Black man as long as he allows others to think for him. A shallow assessment of the situation may prove discouraging, because we appear to be so weak and the opposition seems so "all powerful". Yet we must remember that the Creator is the only one who is all-powerful and invincible. **Western man only appears to be firmly entrenched as the "gods of this world". With all their material riches, advanced technology and seeming control of the situation, they are not.** The spiritual capacity for connecting to the Creator possessed by African Americans makes them the strongest force on the planet at this time.

I am grateful to see African Americans excelling in sports and entertainment however it is time we excelled in the one area that matters most. That area is not politics, nor is it to be found in the financial world, the Black community needs those who are willing to excel in the area of religion. Let us take religion to new heights. Let's us be stars for the Creator.

Blacks must adopt the attitude of David in the scriptures regarding the giant of materialism and capitalism and spiritual wickedness, David said *"to the men that stood by him...what shall be done to the man that kills this Philistine, and take away the reproach from Israel? For who is this uncircumcised Philistine, that he should defy the armies of the living God"?* I Samuel 17:26

To be uncircumcised biblically is to be a heathen. Western man continues to display the attributes of the heathen. **To be ruled and intimidated by heathens is a reproach.** The spiritual rebirth and regeneration of African American peoples would change the balance of power in this world. You have heard and perhaps believe, that "he who owns the gold, makes the rules". That is a lie and a misrepresentation of reality. **It is declared unto you this day and is true, that "Spirit rules" even in the material realm. They that truly have the Spirit of God shall rule".** Euro-Christianity will not grant us that Spiritual power. We must adopt an African spiritual frame of reference. And with the smooth stone of Spiritual Truth and reality and trusting in the Creator to guide our efforts, as David, we will be victorious. **This worlds system is doomed because it was built on a shaky foundation called falsehood (untruth).**

Returning to the Roots of Wisdom

We must face the fact that the knowledge base provided by Euro-Christianity is corrupt and will not produce the fruit desired. You cannot get bitter and sweet water from the same fountain. We must seek a new understanding of the ancient wisdom to reach a new level of awareness. There is a bird in Africa called the Sankofa bird it is depicted with its head looking backward. It symbolizes the need for us to return to our roots. We must do this not only culturally but spiritually as well. It is understood by many Black people that no forward progress can be made without first reaching back to reclaim that which was viciously beat out of the slave, his spirituality. Many within the Black Church, both ministers and lay-people, have adopted African names and are wearing African garments to Church service. **This is evidence of our beginning to break the cultural shackles. This goes far in breaking the cycle of self-hatred and the dysfunctional mindset of Black Inferiority**. Yet, we must understand that included in the culture is a mind-set, an African paradigm and perspective.

We are free men and women, why not exercise that freedom and choose to be yourself for once. We have tried to be someone else; by now we should know, it doesn't work. We must go beyond morality to spirituality. This does not discount the need for moral commitment and righteousness. However we must return to our roots and adopt an African Spiritual frame of reference if we would be spiritually free.

Christianity Creates Confusion and Division Among Blacks

In the movie Sankofa, Joe who had been fathered by a European, that had raped his Black mother, chose to embrace the religion of the one who raped his mother. **He symbolizes those of us that have chosen to embrace Christianity. Early Western man raped the people of Africa spiritually and put a foreign seed in their minds.** Throughout the movie, we observe the confusion the teachings of the slave master (the foreign seed) create within Joe. Though he longed for love, he rejected the Black woman who loved him. Eventually his confusion led to him murdering his own mother. As he choked her he called her a demon because of what he had been taught by Christianity. The reason for this twisted scene in his life was all because he embraced a foreign teaching. An African frame of reference is required for African minds. Without it, Blacks commit genocide. African Americans are like salt-water fish in fresh-water. This means, in such an environment, Blacks can never really be their true selves nor can they survive.

Now that we have established the fact that the authority of Christianity is **European in nature, what must we do? Is that acceptable?** With all the negative spin that has been put on the culture and history of African people, we have learned to distrust and reject the wisdom of our own people. This must cease! **We must embrace an African spiritual frame of reference for viewing the world, our God and ourselves.**

Today, Europeans still apply Western concepts to African people. The use of Western concepts to teach and test Black children, still prevails in the public education system. There, African American youth are tested by educators according to European standards, as though they were European children. Western man too often lack the capacity to look through 'black eyes' and understand the black experience, nor for the most part have they shown a true desire to look.

Time For A New View

It is difficult to maintain a system of "White Supremacy" with evidence of this nature illustrating that an African nation had surpassed even contemporary European knowledge on such a profound subject. **European scholars, after attempting to white-wash parts of African in order to stake a claim on the advance knowledge of African people and upon failing miserably, resorted to presenting the "space men" theory of how the Africans came into such delicate knowledge. This unbelief is founded, not in the impossibility of such accomplishments by Africans, but based entirely on the racist ideology of those who come to such frivolous conclusions.** As with the pyramids the knowledge and wisdom of Ancient Africa continues to baffle and fascinate the mind of the European scholars and scientist. White Supremacy is based on a "white lie" and a big one at that. For this reason, as you read it is crumbling. It cannot stand the light of Truth.

In its place we must erect a new view, a true view. Afro-centrism without truth will not suffice. However an African Spiritual frame of reference will provide a vessel to take African Americans safely to the Promised Land. To

liberate that mind is the key to Black Salvation. It starts with thinking for oneself. Black man free your mind and your destiny will follow.

Chapter 8

REVERSING THE REVERSAL

BREAKING THE SHACKLES THAT BLIND

"There are a people, now forgotten, discovered, while others were yet
Barbarians, the elements of the arts and sciences. A race
of men rejected now for their black skin and wooly hair
founded, on the laws of Nature, those civil and
Religious systems, which still govern
the universe.
Count C. Volney
French scholar
1787

True Confessions

The majority of the statements and quotes in this chapter are described as "true confessions" because in this chapter the perpetrators speak for themselves. **We will let Western man speak for himself for the most part with occasional comments. Here we will examine the lies that have been fostered about both Western man and Africans. "Truth though crushed to the earth will rise again".**

In the opening of his book, *"The Iceman Inheritance"*, by Michael Bradley a European from Canada, we find this statement;

"THIS BOOK IS RACIST.
FOR AMONG OTHER THINGS, I WILL ATTEMPT TO SHOW
THAT RACISM IS A PREDISPOSITION
OF BUT ONE RACE OF MANKIND – THE WHITE RACE.
I BELIEVE THAT I CAN SHOW THAT OUR CONVERGING CONTEMPORARY
CRISES, LIKE RACISM ITSELF,
HAVE THERE ORIGINS IN THE PREHISTORY
OF THE WHITE RACE ALONE.
WE ATTRIBUTE VARIOUS THREATS TO OUR SURVIVAL
TO MAN'S FOLLY...BUT THIS IS A CONSCIOUS AND SELF-PROTECTING
EUPHEMISM.
NUCLEAR WAR, ENVIRONMENTAL POLLUTION,
RESOURCE RAPE...ALL ARE
THE RESULT OF PECULIARLY CAUCASOID BEHAVIOR,
CAUCASOID VALUES,
AND CAUCASOID PSYCHOLOGY.
THERE IS NO WAY TO AVOID THE TRUTH.
THE PROBLEM WITH THE WORLD IS WHITE MEN.
IF THIS INSIGHT HAS GENERALLY ESCAPED US
IT IS ONLY BECAUSE WE CAUCASOIDS
HAVE DICTATED MUCH HISTORY,
WRITTEN MOST OF IT, AND JUDGED IT
IN TERMS OF OUR OWN SELF IMAGE".

I could not have done a better job of summing up what has occurred. In writing history, it is true, and most of us know it, history is really his-story. Yet, this process can be reversed if we are honest and courageous enough to face the challenge. Blacks must learn how to trust their own scholars again. This is not a racist position; it is simply the truth. Perception is everything, even a lie repeated often enough and long enough will eventually be accepted as truth. Do you not perceive that Truth has been turned upside down? Everything got reversed. What was good was called evil and that which was evil was now called good.

Today the education system teaches that civilization began in Rome and Greece. While the Church continues to teach that Western man is God's chosen people divinely ordained to bring civilization and religion to the world. We believed it. This misperception must be eradicated and permanently erased from the memory of man. The validity of the Spiritual base of knowledge bestowed on humanity by the ebony people of the Nile Valley must be established as true.

PART I

REVERSAL #1

"Indeed, history has been very kind to Europeans because they have written it and in many instances, it has been the fiction (lie) agreed upon. Because of a global system of miseducation which currently exists, the average person honestly believes that civilization began in Europe, and that the rest of the world waited in darkness for the Europeans to bring them the light. For more than 500 years, Europeans have controlled and manipulated the image and information of the world". *Nile Valley Contributions To Civilization*, Anthony T. Browder, pg.37

The Beginning---How White became Right

The names of the races that made up the early nation of Europeans are numerous. They were called Visigoths, Ostrogoths, Sycthians, Vikings, Teutonics, Francs, Angles, Saxons, Vandals, Danes, and the Lombards. Many of these people combined to become the Greek and Roman nations. These are the earlier names of the English, Spaniards, Germans, Italians, Russians, Dutch, French, British and Portuguese people. The names were changed in the reversal, the great cover-up. Let's look at what Western man has to say about his roots. We will begin with the Greeks and Romans.

"The invaders of Aegean civilization were the Greeks-a tall blond, barbarous, Indo-European people from the north. Slowly and thoroughly (about 1600-1000 B.C.) they conquered and occupied Greece, Crete, the Aegean islands, and West Asia Minor. But the Greeks gave the chief stamp to a new and better civilization, which arose gradually". *Visualized Units in Ancient and Medieval History*, Russell E. Fraser & William D. Pearson, pg. 28

"Greeks were, as a race, observant, acute-minded, versatile, open to new ideas, and probably more highly imaginative than any other people of history. Their services to civilization were, above all, intellectual and artistic". *Visualized Units in Ancient and Medieval History*, Russell E. Fraser & William D. Pearson, pg. 31

"The Greeks proved that they were intellectually superior to other races. About 950 B.C. a few Greeks learned the Phoenician alphabet, modified it in their own way, and before long many of them were writing clear and forceful Greek language. The most brilliant achievements of the Greek mind belong to a later period, but were rooted in the work of early poets, philosophers, and artists, especially of those between 700-500 B.C.". *Visualized Units in Ancient and Medieval History*, Russell E. Fraser & William D. Pearson, pg. 35

"Real philosophy arose and reached its highest development among the Greeks". A philosopher is a student of causes, nature, and system. *Visualized Units in Ancient and Medieval History*, Russell E. Fraser & William D. Pearson, pg. 52

"The religion of the Greeks… was polytheism, free, on the whole from degrading practices, although it had little connection with right conduct. The divinities, which were numerous, resembling superior mortals, possessed the usual weaknesses of mortals, and lived on intimate terms with men. After death a dreary existence in the underworld awaited all except a few great heroes, who entered 'Elysium' (a paradise). About the Greek religion clustered a multitude of varied and beautiful myths, an acquaintance with which has long been considered a part of education of cultured people". *Visualized Units in Ancient and Medieval History*, Russell E. Fraser & William D. Pearson, pg. 30-31

"Greece is a very small land, a peninsula, the southern part of which is a separate peninsula…a temperate climate, and the soil, which demands fairly hard work, produced a hardy people. Greece suffers so little from calamities of nature, such as floods and droughts, that its people were free from overpowering superstitious fears. The varied and harmonious beauty of the country explains, in part, the Greek artistic sense…they became great traders and colonizers, 'citizens of the world'. Greeks called themselves 'Hellenes' from a mythical common ancestor and the Greek word 'Hellas". *Visualized Units in Ancient and Medieval History*, Russell E. Fraser & William D. Pearson, pg. 27

"Education and training was almost entirely military, with emphasis on obedience. Respect for elders, endurance, and patriotism. Men between the ages of seven and thirty lived in barracks, and even until sixty took their meals at public messes. **Every man's first duty was to be a soldier; cripples and weaklings were not tolerated. Training was from seven years old to twenty, most active service from twenty to thirty".** *Visualized Units in Ancient and Medieval History*, Russell E. Fraser & William D. Pearson, pg. 36

"Family life left, on the whole, much to be desired. The respectable woman led a very restricted life at home, seldom appeared in public, and even kept to her own rooms when guests were present, unless these were relatives or quite intimate friends. She managed the home and reared the children, with whom the father had few contacts. **Formal education was for boys only; the girls played with their dolls and remained with their mothers till marriage".** *Visualized Units in Ancient and Medieval History*, Russell E. Fraser & William D. Pearson, pg. 55

"The establishment of the Roman empire ushered in a prolonged period of peace, harmony, and order after a most dreadful period of war, discord, and disorder. The Empire unified, blended, and, in great part, refined and modified the most important movements of ancient times, and began to transmit to later times what was the best in ancient life". *Visualized Units in Ancient and Medieval History*, Russell E. Fraser & William D. Pearson, pg. 105

"Roman commerce introduced into Roman life a higher degree of culture and comfort. The Greek language, art, literature, and philosophy had an especially refining effect on many opened minded Romans". *Visualized Units in Ancient and Medieval History*, Russell E. Fraser & William D. Pearson, pg. 88

"Unless corrupted by outside influences, the Romans were industrious, home-loving, simple and frugal in their habits, patient, orderly, reverent of the gods, courageous, honorable privately and publicly, stern in discipline, and patriotic. They were, however, crude and stubborn, and scorned learning, the fine arts and many niceties of civilized life. Frugal habits led sometimes to miserliness, and patriotism to cruelty". *Visualized Units in Ancient and Medieval History*, Russell E. Fraser & William D. Pearson, pg. 77

"Roman houses were at first small, crude huts of one room, with a hole in the roof for chimney and skylight. Other rooms were added later, leaving the former hut a central hall. Furniture was simple-wooden couches, tables, and stools". *Visualized Units in Ancient and Medieval History*, Russell E. Fraser & William D. Pearson, pg. 77

"Roman religion was unimaginative, and its practice consisted mostly of the strict observance of ceremonials. **It was intimately connected**

to state affairs, and one of the important duties of the king was to offer sacrifice on behalf of the people. Important features were a deep veneration of ancestors and an indifference to life after death. The gods who were numerous, stood apart from men, and few myths were connected with them. The priests were active men of special functions. **Such were the pontiffs, who had general charge of all religious matters, and the augurs, who sought and interpreted omens from the actions of birds, from signs and wonders, and the appearance of entrails of sacrificial victims.** The Romans finally added to their religion much of the Greek religion, including the beautiful Greek myths". *Visualized Units in Ancient and Medieval History*, Russell E. Fraser & William D. Pearson, pg.78

Within these quotes we find examples of gross misrepresentations. As Western man practices his self aggrandizement, he must depart from the truth. We have seen his true history and have learned that such descriptions are merely distortions used to deceive other people.

Such statements as: "The Greeks gave the chief stamp to a new and better civilization." And that they: "were open to new ideas,"…"their service to civilization were, above all, intellectual and artistic,"…"The Greeks proved that they were intellectually superior to other races,"…"Real philosophy arose and reached it's highest development among the Greeks,"…"its (Greece) people were free from overpowering superstitious fears,"…"The establishment of the Roman empire ushered in a prolonged period of peace, harmony, and order," we know to be all false.

Once again we see how Western mans sordid past was concealed with lies as he grappled with claiming the inheritance and history of the African nation. Perhaps the jealous nature of the Greeks was a factor in their coveting the greatness of African civilization. **Like Jacob in the Scripture who out of jealousy covered himself with the clothing of his brother Esau and made himself to smell like him in order to deceive his father, we see Western man clothing himself in the likeness of the African in order to deceive the world and lay claim to Africa's blessing and inheritance.**

A people who from the age of seven were preparing for war and to whom war was a favorite pastime and business, could not and did not usher in any period of peace or harmony. As we shall see in Part 2, "a long period" is relative for there were very few years when there were no wars in early Greek and Roman history.

Note: **The religion of both the Greeks and Romans was polytheistic meaning they worship many gods. Note also that these gods resembled the men that had made them.** As we have seen it would be difficult for a people who had worshiped numerous gods to accept the African worship of one God. Evidently they wanted to keep their idol gods, for they brought them to Christianity. They could not understand the three attributes of the Creator illustrated in the symbolic imagery of the Trinity of Father, Mother and Son as taught by the African priest. They had to add a god that resembled them as they were accustomed to doing. **Making one God into three gods was a difficult task but Western man managed.**

PART 2

REVERSING THE REVERSAL

Let us continue with Western man's testimony as he begins to give a more accurate view of the early Greeks, Romans and the others who represent Western man's ancestral lineage. We have also included a few observations from some distinguished Black scholars. Afterward we will provide a summary of the material presented.

'The Greeks never combined into one great, united state-a chief defect in their civilization. The cause of this lay partly in geography and partly in the Greek nature. The Greeks were peculiarly patriotic locally, and jealous and suspicious of foreigners..." *Visualized Units in Ancient and Medieval History*, Russell E. Fraser & William D. Pearson, pg. 29

"Primitive Hellenic civilization (about 1100-750 B.C.) is called Homeric, because of the Homeric Poems, the 'Iliad' and the 'Odyssey'...the Iliad deals with a ten-year war of the Greeks against Troy, the Odyssey with the adventures of Odysseus, one of the Greek heroes before Troy, while returning home". *Visualized Units in Ancient and Medieval History*, Russell E. Fraser & William D. Pearson, pg. 28

"Dark spots in Athenian life. (1) Women were assigned a low position. (2) The greater benefits of civilization were based upon slavery. (3) The dignity of honest toil had little appeal. Manual labor, except agriculture, was thought somewhat degrading. (4) Morality was lower than we should expect from people so highly developed. For example, many men were not ashamed of lying to serve their own ends. (5) There was little progress in sanitation and in providing ordinary comforts and conveniences". *Visualized Units in Ancient and Medieval History*, Russell E. Fraser & William D. Pearson, pg. 57-58

"Development in government was along certain lines in each city. The Homeric councils of nobles gradually stripped the king of power and set up an oligarchy, rule by a few. Oppressive rule by the oligarchy led to its overthrow and the establishment of tyranny, that is rule by a tyrant, usually a man who championed the people against the oligarchy and usurped supreme power. Many Greek tyrants were wise, just rulers". *Visualized Units in Ancient and Medieval History*, Russell E. Fraser & William D. Pearson, pg. 34-35

"All hard work was done by the helots (descendants of the original inhabitants subdued by the Dorians), who were made state slaves, who often were killed off in cold blood when they grew too numerous". *Visualized Units in Ancient and Medieval History*, Russell E. Fraser & William D. Pearson, pg. 36-37

"A rebellion headed by Cylon was unsuccessful, but led to the concession of a written code of laws. This (621 B.C.), the work of Draco, was so cruel that it was said to have been written in blood". *Visualized Units in Ancient and Medieval History*, Russell E. Fraser & William D. Pearson, pg. 37

"When a violent revolution threatened, Solon a noble renowned for justice and respected by all classes, was appointed sole Archon with full powers to remodel the constitution and draft new laws. Solon's reforms completely satisfied no class, and from the constant strife of factions and clans resulted in the twenty-year tyranny of Pisistratus. But he was a democratic tyrant..." *Visualized Units in Ancient and Medieval History*, Russell E. Fraser & William D. Pearson, pg. 37-38

"In Athens, Themistocles, a radical democrat, a man of outstanding ability and personality, became a leader, and induced the Athenians to build a fleet. But in a Greek council held at Corinth, in which the Greeks tried to repress their natural jealousies of each other, Sparta was chosen leader to repel a new and greater Persian invasion under Xerxes, son of Darius". *Visualized Units in Ancient and Medieval History*, Russell E. Fraser & William D. Pearson, pg. 40

"The Romans were unable for a while to deal successfully with the many new and difficult problems of rule and social changes that arose from their conquests. There followed an epoch of instability, insecurity, corruption, class-strife, and civil war. These evils were evident about 200 B.C., and in full swing about 150 B.C." *Visualized Units in Ancient and Medieval History*, Russell E. Fraser & William D. Pearson, pg.87

"Rule of the provinces by absolute governors, who had held high offices at Rome, was begun during the fever or conquest. **The provincials were, for the most part, fearfully oppressed. They paid huge tributes, were disarmed, and were subject without warning to outrageous violations of person and property**". *Visualized Units in Ancient and Medieval History*, Russell E. Fraser & William D. Pearson, pg. 87

"The government (Roman) fell into the hands of the wealthy, selfish, and corrupt capitalists (knights), who plundered the provincials. They disregarded treaty obligations with their Italian subjects, and tyrannized over poorer Roman citizens". *Visualized Units in Ancient and Medieval History*, Russell E. Fraser & William D. Pearson, pg. 87

"Serious blots upon the Empire were: slavery; the inhuman sports of the gladiatorial games; deliberate killing of unwanted children, especially the poor; frequency of suicide, especially among the upper classes, for whom, until the spread of Christianity, there was no real spiritual relief; wanton and extravagant habits among the wealthy; misdirected state charity which encouraged idleness among the masses; and a decline in the sanctity of marriage and of family life, **which made divorce quite common**". *Visualized Units in Ancient and Medieval History*, Russell E. Fraser & William D. Pearson, pgs.113-114

"The Empire almost broke up in the third century because of uncertainty about the succession to the throne and the need of new methods in government to fit the changed conditions. **There were constant civil wars and a rapid succession of emperors, most of whom were weak or evil. It then entered into a final decay, for it had become worn-out from many causes**". *Visualized Units in Ancient and Medieval History*, Russell E. Fraser & William D. Pearson, pg. 117

"The Vandals, Burgundians, and Anglo-Saxons. **The Vandals were so savage that 'vandalism' has come to mean 'useless and willful destruction'.** They crossed the Rhine; plundered Gaul and Spain; and were driven by the West Goths into Africa, where they set up a kingdom, with Carthage as capital. Later, under their leader, Genseric, they attacked

Adisa Franklin

Italy by sea and sacked Rome". *Visualized Units in Ancient and Medieval History*, Russell E. Fraser & William D. Pearson, pg. 123

"The Franks were a race of tall, fierce, blond warriors, who finally became the most powerful of the Teutonic invaders of the Roman Empire. They settled at first along the middle Rhine and the Rhine near its mouth as groups of loosely allied tribes, governed by chiefs and democratic assemblies of warriors. **Each man's importance in assembly was determined by his military prowess alone.** They were respected by their Roman subjects, because they became orthodox Christians and friends of the pope. **The Frankish state was broken into four main divisions, torn by constant warfare".** *Visualized Units in Ancient and Medieval History*, Russell E. Fraser & William D. Pearson, pg. 141

"He (Charlemagne) defeated the barbarian Slavs and Avars to the east, and carved from their territory the Avaric Mark, a 'buffer' state. **His greatest wars were against the heathen and savage, but the Teutonic, Saxons of North Germany".** *Visualized Units in Ancient and Medieval History*, Russell E. Fraser & William D. Pearson, pg. 144

"Conditions in Germany and Italy were especially bad. Germany was broken into numerous, really independent states, large and small; **Italy was torn by rival rulers fell into a condition of lawlessness and disorder".** *Visualized Units in Ancient and Medieval History*, Russell E. Fraser & William D. Pearson, pg. 146

"A fierce horde of Vikings or Northmen-Teutonic barbarians from Scandinavia-descended upon central and southern Europe with great fury during the ninth century". *Visualized Units in Ancient and Medieval History*, Russell E. Fraser & William D. Pearson, pg. 148

"Feudalism was a form of government, highly decentralized. Feudal law was Europe's only law. Feudal lords were Europe's real rulers. Feudalism was a military system. The whole organization served as a base for the support of the armed horsemen, who in turn maintained the existence of the organization. **The Feudal noble regarded warfare as both business and pleasure. Any occupation other than war he regarded as beneath his noble position. When not engaged in fighting he feasted, drank heavily, engaged in tests of his warlike skill in tournaments, hunted with hounds or falcons, gambled or listened to news or ballads told and**

168

sung by traveling minstrels". *Visualized Units in Ancient and Medieval History*, Russell E. Fraser & William D. Pearson, pg, 150-151

still taken't

From the pen of Bishop William Montgomery Brown: **"For the first two or three thousand years of civilization, there was not a civilized white man on the earth.** Civilization was founded by the swarthy races of Mesopotamia, Syria and Egypt, and the white race remained so barbaric that in those days an Egyptian or Babylonian priest would have said that the riffraff of white tribes a few hundred miles to the north of their civilization were hopelessly incapable of acquiring the knowledge requisite to progress". *What They Never Told You In History Class,* Indus Khamit-Kush, pg. 255

"Half of recorded history had passed before anyone in Europe could read or write. In contrast…the priests of Egypt began to keep written records between 4000 and 3000 B.C…." *A History of the Modern World,* R.R. Palmer and J. Colton, pg. 13

"While men in Europe were still savages, marvelous civilizations existed in Egypt, located in northeastern Africa". *Visualized Units in Ancient and Medieval History*, Russell E. Fraser & William D. Pearson, pg. 7

Dr. Diop notes that: "Egypt was the cradle of civilization for 10,000 years while the rest of the world steeped in barbarism". *What They Never Told You In History Class,* Indus Khamit-Kush, pg. 30

As we can see from the partial list of wars below Western man has exhibited his warlike nature and propensity for violently taking what does not belong to him throughout history.

TABLE OF IMPORTANT DATES (Of Western Wars)

	B.C.	
538		CAPTURE OF BABYLON BY CYRUS THE GREAT
490		BATTLE OF MARATHON
480-431		BATTLES OF THERMOPYLAE, SALAMIS, AND HIMERA
431-404		THE PELOPONNESIAN WAR
413		DEFEAT OF THE ATHENIANS AT SYRACUSE
390		BURNING OF ROME BY THE GAULS
338		BATTLE OF CHAERONEA
331		BATTLE OF ARBELA

264-241	THE FIRST PUNIC WAR
218-202	THE SECOND PUNIC WAR
207	BATTLE OF THE METAURUS
146	DESTRUCTION OF CARTHAGE AND CORINTH
58-50	CAESAR'S CONQUEST OF GAUL
48	POMPEY DEFEATED AT PHARSALUS BY CAESAR
44	ASSASINATION OF JULIUS CAESAR
31	ANTONIUS DEFEATED AT ACTIUM BY OCTAVIUS

A.D.

9	BATTLE OF THE TEUTOBERG FOREST
325	COUNCIL OF NICEA
378	BATTLE OF ADRIANOPLE
410	SACK OF ROME BY ALARIC
451	BATTLE OF CHALONS
486	BATTLE OF SOISSONS
732	BATTLE OF TOURS
1066	BATTLE OF HASTINGS; NORMAN CONQUEST OF ENGLAND
1095	CRUSADES BEGIN
1346	BATTLE OF CRECY
1381	PEASANT UPRISING UNDER WAT TYLER
1431	JOAN OF ARC BURNED AS WITCH
1453	CONSTANTINOPLE TAKEN BY TURKS, HUNDRED YEAR'S WAR ENDS
1455-1485	WAR OF THE ROSES
1571	TURKS DEFEATED AT LEPANTO
1588	SPAIN'S ARMADA DESTROYED
1618-1648	THIRTY YEAR'S WAR
1642-1648	CIVIL WAR IN ENGLAND
1756-1763	SEVEN YEAR'S WAR
1775-1783	AMERICAN REVOLUTION

Visualized Units in Ancient and Medieval History, Russell E. Fraser & William D. Pearson, pg. 291-292

Let's summarize what has been presented here and see if these are the people Blacks should continue to trust to lead them to spiritual maturity and to create a civilized society: WHITE PEOPLE:

(1) Never once have they created a unified and civilized society

170

(2)   The Greeks were a jealous and suspicious people

(3)   Greek women were assigned a low position in Western society

(4)   The greater benefits of society were based on slavery. They were a lazy people who shunned "honest" labor.

(5)   They were a people that lacked morals. They accepted lying and deceit as a means of achieving their goals.

(6)   They were unsanitary and crude in their living habits and environment.

(7)   Their emperors and kings were despots and tyrants. They are described as utterly evil, corrupt and cruel. They almost always oppressed the people even though from the fourth century on they were confessing Christians.

(8)   Western man's history is a history of constant warfare.

(9)   Conditions for the average man and women in Western society, has always been oppressive and the common man has always been exploited.

(10) All of Western man's ancestors: The Vandals, Franks, Saxons, Teutons, Slavs, Visigoths, Sycthians, Vikings, Danes, Lombards, Angles, and Ostrogoths were savage barbarians who worshiped many gods.

White Supremacy Theory is Bankrupt

According to Western mans own testimony, his history is more barbaric and savage than any other people on the planet. In addition his contribution to peace, harmony and enlightenment has been practically non-existent.

From the Romans and their sordid gladiator sports and heathen emperors to the vicious Vikings who terrorized the seas. From wicked Protestant and Catholic Kings and Queens to the corrupt priest of the "Unholy Crusades". From the witch hunts of early Christians to the oppression of the masses for material gain by the Christian Feudal Lords. From taking humans as chattel in Africa: To the violent taking of the America's from its native people. From the White cowboys that terrorized the early Americans to the White gangsters who murdered thousands on America's city streets. **We have inherited the legacy of Western mans true contribution to civilization i.e. violence and aggression.** Western man has sown to the wind and we are reaping the whirlwind. Those that love peace and are humane find nothing to glory in the accounts of Western man's history.

We find also in Western man's history the seeds of the chaos we are experiencing today. The world is still at war. Western man is yet to create a truly unified society. Many still shun honest labor and believe that the masses should provide for their extravagant lifestyle. Morals are still glaringly absent from Western culture and lying and deception are still acceptable means for achieving goals. Women are still relegated to an inferior position in society. Perhaps the greatest tragedy is that we are still worshipping idol gods.

PART 3

this is what they think of us!

REVERSAL #2

Now we will turn our attention to what was falsely said and promoted about the history, nature, contribution and abilities of Black people. Let's view how Western man tried to portray Africans in their likeness.

The following quotes are taken from the book *What They Never Told You In History Class,* Indus Khamit-Kush, pgs. 2-8

> Billy Graham, evangelist:
> "Stephen, if it weren't for you wretched Britishers, we wouldn't have any Negroes in this country anyway; we wouldn't have this mess". To Stephen Olford, 1940,

> Charles Seignobos, professor-History of Ancient Civilization:
> "Almost all civilized peoples belong to the white race. The people of other races have remained savage or barbarian, like the men of prehistoric times".

> G. Culvier, producer, the Animal Kingdom:
> "The Caucasian, to which we ourselves belong, is chiefly distinguished by the beautiful form of the head, which approximates to a perfect oval... From this variety have sprung the most civilized nations, and such as have most generally exercised dominion over the rest of mankind.

> G. Culvier, producer, the Animal Kingdom
> The Negro race is confined to the south of Mount Atlas. Its characteristics are black, wholly hair, and flattish nose...In prominence of the lower part of the face and the thickness of the lips, its (characteristics) manifestly approaches to the monkey tribe. The hordes of which this variety is composed have always remained in a state of complete barbarism".

> E.B. Reuter, author-American Race Problems:
> "without ancestral pride...even a tradition of historical unity or racial achievements...the whole record of the race was one of servile or barbaric status".

Thomas W. Hardwick, U.S. Congressman:
"And who is the Negro that he should dispute this demand? A race that never founded a government or built a state that did not soon lapse into barbarism, a race that never yet made a single step towards civilization, except under the fostering care and guidance of the white man; a race into whose care was committed one of the three continents, and who has made it, ever since the remotest of times, a land of utter darkness, until today the nations of Europe, in the onward march of irresistible civilization are dividing his heritage, the greatest of the continents among themselves…".

Charleton Coon, professor-The Origin of Races:
"If Africa was the cradle of mankind, it was only an indifferent kindergarten. Europe and Asia were principal schools".

Hugh Trevor-Roper, scholar-The Rise of Christian Europe:
"It is European techniques, European examples, European ideas which have shaken the non-European world out of its past-out of barbarism in Africa…"

Dr. Livingston, doctor:
"We come among the Africans members of a superior race and servants of a Government that desires to elevate the more degraded portions of the human family".

Albert Schweitzer, M.D.:
"The Negro is a child, and with children nothing can be done without the use of authority. With regard to the Negroes then, I have coined the formula: I am your brother, it is true, but your elder brother".

Dr. Robert Bennett Bean, doctor
"Having demonstrated that the Negro and the Caucasian are widely different in characteristics, due to a deficiency in the Negro brain, a deficiency that is hereditary…we are forced to conclude that it is useless to try to elevate the Negro by education or otherwise"

William Shockley, Nobel Peace Prize winner-Lesser Breeds:
"Since Negro intelligence is naturally…low…let's give blacks cash incentives not to breed. A voluntary sterilization program for people of low intelligence".

173

Richard Nixon, president:
"America's blacks could only marginally benefit from federal programs because 'blacks are genetically inferior to whites'".

R.B. Carttell, professor-The Origin of Civilization:
"...that savages, including the whole Negro race, should on account of their low mentality an unpleasant nature, be painlessly exterminated".

Did these learned men not know? Or were they suffering from the disease of racism? What can we say of such sick caricatures of a noble race by educated men?

"The discovery that the earliest civilization and, therefore, the most advanced nation was in Africa led white scholars to do a quick turn-about, going far beyond transforming the indigenous people into whites: They now made Africa the birthplace of the entire human race and, to please God, rushed back to Noah's sons again for a theory of racial origins and dispersions-but now from Africa-over the earth. Western scholars, in the absence of solid facts, do not hesitate to use myths and legends if these serve their purposes". *The Destruction of Black Civilization,* Chancellor Williams, pg. 31-32

"No history of humankind has been as distorted as that of Africa and the Africans. A good job has been done in trying to convince Africans living in the Americas, West Indies and Europe that their 'true' history started with the ships which carried them into captivity and servitude". *No More Lies About Africa,* Chief Musamaali Nangoli, pg. 4-5

"Africa was for generations presented to the outside world by her ruthless invaders as the 'dark continent' inhabited by savages, intellectually lacking, unchristian and morally uncivilized. Hence, the Africans outside Africa could hardly be blamed for not wanting to be reminded of, or associated with Mother Africa. The story of the 'history' of their forefathers was more than they could stomach"! *No More Lies About Africa,* Chief Musamaali Nangoli, pg. 6

This prevailing sentiment among learned and influential Whites is a symptom of the disease state of mind created by perpetuating falsehoods. It is the reason there is no regard for the person who is by nature and appearance a member of the race described above. We must not forget however that this

174

sentiment was created by the Christian Church who taught for centuries that Blacks were the son's of Ham who were cursed by God and commanded to serve his brother. **It was Christianity that created the model for the erroneous doctrine of White Supremacy.** Once created the sentiment was self perpetuating as books like "The Bell Curve" by Charles Murray and Richard Hermstein was released seeking to give scientific validity to the erroneous "Hamite" theory.

PART 4

REVERSING THE REVERSAL

The Only True Civilization

What I am about to share should be made a part of the early instruction and information given to every child especially African American children. Remember its purpose is not to make the Black child feel superior to the White child but to give both children a realistic and accurate picture of the history of humanity. In reversing the reversal we will right the wrong that is continually heaped on the Black race because no one believes it has ever contributed anything of significance and that Blacks are the sort of people that are portrayed in the media. No longer must the Black race allow the myth about their past to be perpetuated within the Churches or schools of America. We must tell our own story if it is to be told. Let us begin by viewing the efforts of two courageous Black men who took a stand for the truth and won.

LET THE TRUTH BE KNOWN: AFRICAN AMERICANS COME FROM GOOD STOCK.

"In the early 1970's these biases were scholarly, intellectually and scientifically challenged by two sons of Africa, the late Senegalese multi-disciplinarian Dr. Cheikh Anta Diop and his associate from Gabon, Dr. Theophile Obenga".

"Drs. Diop and Obenga both presented papers at the Cairo Symposium which unequivocally destroyed the myths of racial inferiority. From January 28, through February 3, 1974, the United Nations Educational, Scientific and Cultural Organization (UNESCO) sponsored the symposium, which was held in the capital of Egypt. The symposium was attended by 20 of the most prominent Egyptologist in the world who assembled to debate, among other topics, the race of the ancient Egyptians".

"Dr. Diop was a brilliant scientist who held degrees in Egyptology, physics, linguistics and anthropology. He was regarded by his contemporaries as the 'pharaoh' of African studies. Dr. Diop presented a paper entitled Origins of Ancient Egyptians and argued, irrefutably, that there were 11 categories of evidence to support the thesis that the ancient Egyptians were indigenous 'black' Africans".

"Dr. Obenga's paper was entitled The Peopling of Ancient Egypt and the Deciphering of the Meroitic Script. He provided data which confirmed the existence of substantial linguistic relationship between the ancient Egyptian language and traditional African languages. The papers presented by Diop and Obenga were virtually unchallenged by the other scholars present." *Nile Valley Contributions To Civilization*, Anthony T. Browder, pgs. 19-20

The people of Africa for centuries maintained a society of civilized people that reflected the wisdom of an advanced people. They were a very humane people!

white people literally run everything)

"Once upon a time in Africa, we paid no taxes, there was no crime, there was no police, there was no inflation, there was no unemployment, men did not beat or divorce their wives, then the white man came to improve things". *No More Lies About Africa,* Chief Musamaali Nangoli, pg. 18

"In comparison, however, with most other ancient peoples, the Egyptians were a kindly, sunny-dispositioned, and just race. For example, they granted women greater rights and freedom than any other Eastern (or Western) people". *Visualized Units in Ancient and Medieval History*, Russell E. Fraser & William D. Pearson, pg. 10 (Brackets mine)

"Soon after initiation, one must get married in Africa…It is considered abnormal, unnatural and ungodly not be married. The decision isn't left to the individual as such, but to the entire society. It is considered abnormal because it is ABNORMAL to live without the opposite sex; it is unnatural because man and woman need each other for their physical and emotional needs and it is considered un-godly because God made man and woman and commanded that they unite in marriage to reproduce mankind. On these grounds, Africans uncompromisingly regard marriage. No ifs and buts. One gets married or risks the wrath of the community". *No More Lies About Africa,* Chief Musamaali Nangoli, pg. 26

"In modern times, the woman in Africa remains a powerful figure. She is the essence of being and existence. A man is not considered a man in Africa unless he has a woman besides him. A home without a woman is looked down upon and often the object of ridicule by society. The home is shunned by people because it is considered unblessed hence cursed. Who in his right mind would want to visit a home not graced by the presence of a woman? Africans would ask". *No More Lies About Africa*, Chief Musamaali Nangoli, pg. 38

"A man who beats up his wife is considered by society to be weak in mind and utterly lacking in moral character. How dare you beat up on God's finest creation? Society wants to know. The woman is yesterday, today and tomorrow"! *No More Lies About Africa*, Chief Musamaali Nangoli, pg. 39

"Children are a big exultation in African society. There coming is always awaited by society and by individual communities in particular. To say nothing about the pride a family feels with this blessing. Children in Africa don't stay children for very long. They are encouraged to assume adult roles in society as a way of testing their character. Respect for adults can't be over emphasized. Children are not expected to talk back to adults in African society. It is a cardinal sin for a child to engage in an argument of cross words with his elders. The reason being that the adults saw the sun first". *No More Lies About Africa*, Chief Musamaali Nangoli, pg. 42

"Sex was considered sacred in African society. To engage in it was seen as a commitment to each other. Casual sex was despised and frowned upon. Africans believed that sexual intercourse is the ultimate in male and female relationships. It seals and solemnizes it at the same time. Thus, if a man has sex with a woman, according to African custom, she becomes his wife by this single act". *No More Lies About Africa*, Chief Musamaali Nangoli, pg. 49

"Homosexuality is taboo in African society. Ten years of exhaustive research across the continent didn't produce any evidence of homosexuality having been a part of African life. Indeed hardly any translation of the word 'homosexual' exist in African languages. Africans have a name for almost everything they do that is a part of their culture. The absence of direct translation for the word could only suggest that homosexuality

177

was never a part of African culture". *No More Lies About Africa,* Chief Musamaali Nangoli, pg. 50

"Divorce was never allowed or encouraged in ancient African society, save in the most extreme cases. Everything possible was done to save a failing marriage. This stemmed from a long held belief that the act of marriage, was God's wish. To destroy it therefore, was the most ungodly thing for man to do". *No More Lies About Africa,* Chief Musamaali Nangoli, pg. 51

"Scholars have always agreed that religion permeates every dimension of African life. In spite of their many and varied religious systems the ubiquity of religious consciousness among African peoples constitutes their single most important common characteristic. Thus, John S. Mbiti's claim that secularity has no reality in the African experience is affirmed by all scholars of African religion. None perhaps, has expressed this point better than he:

'Wherever the African is, there is religion: he carries it to the fields where he is sowing seeds or harvesting a new crop; he takes it with him to the beer party or to attend a funeral ceremony; and if he is educated, he takes religion with him to the examination room at school or in the university; if he is a politician he takes it to the house of parliament. Although many African languages do not have a word for religion as such, it nevertheless accompanies the individual from long before his birth to long after his physical death'. *The Spirituality of African Peoples,* Peter J. Paris, pgs. 27-28

"But when we come to consider the history of man, was not the African a power, was he not great once? Yes, honest students of history can recall the day when Egypt, Ethiopia and Timbuktu towered in their civilizations, towered above Europe, towered above Asia. When Europe was inhabited by a race of cannibals, a race of savages, naked men, heathens and pagans, Africa was peopled with a race of cultured African men, who were masters in art, science and literature; men who were cultured and refined; men who, it was said, were like gods. Even the great poets of old sang in beautiful sonnets of the delight afforded gods to be in the companionship with the Ethiopians". *No More Lies About Africa,* Chief Musamaali Nangoli, pg. 143

As we have seen, at one time Blacks lived in harmony with each other and the universe. Our family structure was sound. We did not abuse our women and they were well respected. Our children were esteemed gifts from the Creator and they respected their elders. Sex was sacred rather than merely a source of physical pleasure for a people that have lost (forgotten) their divinity. Homosexuality was taboo! Divorce was not allowed. We didn't abort our children! We respected our ancestors. Our culture was rich in spirituality; we reverenced the Creator in everyone and in every action. Can we not do this again? Certainly we can! We have only begun to examine the glorious dynasties of Africa that predate Western man's history by thousands of years.

All Black people may not have been kings and queens like King Rameses II and Tutankhamen or Queen Hapshesut and Nefertiti, but all African Americans are connected by DNA to these royal families and communities. Theirs was a community that esteemed the highest virtues of man as priority. As stewards of the fertile Nile Valley they kept the garden and dressed it in righteousness and the love of God manifested in the love for man and all of God's creation. To them man was the crown of God's creation and they acted accordingly. **Blacks have no reason to be ashamed of their roots and no cause to disassociate themselves from their past and their ancestors.**

PART 5

THE TRUTH IN BLACK AND WHITE

In this section we will compare the African and Western world views. Of course in doing so it is presumed that the reader knows that what we are referring to is general dispositions and as our Western scholars put it "natural tendencies". Of course today with the mixing of cultures you have Blacks and Whites that exhibit the characteristics normally assigned to the opposite race.

AFRICAN   EUROPEAN

- ONE WITH NATURE.............................CONTROL OF NATURE
- SURVIVAL OF THE GROUP..............SURVIVAL OF THE FITTEST
- COOPERATION......................................COMPETITION
- INTERPERSONAL INTERDEPENDENCE.....INDEPENDENCE
- COLLECTIVE RESPONSIBILITY..............INDIVIDUAL RIGHTS
- SEX EQUALITY...........................SUBORDINATE FEMALE
- PACIFIST MORALITY...........................WARRIOR MORALITY
- FAMILY LOVE (EXTENDED)..........SELF CENTEREDNESS

- MORAL RIGHTEOUSNESS...............POLITICAL EXPEDIENCY
- SPIRITUALISM......................................MATERIALISM
- SIBLING RESPONSIBILITY.....................SIBLING RIVALRY
- COLLECTIVE PROPERTY.......... .LAND AS PRIVATE PROPERTY
- ALL CHILDREN RAISED.................EXCESS BABIES KILLED
- LOVE OF STRANGERS...................FEAR OF STRANGERS
- GENTLE, FORGIVING................HARSH, NON-FORGIVING
- LARGELY SEDENTARY........................NOMADIC
- NO NOTION OF GUILT................DEEP SENSE OF GUILT
- NO NOTION OF ORIGINAL SIN...............ORIGINAL SIN
- BENEVOLENT GOD...................MALEVOLENT GOD

European Thought, Values and Ideas Dominate

the African American Psyche

Looking at this comparison in the light of what we have learned we must admit that it is accurate. This difference in nature is demonstrated in the way Western man can drop tons of bombs on innocent people to gain that for which they lust, temporal power and wealth. As long as it is politically expedient, which means they have made it legal, it is justified. It is their fear of strangers that leads them to conduct themselves in this manner. **No honest person can examine the list above and not conclude that European values, thoughts and beliefs dominate the values and beliefs of the people of the world and particularly Americans. This is because Western values and world outlook permeate all of the institutions of Western societies.**

These same values are hidden in the doctrines and dogmas of Christianity but seen in its fruit. Christianity promotes materialism which is why such phrases as "money cometh" are so popular among Christians. Those that will not accept its doctrines are condemned. In many instances it has used military force as a means to achieve its ends. As we have seen it promotes sexism. Survival of the fittest, independence, individual rights, competition rather than cooperation are all Western man's values. And it is these values that must be seen as unwholesome, undesirable and that which needs to be rejected by Blacks. It is from Western man's world view and values that Blacks must seek to liberate themselves. These values are the root cause of the division and dysfunction, chaos and confusion as well as the darkness and death within the Black community.

Africans were falsely labeled savage, barbaric, pagan, animist, heathen, and polytheist to discredit and dehumanize them. That was the beginning of the reversal. Somehow, because Africans were labeled such, it justified the overthrow and destruction of their nation. Somewhere, the account of the records got switched and the savage destruction of Black civilization became a noble cause inflicted by a noble and godly people. Ironically it was the real barbarians that claimed they were on a mission to civilize a people that were already civilized. More than any other sector of our people, it is the African American Christian who has bought the hype. Many Black churches regard having a ministry in Africa in the same light as their White counterparts. This perception must be reversed. We must honor our ancestral parents and once again claim our inheritance that we may receive our blessing. The wisdom of Africa is the inheritance. Africa is still the "Motherland".

PART 6

HEALING---LIBERATING BLACK MINDS

The only way for Blacks to heal is to reclaim their right minds. This can only be done by returning to the wisdom and the way that was lost. We are free to be ourselves today regardless of social pressures to keep the Black man from expressing his African heritage. Despite this fact there is no one who can limit Black minds but Black people. African people can reclaim their African mind and find there solace, inspiration and guidance. What was taken away can be regained. Only we must take the responsibility for getting the job done.

"The term 'Conceptual Incarceration' has been used by Dr. Asa G. Hilliard to describe the mental condition which affects the thinking processes of millions of peoples of African descent. Dr. Hilliard, an educational psychologist and historian, suggests that victims of fabricated histories are often confused, isolated and disorientated as a result of a loss of historical continuity". *Nile Valley Contributions To Civilization*, Anthony T. Browder, pg. 21

"Hand in hand with the enslavement of African people came the destruction of African civilization and the loss of a culture, which the European would later say never existed". *Nile Valley Contributions To Civilization*, Anthony T. Browder, pg. 36

Carter G. Woodson, historian-The Miseducation of The Negro:
"If a race has no history, if it has no worthwhile traditions, it becomes a negligible factor in the thought of the world, and it stands in danger of being exterminated". *What They Never Told You In History Class,* Indus Khamit-Kush, pg. 8

"The transformation of enslaved people from African to Negro to Colored to Black and currently, to African American, has been quite an evolution. In eighteenth century America, 'free blacks' saw themselves as African and incorporated their ethnicity into newly created institutions. Richard Allen...founded the Free African Society in 1787 and the African Methodist Episcopal Church (AME) in 1794. After emancipation in the mid nineteenth century, black Americans no longer identified with the term 'African' and began to refer to themselves as 'Colored' or 'Negro' in order to distinguish themselves from Africans living in Africa and elsewhere. Some of the black institutions that developed in the twentieth century began to reflect this new orientation in name-such as the National Association for the Advancement of Colored People (NAACP)". *What They Never Told You In History Class,* Indus Khamit-Kush, pg. 28

"Identification with one's past (history) is an important step towards mental liberation, but the process must begin with the identification and use of your correct name. Noted historian Dr. John Henrik Clarke provides us with a working definition of history: 'History is the clock that people use to tell their political and cultural time of day. It is a compass that people use to find themselves on the map of human geography. The role of history is to tell a people what they have been, and what they are and where they are. The most important role that history plays is that it has the function of telling a people where they still must go and what they still must be". *What They Never Told You In History Class,* Indus Khamit-Kush, pg. 29

"A nationwide telephone survey of 759 African Americans, conducted by the Joint Center for Political Studies in the fall of 1990, disclosed the following: Despite the increasing use of the term African-American, most Black Americans still prefer to be called Black; 72 percent preferred to be called Black; 15 percent preferred African-American and 2 percent Negro, with the rest giving no opinion or other response". *What They Never Told You In History Class,* Indus Khamit-Kush, pg. 28

Blacks Must "HEAL THEMSELVES" First —yes!

Blacks cannot cure white people. Blacks cannot make Whites love them. Blacks believe they can change how Whites look at them. They believe that if they just love Whites and show White people that they are civilized and moral beings they will be worthy of their respect. It is not working for the vast majority or Whites. Loving self rather than loving your enemy is the answer for Blacks. This is not to say that white people are the enemy of Black people. The truth is that most White people have been duped as well, which is the reason that in general the relationship between Blacks and Whites is dysfunctional. It is convenient for those who rule to keep Whites and Blacks at odds with each other. However, Blacks must realize that you cannot truly love someone else until you have loved yourself. Loving themselves will give Blacks the spiritual power for their love to be affective on others. **African Americans must first heal themselves; the physician must heal himself first. For this reason, Blacks must assume a race first attitude.**

African Americans can no longer rely on Europeans to instruct them in the knowledge of God. If Black people are to heal and once again be a beneficial influence on humanity, this tendency must be reversed. Before that will occur, the story has to be told. **Black youth must learn about their true history at home, in school and in church. African Americans must reclaim their history and culture if they are to heal.** We know now how Africans came to hate themselves and their identity. Let us show that we know how to teach ourselves to love each other. Stand up Black man and be African.

Reversing the Reversal

The key to reversing the reversal is; understanding that the lies and falsehood permeate all the institutions of our society. The cornerstone of this deception however is in the racist and otherwise faulty religious dogmas and views. New institutions must replace the old; institutions that recognize the divinity in man and that teach man again how to live in peace with each other and in harmony with the universe.

We must teach our children the truth that it was Western man that was the heathen of antiquity and that it was they who worshipped many gods (false gods). We must teach the children that the Africans were the true Fathers of Civilization. To make this information common knowledge will go far in overcoming the effects of institutionalized racism, which is based on the vain theory of White Supremacy. The notion of white supremacy cannot coexist with this knowledge. It must not only be taught to our children but teaching this information to European youth will go far in resolving the conflict of race relations. **This is a major "shackle buster". The misinformation that is fostered by the European reversal of history or his-story has done much to, blind Black people to their great potential and to keep Blacks dependent on the authority of others. It is time to break this shackle that blinds, and tell the truth.**

Chapter 9

A DECLARATION OF RELIGIOUS INDEPENDENCE

FREEDOM IS NOT POLITICAL IT IS A SPIRITUAL MATTER

freeing the African Mind use to be a puzzle to me
that is before I realized we've been Sleeping with our Enemy
so I became a Seeker of Truth and knocked on Wisdom's Door
and because of what I found my spirit began to soar
I had to cast down all that was false and reject every lie
that kept me from my freedom and made my spirit seem to die
so I declared my religious independence day or R.I.D.
cause this is where he established his stronghold
and how he got inside of me
I had let the wrong people define who I was and how to get to God
I thought they offered Salvation and Freedom;
instead they put me in a nod
I am still what my Creator made me, and it has always been so
I had just been listening to the enemy who really doesn't know

poem by adisa

"They came heavily armed with Bibles, and through these they would colonize the mind of the African for a long time to come. It was important to Europe after captivity to control the mind of the African. With the mind of Africa firmly in his hands, the white man would be armed with the most lethal weapon with which he would exploit him for a long time to come. Nobody has power over another man unless that person can control the mind of his victim! The white man knew this only too well". *No More Lies About Africa*, Chief Musamaali Nangoli, pg. 72

There was no way for the African slave to know that the religion the white preachers would teach them was corrupted African mythology and cosmology. There was no way for the early Black church leaders to know that the religion they had embraced was the very tool used to justify their enslavement. <u>They did not recognize it to be a "Trojan Horse"</u>. It puzzled them when the white Christians refused to acknowledge them as brothers in Christ and to treat them accordingly. It was no way for them to know that hidden in the doctrines, beliefs and images of the church where the deceptions that would keep their minds bound long after they had fought for and won their political freedom. This "mental shackle" would prove to be more disruptive, divisive and destructive than even the Willie Lynch philosophy of "divide and conquer".

"As well meaning as the missionaries might have been, they were all agreed on and convinced of one thing-that the black man was inferior to the white man in every way". *No More Lies About Africa*, Chief Musamaali Nangoli, pg. 73

Must Break Mental Shackles

"For the weapons of our warfare are not carnal but mighty in God
for pulling down strongholds, casting down ideas
and every high thing that
exalts itself against the knowledge of God" **2 Corinthians 10:5**

"Mental bondage is invisible. Formal physical slavery has ended in the United States. <u>Mental slavery continues to this present day.</u> This slavery affects the minds of all people and, in one way, it is worse than physical slavery alone. That is, the person who is in mental bondage will be 'self-contained'. Not only will that person fail to challenge beliefs and patterns of thought which control him, he will defend and protect those beliefs and patterns of thought virtually with his last dying effort. From the Introduction to the1976 reprint of *Stolen Legacy*, Asa G. Hilliard, III

"it is Africa asserting itself intellectually and psychologically, breaking the bonds of Western domination in the mind as an analogue for breaking the bonds in every other field". *Nile Valley Contributions To Civilization*, Anthony T. Browder, pg. 245

Spirit of Abolitionist gave Birth to Black Church

The spirit of the Abolitionist was born in the Black church. More specifically the spirit of the Abolitionist gave birth to the Black church. The slaves sought in this new religion a means to obtain their freedom. The Abolitionist relied on scriptures for the authority to speak on behalf of freedom. Political liberation was a noble and necessary cause for which the Church to labor. However, the Black Church and the African slave did not know that the Emancipation Proclamation would not really set them free. It only granted them legal freedom, which must be defended. The church however, is mandated to address a higher order of freedom, spiritual freedom. It is the freedom that only rejecting falsehood and acknowledging the truth can achieve.

Most of us sense that all is not right with Euro-Christianity. A little lie leaveneth the whole lump. In order for us to achieve our spiritual freedom, it will be necessary to break the mental and emotional chains that bind us to false religious teachings.

Black Church Sanctioned by White Church

Currently, there is not one Black orthodox Christian Church that is truly independent. The Black Baptist, Church of God in Christ, AME, Church of God, even the Seventh Day Adventist and Jehovah Witness all were sanctioned by the European Church leadership. The Black founders of so-called Independent Black Churches all went to the European for approval. Consequently, each of these denominations teaches fundamentally the same doctrine. **The difference between the Black Church and its white counterpart is surface and in form** only. In fact the fundamental doctrine of the Protestant Church and the Catholic Church are essentially the same.

Martin Luther, the father of the Protestant Church, was the leader of a movement that protested the corruption among the Catholic Clergy. The only doctrinal change made by the Protestant movement is that Martin Luther insisted that scripture be subject to private interpretation. The Euro-Christian "theory of salvation" remains unchanged. There has not been a serious effort among African American Clergy either to independently research or to critically analyze available information regarding Euro-Christianity's doctrines and creeds. This must cease!

"Other leaders, equally ignorant of their heritage, simply do not know which way to lead. They, too, feel compelled to adopt and follow Caucasian ideologies because they do not feel free, equal and competent enough to develop an ideology of their own-an African oriented ideology". *The Essene Book of Creation*, Edmond Bordeaux Szekely, pg. 208

Though it is good to see the Church addressing the physical needs of the community, such as food clothing and shelter, the Church has a higher calling and mandate. As mentioned earlier advancing the cause of freedom from captivity was a noble cause yet there is more to do. As we have discovered the temples in Africa were dedicated to the perfecting of man. This is no different than the mandate of the Church leaders in the Bible where they are instructed to bring the Body of Christ into unity and the believers to that stature of the fullness of Christ. The Church must address the issue of spiritual freedom and spiritual maturity. This most critical charge of the Church has been neglected.

Spiritual freedom is not achieved by accepting and confessing faith in a creed or doctrine. It is achieved when one comes to know the truth about God and self and applies that knowledge to one's life. This is wisdom.

"And you shall know the truth, and the truth shall set you free."

Notice that we do not find the words faith or believe in this "formula for freedom". It is not sufficient to believe that something is true. It is of the utmost necessity that we come to "know" the Truth. The Truth is not in Euro-Christian doctrines and dogma. The Black man must feel free to develop his own spiritual ideology. Many however are so bound to the superstitious beliefs of Christendom that even to talk of not accepting the Bible and the interpretation given to us as the "gospel truth" and Jesus as God is committing blasphemy or some other grievous act of iniquity. By now it is hoped that our readers have been liberated from such childish fears. If so pass it on!

Salvation is deliverance from the corruption that is in this world. The corruption that is in this world is the corruption of the Truth. Acceptance and faith in corrupted Truth or falsehood creates mental bondage. The reason the Truth sets free is it destroys the yoke or bondage of lies. Faith alone will not set one free from the bondage of mental slavery. Because freedom is a spiritual matter, that which is false must be addressed. Even so-called half truths are still Truth that has been corrupted and must be purged from our consciousness.

False Preaching, False Teaching
Wake up yowl
You preachers stop preaching what you teach
Teach the Truth
Wake up Preacher… Harold Melvin, *Wake up Everybody*

Tell My People the Truth

The message of this chapter to African American clergy is, "You have not told my people the whole story. You have not told them the whole truth. You have not known from whence cometh your own faith and in whom you have trusted to lead you to God. You have not weighed and examined it to see if it was even the truth. You have simply believed as you were instructed to do. Believe and not question, this must cease"! No longer must the Black Clergy instruct their followers to just have faith. *"In all your getting, get understanding."* The first thing that needs to be understood is that Blacks are not free. The second thing that needs to be understood is that freedom is essentially a spiritual matter.

"…there is no real freedom for the African person at the moment. Secondly, the absence of this freedom, has to be the result of certain deficiencies. Thirdly, because there is no real freedom for the African person, the next logical question to ask is: what must be done to remove these deficiencies in order to attain real freedom"? *No More Lies About Africa*, Chief Musamaali Nangoli, pg. 145

There are some clergy and lay persons who by their persistence and sincerity have gleaned spiritual insight from the study of the bible. There are signs that many within the Black Church are awakening to the spiritual mission of the Church that needs to be addressed. Yet, because of the fundamental flaw that exists in the current orthodox position on scripture interpretation that which they are taught and teach, is both damaging and limited. **Now that we know that the current doctrines of the Black Church are the erroneous doctrines of Western man we should understand that Blacks need to develop their own. Blacks must declare their religious independence if they are to ever be spiritually free!**

A Declaration of Religious Independence

When one thinks about it in retrospect it is perfectly ludicrous for the Black captive to have embraced the religion of the conqueror. Why would a race of people that are interested in keeping another in subjugation give the captive something that would set him free and empower him? What Blacks were taught put them in bondage declaring their independence from it will have the opposite effect. Let us remove the invisible mental shackles. For Blacks Christianity is a badge of dishonor. Let us make a commitment to define ourselves. As a free people Blacks have the authority to think and believe as they choose. Too few Blacks have exercised that freedom or authority.

> **"Missionary work carefully prepared the African mentality for subjugation".** *No More Lies About Africa*, Chief Musamaali Nangoli, pg. 64

> Dr. Asa Hilliard states that: "Free and critical minds can emerge only by a return to the source-the primary sources. A free and critical mind takes nothing for granted and is not intimidated by 'authorities' who frequently may be more confused than the general public. Free and critical minds seek truth without chauvinism or shame". *Nile Valley Contributions To Civilization*, Anthony T. Browder, pg. 21

It is my sincere hope and desire that by now you are convinced that there is no need to be concerned about becoming independent of Western man's world view and his religious beliefs and superstitions. If you would find peace and live in harmony learn the true spiritual laws of God's creation and the truth about God. **Reject the false god of Euro-Christianity for the one true and living God that needs no partners, he is God all by himself. He is not three in one but one in all.**

> "A factor in the matter, still not understood, is that the Africans tried to bring man in harmony with Nature. Western man tries to defy Nature and often forgets that man cannot start a hurricane or stop one; that before the force of Nature, man is small and puny. The European mind, with all its misconceptions, wants to rule everything, including the elements". *Nile Valley Contributions To Civilization*, Anthony T. Browder, pg. 10

> As stated by Professor John Henrik Clarke, **"The truthful knowledge of African history and the application of that knowledge into a spiritually oriented value system, will serve as the first step toward the continued liberation of African people for generations to come".** *Nile Valley Contributions To Civilization*, Anthony T. Browder, pg. 22

"It represents a revolution of the dynamic against the static; the revolt of freedom against slavery, of wisdom against superstition". *The Essene Book of Creation*, Edmond Bordeaux Szekely, pg. 49

Admitting that we have accepted the authority of Western man by accepting his religion as true when it is false is half the battle. We were programmed subliminally to follow the dictates of what we recognized subconsciously as the Chosen race and fulfill our god given place as the tail and not the head. **Blacks were programmed to never question White authority, to never threaten White security; to never see the beauty of blackness and never to trust the wisdom of Africa.**

> **"The disposition of the many to depend upon the other races for a kindly and sympathetic consideration of their needs, without making an effort to do for themselves, has been the race's standing disgrace, by which we have been judged, and through which we have created the strongest prejudice against ourselves"** –Marcus Garvey. *No More Lies About Africa,* Chief Musamaali Nangoli, pg. 101

In order to be free Blacks must declare their religious freedom. This does not imply that Blacks have no need to be interdependent. All nations of people all need each other. There should be no division in the family of God. Yet African Americans must bring something to the table. It is not time to go along to get along. Black must think for them selves. Determine to declare your Religious Independence Day today!

The House of God the Church has for too long been divided; perhaps as African Americans prepare them selves by becoming truly spiritually free they can bring unity to the House. **It is a great travesty that those who claim to love God, are not able to love each other**. The House of God in reality includes all men some simply do not know their place of residence. When the members of God's House who know where they live demonstrate that they love God by loving God in man, then we can make the world a better place for all men to live. **This is an awesome agenda, but it can be accomplished. It is time to take a stand for Truth and reclaim the African mind. Black churches must become outpost in the battle for the mind of the Black man. Religion is the last shackle that must be broken if Blacks would be free. It is the only thing that lies between freedom and the current dilemma. It is invisible but not invincible. "The gates of hell shall not prevail"; against millions of African Americans who have reclaimed their right minds. Liberate your African mind by rejecting the mind of Western man. We can and must reverse the reversal!!!**

Chapter 10

OPEN LETTER TO THE PIMPS IN THE PULPIT

LET MY SHEEP GO

"For they bind heavy burdens and grievous to be borne, and lay them on men's shoulders; but they will not move them with one of their fingers." **Matthew 23:4**

"As a cage is full of birds, so are their houses full of deceit: therefore they are become great, and waxen rich.
They are waxen fat, they shine: yea, they overpass the deeds of the wicked: they judge not the cause of the fatherless, yet they prosper; and the right of the needy do they not judge." **Jeremiah 5:27-28**

"The heads thereof judge for reward, and the priests thereof teach for hire, and the prophets thereof divine for money: yet will they lean upon the Lord, and say, Is not the Lord among us? No evil can come upon us." **Micah 3:11**

"Is this house, which is called by my name, become a den of robbers in your eyes? Behold, even I have seen it, saith the Lord." **Jeremiah 7:11**

Time To Set The Black House In Order

Now comes the time to address the issue of spiritual abuse in the Black Church. We have spoken quite candidly about the corruption in Western mans Church, now we must do the same for the Black Church. It is time for a new standard among those who are called to spiritually feed the people of God. **Too many**

Pastors are feeding their lust and are amassing great wealth for themselves by laying grievous financial burdens on their congregations. These pastors are forever pushing Building Fund Drives in order to build bigger more prestigious church edifices to be admired by competing pastors. **There are too many preachers in the Black Church that are there for the cash rewards and the status such a career bestows on the preacher.** I say career because many are pursuing the ministry because they have gleaned that it is a lucrative career with many bonuses.

"Go ye therefore into all the lands, build great temples to Me, amass great wealth in My name, and make a great name for yourselves among My people and the heathen." Spiritual Abuse 1:1

The pastors that represent this group are a stumbling block for those who are sincere. I therefore address this message to the members of the latter group; the "good shepherds" among the wolves and thieves. **It is time for a new standard and it must be established primarily by those in authority namely the pastors. Pastor, there is only one body or family of God. All sheep are your responsibility not only the ones in your congregation which fall under your direct care. This message is to the pastors that are sincere about the work of the ministry.** Chances are the ones that the scripture and dialogue describes are not likely to read a book such as this and certainly would not be willing to read through this chapter. That's because they serve their own selfish ends and aren't interested in being correct or righteous.

There are many sincere pastors in the ministry. The sincere pastors often have small congregations because the Pastor seeks to be a blessing rather than a burden on his congregation. He is looking for what he can do for them. I served as assistant pastor under such a man. His name is Pastor Dave Forman. Pastor Forman is a humble man that has the interest of people at heart. It was obvious to all who knew him that he is a man seeking to please God by loving and serving his people. He has a deep heartfelt concern for the welfare of the flock he pastures and others. He is humble enough to accept scriptural correction because his ministry is more important than his ego. He sought daily and sincerely to be led of God. I understand that his ministry has grown tremendously, not because he sought to grow but because he sought to serve. It is to men like Pastor Forman to which I write now. Much of the strength and effectiveness of this message depends on the strength of the response of such pastors. They are needed for a major Spiritual Rescue Operation.

It is scriptural to correct those who err among us. I will not bore pastors by repeating well known scripture regarding this subject. Paul in the Bible went from Church to Church admonishing believers and leaders alike. The majority of the New Testament letters for correction and instruction were directed to the various churches and church leaders such as Timothy and Titus.

It will not go away it will only worsen. What am I talking about? **The scourge of preacher pimps, false prophets and fake healers. Devious people that prey on the innocence of Church folk will not stop on their own.**

Spiritual Abuse in the Church must be Addressed

We all are aware of the abuse of corrupt and greedy men that hide behind many of today's pulpits. Do you not care for the people of God who are being manipulated and exploited? If so then that care must lead to concrete actions and not merely words spoken to your congregation condemning such behavior. The problem must be addressed directly. Before proceeding, let us first address the error and misconception that what is about to occur is against the scripture for does not the scripture teach that we should touch not God's anointed. There is no doubt there is a scripture that says those exact words. The problem is that like many other scriptures that are taken out of context and used as weapons, this one is used for defense purposes. In this often misquoted scripture conceals the questionable defense for undesirable actions by pastors that should be questioned in the church. I hope you caught it. The last scripture quoted was written by the author;

"Go ye therefore into all the lands, build great temples to Me, amass great wealth in My name, and make a great name for yourselves among My people and the heathen." Spiritual Abuse 1:1

As you can see however it does indeed reflect the sentiments of too many African American pastors. Let's look at one of the scriptures such pastors hide behind.

"When they went from one nation to another from one kingdom to another people; He suffered no man to do them wrong: yea, he reproved kings for their sakes; Saying Touch not mine anointed, and do my prophets no harm." **Psalms 105:13-15**

Touch Not My Anointed Offers no Protection For False Teachers

This text as can be readily seen refers to the doing of physical harm to the prophets of God. Three things: first the person in question has to be a true man of God and second this scripture is totally irrelevant in regards to the issue of questioning the teachings or actions of any of the preacher pimps, and lastly and perhaps most importantly that God does not anoint lies and half truths. The anointing that most Church attendees experience is actually emotionalism. Some pastors and teachers even go so far as to imply a divine threat to those who would question their teachings. I am sure the "Money Cometh" group will not appreciate what is being said here. Listen to this statement by Kenneth Copeland.

> Prominent "faith" teacher Kenneth Copeland affirmed in his message, "Why All Are Not Healed": There are people attempting to sit in judgment right today over the ministry that I'm responsible for, and the ministry that Kenneth E. Hagin is responsible for…Several people that I know had criticized and called that faith bunch out of Tulsa a cult. And some of 'em are dead right today in an early grave because of it, and there's more that one of them got cancer."

This obviously is a not so veiled attempt to threaten those who would question this new "deal" to see if it be of God. No pastor or teacher's authority is above question!

> "In addition to certain "word-faith" teachers, such sentiments may be found among various groups involved with shepherding and other forms of authoritarian rule. The leaders of these groups are commonly regarded as having a unique gift and calling that entitles them to unconditional authority. To dispute any of their words or deeds is not distinguished from questioning God Himself. Advocates of such authority assume that Scripture support their view. Their key biblical proof text is Psalms 105:15 (KJV). But a close examination of this passage reveals that it has nothing to do with challenging the teachings of church leaders."

> "Nobody's teachings or practices are beyond judgment—especially influential leaders. Biblically, authority and accountability go hand in hand (e.g., Luke 12:48). The greater the responsibility one holds, the greater accountability one has before God and His people." Christian Research Journal, The Untouchables: Are "God's Anointed" Beyond Criticism? By Hendrik H. Hanegraaff

'It is a sad situation today in many churches that "laity" are content to sit on a pew week after week and assume the opinions of professional clergyman are to be the final authority. They find comfort in this approach because it is safe. Preachers are content to keep it this way because it secures their position in the church. How many times have believers been subject to mishandled scripture with an implicit or explicit "touch not my anointed" if any dared to question? This is in contrast to the biblical injunction to "try the spirits", (1 John 4:1) –Touch Not My Anointed, John R. Anderson, January 1997

"Evil that thrives in this world is not so much caused by those who are evil as it is by good men and women who say or do nothing when their opinion should be voiced and action should be taken." Anonymous

My dear pastor, teacher or lay member; are you a good man or woman? Are there not things occurring in the Church that you know about and therefore should address? The quotes above are from a couple of web sites dealing with spiritual abuse. One of them has had over 25, 000 people to log on their site within a years time. This is indicative of the extent of the spiritual abuse as each one of those people who log on no doubt was prompted to do so because of personal experience or the experience of a loved one. There are thousands of web sites dealing with this travesty within the confines of the Church.

No one is above questioning when he is in a position of authority or teaching others "what thus saith the Lord". God even wants us to ask question of Him. Could the local pastor carry more weight than the God who was supposed to have called him? As we learned in Chapter seven, **there was no known sinner in the first Black Church of Africa. Should we not return to Holiness? There must be accountability in the Church. There should be no place in the pulpit for preacher pimps and false prophets. Who will work for God in restoring Holiness in His House?**

Who Will Build God's Spiritual House?

The men of God are supposed to build a Spiritual House, a House of Unity, and a house inhabited by men and women who have been fed sufficient spiritual food to bring them into spiritual maturity. This means that they are enabled to manifest that measure of the fullness of Christ. Yet all across America, Christians in Black churches are burdened with the massive task of paying off Church mortgages in the millions in record time. Mortgages for these church buildings range from $500,000 to $10,000,000 and higher. **For many believers**

participation in these fund raisers is their only contribution to kingdom building. Very few have actually testified to a non-believer and led such a person to a new life in God. Such fruit is sorely missing among the congregations of all denominations.

> *They hate him that rebuketh in the gate, and*
> *they abhor him that speaketh uprightly.*
> *Forasmuch therefore as your treading is upon the poor,*
> *and ye take from him burdens of wheat: ye have built houses of hewn stone,*
> *but ye shall not dwell in them; ye have planted pleasant vineyards, but ye shall*
> *not drink wine of them.*
> *For I know your manifold transgressions,*
> *and your mighty sins: they afflict the just, they take a bribe,*
> *and they turn aside the poor in the gate from their right.*
> **Amos 5:10-12**

Some of the Black Clergy have enjoyed a time of being "above the law". They have felt and taught they are accountable to God alone and that their schemes should go unchallenged. They have hidden for too long behind the peoples fear generated by the "Touch not God's anointed" teaching of the Black Church. ***"Saying, Touch not mine anointed, and do my prophets no harm" (1Ch 16:22).***

> "Many would say that to be critical of other Christians is to sit in judgment of them, and that is God's role. But we must understand that we are in covenant relationship with other members of the body. To clearly see error and say nothing about is to abdicate ones' responsibility as a believer. *Imitation of God*, Dr. Frederick A. Hogan, pg. 1

> ***All scripture is given by inspiration of God, and is profitable for doctrine, for***
> ***reproof, for correction, for instruction in righteousness:***
> ***That the man of God may be perfect, thoroughly furnished***
> ***unto all good works.***
> **II Timothy 3:16-17**

It is because of their lust for worldly things that these transgressions against the children of God are made. Although they appear to be "religious", on the inside they are ravenous wolves, who deal falsely with the people of the church. These false leaders, perpetrators of righteousness, drain the life out of the body of God. Their leadership is vain. The most important project in these churches is the "Building Fund" and the fund-raising efforts to raise money to "burn the mortgage" sooner. These are material goals and are not necessarily "inspired" of God. The house that the Creator commissioned these leaders to build goes neglected.

> *But Solomon built him an house.*
> *Howbeit the most High dwelleth not in temples made with hands;*
> *as saith the prophet,*
> *Heaven is my throne, and earth is my footstool: what house will ye build me?*
> *saith the Lord: or what is the place of my rest?*
> *Hath not my hand made all these things?*
> *Ye stiff-necked and uncircumcised in heart and ears, ye do always resist the*
> *Holy Ghost: as your fathers did, so do ye.* **Acts 7:47-51**

Electronic Evangelism

Today, evangelism for the most part is done electronically. The picture of the witnessing Christian is a misnomer. We live in the age of "Electronic Evangelism". **Though Christians speak of a "personal Savior", there witness of that Savior, is very "impersonal".** The Jehovah's Witness, who do not consider themselves to be Christians are an exception to this rule. Though considered a cult by mainstream Christendom they appear to be the only ones who do as the scripture suggest Christians do, that is be a witness to the lost. Although they claim autonomy, they have fundamentally the same "original sin theory" and "plan of salvation" as the orthodox Christians.

> *"You have wearied the Lord with your words;*
> *Yet, you say, 'In what way have we*
> *wearied Him? In that you say, every one that does evil is good*
> *in the sight of the Lord, and He delights in them', or, 'where is the*
> *God of Justice?* **Mal. 2:17**

Lavish Lifestyles of Clergy Unjustified

Instead of lavish lifestyles, members of the Black Clergy could take their wealth and the many other assets of the church and truly be about the salvation and rescue of a people. The lavish lifestyles are not justified and are often symptoms of pastors who are walking in the flesh. While they preach about robbing God they are robbing God's people. According to the scriptures in which they teach from, it is said that God put such leaders in the church and charged them with the responsibility of bringing the members of His body into the *"Unity of the Faith"*, and to grow them to that *"measure and stature of the fullness of Christ"*. This aspect of the mission of the Black Church must become

199

the priority. Currently, this remains on paper only, while many clergymen pursue their material fantasies and their lust for power and prestige. This must cease! And if you will not do the job given to you by the same scriptures you gather tithes with, why ask for pay at all; maybe preaching isn't the career for you.

> "Many black, non-denominational, Pentecostal or full gospel pastors have begun to teach a prosperity-type message in addition to their gospel message. Part of this message is teaching the flock that the pastor is worthy of the best and is justified to spend whatever it takes to maintain the best for him." *Imitation of God*, Dr. Fredrick A. Hogan, pg. 14

> "Many pastors believe that their obligation is to preach or teach the Word, counsel individuals of the church (whether they are qualified to do so or not) and lastly, to amass all the wealth they can." *Imitation of God*, Dr. Fredrick A. Hogan, pg. 19

"For they that are such serve not the Lord...but there own belly; and by good words and fair speeches deceive the hearts of the simple."
Romans 16:18

> "The ends you serve that are selfish will take you no further than yourself; but the ends you serve that are for all, common, will take you even into eternity". *No More Lies About Africa,* Chief Musamaali Nangoli, pg. 135

The outstanding characteristic of all abusive churches is the presence of fake healers, false prophets and preacher pimps all pretending to work for God while they con the innocent out of cash they actually worked for. For the believers it is "hard" earned cash. Many are our seniors and most are single mothers in which they take advantage of. These men follow their own desires and depend on their own understanding for guiding those who would follow them. They pollute the table of the Lord that the believers come to feed on.

"Woe unto you, scribes and Pharisees, hypocrites! For you devour widow's house, and for a pretense make long prayer: therefore you shall receive the greater damnation. Woe unto you, scribes and Pharisees, hypocrites! For you compass sea and land to make one proselyte, and when he is made, you make him twofold the child of hell than yourselves." Matthew 23:13-15

*

"For I know your manifold transgressions, and your mighty sins: they afflict the just, they take a bribe, and they turn aside the poor in the gate from their right." **Amos 5:12**

"Most victims are women, and many of these women are single parents. Most of these women have been hurt emotionally and are lonely. An abusive leader is a poor substitute for a mate, but at least it is someone who periodically gives them attention and recognition. These victims crave the leader's attention and will do anything to get it. They are present at every service and make themselves available for almost any menial task. They sometimes take over duties of the leader's spouse, not as service onto the Lord, but unto the leader." *Imitation of God*, Dr. Fredrick A. Hogan, pgs. 38-39

I know Dr. Hogan personally and even grew up with him and know him to be an ethical leader. He has since writing this book entered the ministry and is Pastor of a local congregation to my knowledge. I am also familiar with the context of his comments. He was himself a member of an abusive church in which all church assets totaling nearly seven million dollars was in the name of his pastor, pastor's wife and pastor's mother. The pastor's entire family was on the payroll. There were no other paid church employees. This pastor took the Lord's money and bought himself a personal mansion with only the consent and knowledge of a few in the congregation; his hand picked devotees. He bought his house before building the six million plus house of the Lord now owned by his family exclusively. Both he and his wife drive expensive vehicles which they often trade for the latest luxury vehicle. I believe this pastor to be truly gifted. However I also believe that he has gradually come to abuse those gifts exchanging them now for filthy lucre and power. Someone has to care as Dr. Hogan did. He wrote a book, what will you do?

Who is wise, and he shall understand these things? Prudent, and he shall know them? For the ways of the Lord are right, and the just shall walk in them: but the transgressors shall fall therein. **Hosea 14:9**

"Woe unto the pastor that destroy and scatter the sheep of my pasture! Saith the Lord. Therefore thus saith the Lord God of Israel against the pastors that feed my people; ye have scattered my flock, and driven them away...behold, I will visit upon you the evil of your doings, saith the Lord." **Jeremiah 3:1-2**

Is There No Balm In Gilead?

It is because of wicked pastors that prey on their flocks that many have left the church feeling safer and more at peace at home. For those who remain in the church they must be rescued. Jesus would not leave them comfortless, why should those who claim to follow him ignore the money changers in the temple? When will saints rise in righteous indignation and remove these spots from their feast.

"Is there no balm in Gilead; is there no physician there? Why then is not the health of the daughter of my people recovered? **Jeremiah 8:22**

Good Shepherds will Risk own Life, for the Life of the Sheep

The most difficult aspect of having to discuss the corruption and darkness in the church is that for most black Christians, the sentiment is, "If you can't go to the church, where can you go; and if you can't trust the preacher, who can you trust". **The church is a very essential aspect of a large number of African American's lives. Believe me I am interested in preserving what is good in our only institution.** The good shepherd cares for the life of the sheep, more than his own comfort and safety. As in the natural world, where shepherds are called upon to face bears and lions to protect the life of the defenseless sheep, so to "Spiritual Shepherds" must face whatever danger is required to assure the safety of the sheep. Spiritual shepherds will recognize that, all of the sheep deserve and require their protection, and not just the sheep of their individual flock. Most importantly, it is required of the shepherds by the scriptures they teach from, that they be God's mouth-piece; the ones to put the light on the darkness of those who are falsely representing themselves.

"I am the good shepherd: the good shepherd gives his life for the sheep. But he that is an hireling, and not the shepherd, whose own the sheep are not, seeth the wolf coming, and leaves the sheep, and flees: and the wolf catches them, and scatters the sheep. The hireling flees, because he is a hireling, and cares not for the sheep." **John 10:11-13**

*

"For I know this, that after my departing shall grievous wolves enter in among you, not sparing the flock." **Acts 20:29**

*

So you, O son of man, I have made you a watchman for the house of Israel;

therefore you shall hear a word from my mouth, and warn them for me. When I say to the wicked, O wicked man, thou shall surely die; and you do not speak to warn the wicked from his way, that wicked man shall die in his iniquity; but his blood will I require at your hand. Nevertheless if you warn the wicked to turn from his way, and he does not turn from his way, he shall die in his iniquity; but you have delivered your soul." **Ezekiel 33:**

*

Never forget that man is the agent by which the Creator gets His work done. We must be his hands and mouth. When one assumes the position of Pastor he or she has taken on an awesome responsibility. Pastors are spiritually responsible for those who they see are in need of correction. Man is the agent the Creator uses to speak and correct those that are in error and therefore danger. Someone must be "willing" to "do" the will of God. Someone must be willing to be the vessel that is fit for a holy work, and deliver those who have fallen prey to false prophets and preacher pimps.

"The Spirit of the Lord is upon me, because he has anointed me to preach the gospel to the poor; he has sent me to heal the brokenhearted, to preach deliverance to the captives, and recovering of sight to the blind, to set at liberty them that are bruised, To preach the acceptable year of the Lord." **Luke 4:18-19**

Do you have the Spirit of God on you? Are you allowing God to use you? Or do you live in fear? If you are afraid to do what God would have you do; ask yourself, 'where did I get this fear from' because we know that *"God has not given us the spirit of fear"*. As ministers of God you belong to a royal priesthood. There is a standard that you must uphold. Do not forget that in the first Black Church there was not even a mention of sinners. They had set themselves aside (sanctified) for Gods work. Today's church congregations will overlook almost anything. Forgiving is important but pastors who stand in the pulpit presuming to speak for God should uphold a standard.

"But you are a chosen generation, a royal priesthood, a holy nation, His own special people, that you may proclaim the praises of Him who called you out of darkness into His marvelous light." **1 Peter 2:9**

It is time for a new standard in the Black Church. Of course in light of the recent crises within the Catholic Church many of us would hope that there are radical changes made there as well. **Humanity can no longer afford to be stumbling in the darkness and only the Church can bring the light of hope. This places a**

203

great responsibility on the shoulders of Religious leaders. However, if pastors are walking in the Spirit, they will not use carnal methods to achieve spiritual ends. They will trust the Spirit to honor their word as they speak to the mountain of darkness and command it to be cast into the sea. Some are heeding the call. There is a movement of the Spirit in the entire world and particularly in the Church.

The work that needs to be done is of a spiritual nature. Therefore it cannot be done in the flesh or natural. Those ministers who operate in the flesh will be ineffectual in the battle for the minds of African Americans. We must recreate a holy nation of priest (pastors) in these dark days. The reason we must do it: Because Spiritual abuse is the worst kind of abuse. It disturbs the critical relation between the Creator and His creature. Man's faith in his Creator is often shattered when impacted by the "unholy priesthood".

The Worst Abuse is Spiritual Abuse

Today, abuse is quite widespread. We read reports about it daily and view examples on the evening news. We hear about workers being abused by their employers, women that are abused by their husbands and lovers and children who are abused by their parents, relatives and strangers. **As tragic as all abuse is, the worst abuse is spiritual abuse. Spiritual abuse comes between man and his Creator and negatively affects this most vital connection. Spiritual abuse is abuse of the worse kind.** It is the lowest form of abuse. It is taking advantage of people who are lost, confused, weak and already bruised. It is the worst of abuses because it affects the perceptions of God of those who are abused. Some never recover from the devastation of this type of abuse and go to their graves angry with God. The first order of business is to get a working definition of the abusive leader and church. We will use a definition found in the *Imitation of God* by Dr. Fredrick A. Hogan:

"The general definition of spiritual abuse…is from Johnson and Van Vonderen's book The Subtle Power of Spiritual Abuse…is stated as follows:

"The mistreatment of a person who is in need of help, support, or greater spiritual empowerment, with the result of weakening, undermining or decreasing that persons spiritual empowerment". *Imitation of God*, Dr. Frederick A. Hogan, pg. 8

"This definition will include most situations in the church, but for the purpose of this work, a more specific definition is as follows:

"When a pastor or pastor-endorsed leader uses his or her spiritual authority to control or manipulate". *Imitation of God*, Dr. Frederick A. Hogan, pg. 8

"This manipulation and domination can take on many forms. Some of the more common forms of spiritual abuse are when authority is used to force the giving of finances, or forcing strict attendance at church, or to control information-gathering from members about other members, or to force others to try to live up to some super spiritual standard". *Imitation of God*, Dr. Frederick A. Hogan, pg. 8

Preacher Pimps Cause More Harm Than Good

The condition of the people after becoming involved with an abusive religious leader is often worse than when they came to the leader. Instead of becoming spiritually empowered they become emotionally handicapped. The pastors are the only ones who "appear" to be empowered. They are only empowered temporally, and such power is not of the kingdom so it is vain.

Some Christians advance the theory that if people are in an abusive church, they should leave. This sounds simplistic and logical enough. This however, is not an African attitude or perspective. It is a reflection of the European ideology of "rugged individualism".

The major reason for the "gullibility of believers" is their sincere desire to please God. As I, they too want to hear their Creator say, "well done thy good and faithful servant". The second major reason is that pastors are naturally trusted by believers. Unfortunately, because of abuse in the Church, these sterling characteristics are manipulated and taken advantaged of. Their innocence is robbed as they are raped financially, physically and emotionally. This is tragic because the second reason for the believer's gullibility is their emotional condition. Most people that seek church membership do so under hardship and duress. They go to church to "get their life together". Instead of finding a place of solace and comfort they find wolves in sheep clothing waiting to devour their substance (wealth). Oftentimes these wolves even take physical advantage of women in the church.

The scriptures use sheep to describe believers, because the characteristics of believers and sheep are nearly identical. Sheep are the most innocent and defenseless animal in the animal kingdom. They will follow a shepherd to the slaughter without even a complaint. We have seen this behavior in several religious groups or cults. In these groups, innocent men, women and children are led to commit suicide. Though these are extreme examples, they demonstrate the extent of the gullibility of believers, the sheep of the church. If sheep are not led to pasture, they would starve. They are wholly dependent on their shepherds for their safety, sustenance and survival. They are dependent on their shepherds for every vital aspect of their lives.

The sheep of Christianity are no different. Perhaps, this is the reason Jesus is recorded as asking Peter three times, if he loved him. After each answer from Peter, Jesus instructed Peter to "feed his sheep". He made it known that it was an intimate connection between loving him and feeding the lambs of God.

"So when they had dined, Jesus saith to Simon Peter, Simon, son of Jonas, lovest thou me more than these? He saith unto him, Yea, Lord; thou knowest that I love thee. He saith unto him, Feed my lambs.
He saith to him again the second time, Simon, son of Jonas, lovest thou me? He saith unto him, Yea, Lord; thou knowest that I love thee. He saith unto him, Feed my sheep.
He saith unto him the third time, Simon, son of Jonas, lovest thou me? Peter was grieved because he said unto him the third time, Lovest thou me? And he said unto him, Lord, thou knowest all things; thou knowest that I love thee. Jesus saith unto him, Feed my sheep". **John 21:15-17**

The Abuses in The Black Church

Pastors of abusive churches follow their own desires and depend on their own understanding for the manipulating of those that follow them. They are manipulators because ultimately they serve only their selfish desires. The reason for this is seen in their true desires, which are almost entirely material. These are the flamboyant pastors that are often difficult to distinguish in their style of dress from the hustlers in the streets. They drive the fanciest cars and wear the most expensive clothes available as their use of church funds for personal items are usually subject to their discretion only. They pollute the table that the believers feed on. Because of these pimps in the pulpit many are bruised and their love for their Creator grows cold.

"But ye have profaned it, in that ye say, the table of the Lord is polluted; and the fruit thereof, even his meat, is contemptible". **Malachi 1:12**

*

"And many false prophets shall rise, and shall deceive many.

And because iniquity shall abound, the love of many shall wax cold".
Matthew 24:11-12

Money Cometh

Now we must focus on the center of corruption the tithe and the offerings. There are many abused scriptures but the scriptures around tithes and offerings seem to be the most abused. Many of today's "Word Churches" are beginning to focus a lot of energy into getting believers blessed. On the surface this appears to be a worthy cause. The leaders of this movement declare they are tired of God's people living in poverty and want to show believers how they can be "biblically blessed". They reason that the testimony of people who lack abundant resources is weakened because it does not give any glory to God. So they began to preach that it is God's desire that His people prosper. They have produced numerous scripture to support their theory and have stirred quite a number of people up as there are quite a number of people today in need of financial blessings.

I call this crowd the "Money Cometh Crowd'. They claim they want to make Christians look good to the unbelievers by teaching them how to claim the finances of the "people of the world". When they say "money cometh" that is supposed to bring the finances of the so-called ungodly into the hands of the Saints where it belongs. One popular leader of this new movement is a Black author by the name of Dr. Leroy Thompson, Sr. He testifies that he received those words from God for God's Church. I guess God is still speaking with the King James dialect since His "Word" is written in it. Listen to his testimony.

> "More than a year ago, the Lord gave me this revelation of 'Money cometh'. At first, I thought He gave it to me just to bless me and my family, because 'money cometh' began working mightily in our lives...But soon after I received this revelation...God began dealing with me about sharing it with the Body of Christ. The Lord wants me to establish a money-covenant with believers...God has given me the assignment to teach the Body of Christ about prosperity. He wants His people to know that it is His will and good pleasure to prosper them. And God wants the Body of Christ to take back what the devil has stolen."

> "There is no side door to God's blessings. In other words, you can't creep in a side door by prayer when He told you to give. You can't pray past giving! If God said, 'Here's what you're to do. I want you to give,' and you say, 'No, I'm going to pray; praying is really spiritual,' then 'Money cometh' won't work for you."

"I tell you, you ought to think about prosperity all the time. You ought to think about abundance."

"So the blood and money do go together! Somebody said, 'Oh, no. communion---the Lord's Supper---and being wealthy don't go together. But, yes, Jesus became poor and He died that you might become rich (2 Corinthians 8:9)."

"The Body of Christ needs this message. Too many in the Body are broke. Many have a false prosperity or a false front. In other words, they over-buy to prove they have money. But, really they're broke."

"Some people hear Malachi 3:10 preached, and they get happy. They say, 'Okay, I'm going to tithe!' They tithe for two weeks. Then when they go to counting up their bills they say, 'I just can't tithe anymore.' For ten cents, they are holding back their promotion. Robbed because of a dime! If that describes you, the devil is stealing from you. He has his hand in your pocket. While you're stealing ten cents from God, the devil is stealing ninety cents from you. Why? Because when you don't give God ten cents, then that other ninety cents belong to you and the devil."

Make Sure God Said It Before You Believe It

While this may sound like sound doctrine it is not. It is doubtful that God gave him the revelation or the assignment. The scriptures this man professes to teach out of insist that man ought to meditate on all the words of God continually and always, yet he tells believers they should think about money all the time. The Scriptures teach that man should make seeking the Kingdom of God first yet Dr. Thompson teaches the Body of Christ that they should make prosperity; the getting of things (wealth) first.

Then he stoops lower than low and says, "Jesus died so that you could become rich". I know the rich man in the bible that was rebuked by Jesus and told that it was hard for a rich man to enter heaven wishes he would have been living today under Jesus new covenant. This of course is ludicrous but shows the level of corruption these people are willing to indulge so that money would cometh their way. Dr. Thompson wrote a three hundred and thirty six page book explaining his new "revelation" from God and making a defense of its obvious departure from sound doctrine. Someone should direct Dr. Thompson's attention to a couple of scriptures that he has obviously overlooked.

"Love not the world, neither the things that are in the world. If any man love the world, the love of the Father is not in him. For all that is in the world, the lust of the flesh, and the lust of the eyes, and the pride of life, is not of he Father, but is of the world. And the world passes away, and the lust thereof; but he who does the will of the God abides forever." **1 John 2:15-17**

*

"But seek first the Kingdom of God and His righteousness, and all these things will be added to you." **Matthew 6:33**

We can glean from these passages the error in the "Money Cometh" crowd's philosophy and teaching. They are teaching people to lust after the things of this world. They are teaching Church goers to put the things of this world before the Kingdom of God. They have things backwards and have put the cart before the horse. First seek the Kingdom of God and His Righteousness and then all those things (wealth) will be given to you, totally invalidates putting money first.

It appears that Dr. Thompson's "new deal," his money covenant with the Body of Christ, was cut on the side and has nothing to do with God at all! Instead of teaching believers to go through the front door, through the Kingdom of God, they are teaching how to go through the side door of bribing God to let them keep what they got and allow them to take what unbelievers have. This is a dark creed.

The Tragedy of Carnal Teaching

The tragic aspect of this carnal teaching is that it makes believers fearful of the devil. As Dr. Thompson so eloquently explained, when you don't pay your bill (tithe) to God he sends his bill collector the devil to break your legs and take what money you got since you didn't give Him his. This emotional intimidation which results in the manipulation of millions of African Americans occurs every Sunday. On Sunday an additional ploy is added as believers are made to feel guilty. This is accomplished by allowing the members of the congregation that have fallen for the con game to bring their offering to God first. This little maneuver causes those that are seated during this parade to feel guilty that they are not trusting God like the others.

"As the partridge sitteth on eggs, and hatcheth them not; so he that getteth

riches, and not by right, shall leave them in the midst of his days, and at his end shall be a fool". **Jeremiah 17:11**

Let's take a moment and take a look at this "New Testament Church" ordinance called the Tithe. First we will examine the scripture that relates to this controversial Church ordinance and see if it is of God or just another commandment of men.

"For the priest's lips should keep knowledge, and they should seek the law at his mouth: for he is the messenger of the Lord of hosts.
But ye are departed out of the way; ye have caused many to stumble at the law; ye have corrupted the covenant of Levi, saith the Lord of hosts.
Therefore have I also made you contemptible and base before all the people, according as ye have not kept my ways, but have been partial in the law".
Malachi 2:7-9
*

"If therefore perfection were by the Levitical priesthood, (for under it the people received the law,) what further need was there that another priest should rise after the order of Melchisedec, and not be called after the order of Aaron"?

For the priesthood being changed, there is made of necessity a change also of the law.
For he of whom these things are spoken pertaineth to another tribe, of which no man gave attendance at the altar.
For it is evident that our Lord sprang out of Judah; of which tribe Moses spake nothing concerning priesthood". **Hebrews 7:4-14**

*

"Will a man rob God? Yet have you robbed me. But you say, wherein have we robbed you? In tithes and offerings. You are cursed with a cursed: for you have robbed me, even this whole nation. Bring you all the tithes into the storehouse, that there may be meat in mine house, says the Lord of host, if I will not open the windows of heaven and pour you out a blessing, that there shall not be room enough to receive it. And I will rebuke the devourer for your sakes, and he shall not destroy the fruits of your ground; neither shall your vine cast her fruit before the time in the field, says the Lord of host."
Malachi 3:8-11

Are We Old or New Testament Saints

Its curious how "New Testament" saints like to go back into the "Old Testament" covenants and claim "some" of them for the Church today. The Scripture says that since the priesthood has been changed it was necessary to change the law. **These infamous passages have been used to hold believers hostage for decades but the pressure has really been turned up today so that most of the people that tithe say they do so out of fear that if they don't God will send the devil to take what little they have.** Yet the con men not caring about what little they may have only wish to add what they can to their substantial stash. They are robbing God's people with a promise of prosperity for obedience and the threat of loss for noncompliance. **If people are paying their tithes out of fear that means the pastors are using fear to get them to pay. This is called manipulation.**

> "When asked what was the main reason they gave to the church, over 98 percent of those responding stated, so that God would keep the devil away from their finances. The number two answer was to get more money in return. Only a few people reasoned that they gave because they loved the work of God, suggesting that the objective for giving was either to get more in return, fear of the devil taking their finances or trying to please leadership. God loves a cheerful giver not a fearful giver." *Imitation of God,* Dr. Fredrick A. Hogan, pg. 22-23

The first thing that must be noted from the passages of scripture quoted above is that the entire book of Malachi is written to the corrupt priest of that time who were not giving to God His portion of the offering He had set up for them.

"And now, O priest, this commandment is for you. If you will not hear, and take it to heart, to give glory to my name, says the Lord of Host, 'I will send a curse upon you, and I will curse your blessings, yes I have cursed them already, because you do not take it to heart." **Malachi 2:1-2**

We see here Malachi rebuking the priest for not giving glory to God. They were sacrificing to God the blemished, lame and blind animals. This was viewed as contemptible. In the entire book of Malachi, it was the priest that God was rebuking. It was they that He swore to rebuke the devourer for and allow them to keep the blessing He had bestowed on them in providing a tax on the other tribes labor in exchange for their labor toward the other tribes. It was their job to minister the law to the other eleven tribes. They were the ones chosen to minister before the Lord and to the people. The tithe "Covenant" was with the priest of the Old Testament which was eliminated with the coming of Jesus the High Priest that would end the sacrifice of bulls and bullocks. Any attempt to use this passage in any other way would be taken it out of context.

According to the Bible, the priesthood was replaced by a better priesthood, the priesthood of Jesus the Christ, the High Priest. The old covenant was based on carnal rituals that were a reflection of the new covenant, which was spiritual. In the new covenant, rather than giving a tithe, the believer is to give himself. He or she is to make a living sacrifice by bringing the human personality to the altar to be transformed by the worshipping of the Creator in Spirit and in Truth. We are the tithe in the New Testament church. This is not to suggest that believers are to not support their church financially.

New Testament offerings are to be free will offerings. This can only occur if the offerings are not obligatory. A tithe is an "obligatory" offering. If offerings were left to the individual being led by the Spirit, the corruption of manipulation and exploitation would be minimized. Free will offerings are the only offerings that can be given cheerfully and without obligation or necessity. This is the greatest indictment against the tithe.

Voluntary donations to the church would require the pastor to walk by faith as the believer is instructed to do. Obviously, few pastors have sufficient faith to believe that the needs of the church would be met in this manner. Such a system of donations would free members from the awful and grievous burdens placed on them by unscrupulous pastors looking for a guaranteed income to base their budgets on. A voluntary system would also act as a catalyst for improving the job done by these pastors. Instead of using guilt to "con" the money from believers, the pastors would have to instead demonstrate that they are worthy of financial support. Instead of looking for pastors that preach good sermons, the believer could focus on finding a pastor that produced good fruit.

"Every man according as he purposeth in his heart, so let him give; not grudgingly, or of necessity: for God loveth a cheerful giver". **II Co. 9:7**

Black Clergy Must be Held Accountable

We demand accountability of our teachers, of our police officers, our movie industry, and many others that we recognize have a great deal of influence on our community. **The time has come for the community to hold its religious leaders accountable. The fraternities of clergymen, who are sincerely interested in helping people, should take a stand as well for a new standard.** The ranks of the African American clergy are cluttered with corrupt leaders that prey on Black

Christians. For the most part, the Black religious community is divided. Sunday is the most segregated day of the week. On that day, many crimes are committed against our people "in the name of Jesus" and no one protests. **Preacher pimps, false prophets and fake healers steal from and con our trusting seniors and innocent women out of their hard-earned dollars. The only way to make pastors accountable to God is to make them accountable to God's people. We must stop the robbing of Black people in the name of God! Together we can throw the money changers out of the temple.**

Those that abuse, mislead, confuse, bruise and scatter the lambs of God for filthy lucre (ill gotten wealth) and unearned status should be openly put to shame if they refuse to desist in their crimes within the Church. Good men and women can no longer afford to be silent and afraid to act. The reproach of the entire Black Church should rest on their heads that no other sheep will wander into their pastures of corruption and exploitation. Their evil deeds done in the dark must be brought to the light of public awareness. This is a movement of righteousness. The crooked paths must be straightened and those that have exalted themselves must be abased. **To the preacher pimps, false prophets, and wolves in sheep clothing that masquerade as men of God in the pulpit we must all say, "Let My People Go".**

Chapter 11

TAKING A STAND FOR THE TRUTH

RECLAIMING THE AFRICAN MIND

"Get up, stand up, stand up for your rights
Get up, stand up, once you see the light
Get up, stand up, stand up for your rights
Get up, stand up, don't give up the fight"

Bob Marley

When we see the light, we are moved to take a stand. It gives us the **courage to stand.** We've fallen but we can get up. We must get up. We must take a stand for the integrity of African spiritual wisdom, values and attitudes. It is critical that we come to ourselves and reclaim our minds. This will remove the barriers that prevent us from acting as one. **As we liberate our minds, we will empower ourselves to set the African House in order. Divided the house cannot stand and it is weak. Divided, we will remain in a fallen condition. United the house can and will stand.**

"For over three hundred years the white man has been our oppressor, and he naturally is not going to liberate us to the higher freedom-the truer liberty-the truer democracy. We have to liberate ourselves"—Marcus Garvey. *No More Lies About Africa,* Chief Musamaali Nangoli, pg. 138

we have to do it,
nobody else will!

Spiritual Significance of Million Man March

Those of us, who went to the Million-Man March, experienced "the power of unity". On October 16, 1995 in Washington D.C. and throughout this country, African American men stood up. The experience was unique for Capital demonstrations in that we were not there to demand that the politicians do anything for us. We were there to discuss what we would do for ourselves. That day, one of the respected elders of our community called the men of the village together for a council meeting. On that day, we stood as one. We stood together and vowed to come home and continue to stand. On that day we stood for and demonstrated the power of unity. Because of that stand, the world stood still to see. This was the first major sign to the world that a people that had been put to sleep were waking up. This is not to discount previous marches on Washington. It merely says that the fact that for the first time we were not asking for something was significant. We had decided to throw off the image of the "boy" that others had attempted to create for us. We went to demonstrate that we were men, African men. On that day our show of unity made the world stand still. Unity is the key!

When spider webs unite, they can tie up a lion. Ethiopia

The seed of a great oak was planted that day, and a spiritual quickening occurred that was the rebirth of a nation. Regardless of those that discount the significance of that day, and say nothing has changed, because they haven't. The Million Man March had a profound affect on the Black community and especially those of us who went. The seed has had a chance to incubate in our psyche it is now time to demonstrate that a lot can happen in a day. The time required conceiving each of us took less than a day, less than an hour perhaps less than ten minutes. Yet, as you look in the mirror, some twenty, thirty, or forty years later, you behold the miracle of a single seed.

It is ironic that during the life of Martin Luther King the Government despised him, and many of the Black clergy leadership were too fearful to join in his struggle. Today both of these camps hypocritically celebrate the "Dream", now that they are safe. The dreamer is gone. The Black clergy should have stood with him while he yet lived. Hindsight is always twenty-twenty, whereas insight and foresight often come up short. This must change.

Most of us Know its Time to take a Stand

Many of us know that it is time to take a stand. Some have simply not known where to take that stand. The battle is for the mind, especially the minds of our

216

youth. In our not too distant pass, our right minds were taking from us. Today it is time to take them back. This is the spiritual meaning of the Battle of Armageddon, the final battle of the forces of light and the darkness within. It is not the end of the world but instead the end of an age or era, a dark era. This battle is being fought within each individual and within the larger community of humanity. It is imperative that we stand for that which is true. Much that has been shared in this book, needs to be shared on a mass level. The house is on fire, each one teach one will not work today. Today each one must teach hundreds and thousands.

> "Wake up Africa! Let us work towards the one glorious end of a free, redeemed and mighty nation. Let Africa be a bright star among the constellation of nations". *No More Lies About Africa,* Chief Musamaali Nangoli, pg. 135

African Wisdom Ignored and Rejected by African Americans

The African mind has given so much to humanity that is taking for granted or ignored entirely. Of particular importance to us is the spiritual principles that was used to order their society and relationships. We must become familiar with concepts such as the African concept of MAAT. **Establishing harmony, and unity, achieving inner peace and balance are all based on the level of our awareness of the truth, which is the essential message of MAAT. If we are to find the beauty of life; if we are to experience life and life more abundantly (optimum life) we must live according to the spiritual principles that govern this life and the universe, this is the atonement.** This is the stand we must take. It is the truth, and not a man, which must be lifted up on earth that all men will be drawn to it and be set free. Starting in the year 2004, we must work to establish a spiritual matrix in the Black community based on the Spiritual wisdom of Africa.

Our Greatest Hindrance and Challenge

Unfortunately one of the greatest hindrances to the spiritual awakening and empowerment of African Americans is the emotional and unconscious tie to that which maintains his sleep-like and sheep-like condition. The beliefs of another people have been cleverly and skillfully hidden in the fabric of the Black consciousness so that we claim them as our own. Too many are looking for Jesus to do for them what only they can do for themselves. Our greatest challenge and hindrance lies within us in the form of false beliefs. **The challenge of this chapter and this book is for the reader to shake off this stupor and reject the Trojan horse of the enemy, which is Euro-Christianity.**

Adisa Franklin

White Supremacy has a counter-part called Black Inferiority. Without Black Inferiority, there would be no White Superiority. These two world outlooks form the basis for the dysfunctional relationship shared by whites and blacks. **Rather than focus as we have, on changing racism, a symptom of White Supremacy, our focus should be on eliminating the sickness of Black Inferiority. We cannot force white people to abandon their beliefs. However, we can heal ourselves.**

> "There is always a turning point in the destiny of every race, every nation, of all peoples, and we have come to the turning point of Africans, where we have changed from the old cringing weakling, and transformed into full-grown men, demanding our portion as MEN"—Marcus Garvey. *No More Lies About Africa,* Chief Musamaali Nangoli, pg. 137

Who Can We Look to For A Solution

Every since the Emancipation Proclamation and the Thirteenth Amendment, African Americans have considered the right to vote as a precious privilege. Though important, it too has been over-rated. Initially, Black people were with the Republican Party. We switched when we realized that all we were receiving were promises and rhetoric. While talking of change, the government was responsible for such repressive laws as the Black Codes and the Jim Crow Laws. The Democratic Party has not delivered either. Now many Blacks are switching back to the Republican Party. The government has never provided adequate education or jobs for blacks whether Republican or Democratic.

The political machine that is both Democrats and Republicans is their "machine". What does it take for Blacks to acknowledged, that the machine is corrupt and was never meant to be of any real benefit to Blacks. It is by design. Admit it, 'The solution will not come from the federal government. Besides we all know "What the government gives the government takes away; like affirmative action". **When will we learn? When will we stop believing the hype? Our salvation is not in either political party, it is in us. The Government has not and will not deliver.**

Does Black Church Really Offer a Real Solution?

The sermons and instruction offered by the Black Church fall under the biblical classification of "elementary or fundamental" teachings as recorded in **Hebrews 6:1-3** *"Therefore leaving the discussion of the elementary principles of Christ, let us go on to perfection, not laying again the foundation of repentance from*

218

dead works and of faith toward God, of the doctrines of baptisms, of laying on of hands, of resurrection of the dead, and of eternal judgment. And this we will do if God permits." Another name for this type of teaching is the "milk of the Word". **Though colorful and often preached with great eloquence and enthusiasm, the sermons today more often than not, lack spiritual knowledge. They are almost always based on these elementary teachings of Christianity. This is the reason there are so many twenty, thirty and forty year veteran "Babes in Christ" in the churches.**

Pastors Lack Knowledge and Spiritual Vision

The pastors and teachers blame the followers for this shortcoming in the Church. The truth is that the followers are not receiving the "meat" of the Word. The meat of the Word is spiritual knowledge, wisdom and understanding. Today, the focus is on "faith" and believing in God rather than knowledge of God. In reality, the focus of the Black Church remains temporal rather than Spiritual. Notwithstanding the major issue is making it to heaven. We have seen that there is something fundamentally wrong with both the doctrines of the Church and its practices. The spirit of the prophet and the abolitionist is sorely missing from the rank and file of today's Christians. We praise Fredrick Douglas and others during Black History Month but I believe their spirits are grieved at what we have settled for. In order to take back our minds we will have to take back our Spirituality. What African Americans are in need of is African Spirituality and not European Religiosity. Today's Black Church is hooked on European Religiosity, making them ineffectual in the cause of Black Liberation.

We Must Take a Stand For Truth

Truth can be divided into at least two categories; the first relates to the truth about a specific historical event or occurrence. In the ultimate sense Truth is a Spiritual matter. God and Truth are one. In order to know Truth one must come to know God. **There is only one way to know God and that is to experience God.** For one to experience God one has to know they are one with God and seek to manifest that reality in their lives. This is the only way to experience true freedom. This is the only formula or condition for Sonship, it is not a matter of faith and confession but of knowledge and experience. The Church must get busy preparing people for the real return of the Christ; the return of Christ to man's heart. This is the only way for Christ to manifest on earth. This is the real work of the Church.

Taking a stand for Truth ultimately means making a firm resolution to manifest your godhood. When this is done in conjunction with taking a stand

for that which is true regarding the Black man's true history, a mighty thing will have occurred. When the number of Blacks who take such a stand has reached its critical mass there will be a qualitative change in the lives of the entire race. For this Blacks must reclaim their African minds. This means Blacks must renew their minds with an African Spiritual frame of reference. This is the key to Black Salvation; this is where Blacks must take their stand. This requires new spiritual and educational institutions. This should be our legacy to the generations to come. This is my vision for my people!

In addition the need for unity must be addressed. Whether we have realized it or not the Church is responsible for much of the disunity of Blacks. Orthodox Christians for instance will not work with Jehovah's Witness and vice versa. This must cease. We must come together and reason. The time for large scale action has arrived. There must be a nationwide effort to establish unity in the Black Church. We will unite or perish! It is time for concrete action. No more fragmented programs.

Spirit Man Neglected

All of the Televangelist offer miracles that are for the natural man and have a physical or material matrix as the focus. Healing is for the body. Prosperity is material. Victory over destructive habits, deals with a physical substance abuse problem. **Moral teachings are for the natural man.** At best, the church offers some relief from the trials of life with a message of comfort and a quick connect to a government social program. The Church is serving the needs of the natural man. Food, clothing, shelter, physical health and material prosperity are all creature comforts and concerns of the natural man and have little to do with the spiritual growth and development of believers.

In addition as we have learned the doctrines of Christianity are questionable at best. We know they are not all sound. They need to be examined and weighed to see where they diverge from truth, and try to mix truth with falsehood. We should understand by now that Christianity only has merit on the surface. Until now perhaps Christianity was your best alternative for getting your life together but we can do better. There is a *"more excellent way"*. The time to teach truly sound doctrine is here, but first we must build new models for Spiritual Initiation. This was the function of the Great Mystery Schools of Ancient Africa. It must be the function of the new institution of Spirituality, the new Black Church.

Blacks Need to Convene Their Own Holy Synod

We've come to the fork in the road. There are decisions to be made. Perhaps African Americans should convene their own "Holy Synod" and call together all denominations and non-denominations to come let us reason together, its time to clean house. Every pastor that would teach against a United Church would be unscriptural and impractical. Remember a house divided cannot stand. It is time to stand therefore we must unite. Have you not realize that we have a common destiny. **Leadership must unite in order for the body to unite. Holiness must be restored to the House of God.**

"For whoever exalts himself will be humbled,
and he who humbles himself will be exalted"
Luke 14:11

Those Pastors whose egos will not allow them to humble themselves must step out the way, *"the high places must be brought low and the crooked places made straight".* **This is sacred labor.** There must be a meeting of the heads and a coming together. **Unity is a fundamental doctrine of the Scripture and of Jesus if not of Christendom. Any teaching that fosters division rather than unity is of the anti-Christ.** Any church leader who does not support a movement toward unity is guilty by commission. We all need each other. The Unity of Life is a fundamental African doctrine based on the knowledge that God the Creator of all life, is the one life in all life.

"And now I am no more in the world, but these are in the world, and I come to thee. Holy Father, keep through thine own name those whom thou hast given me; that they may be one, as we are one." **John 17:11**

*

"For the body is not one member, but many. If the foot shall say, because I am not the hand, I am not of the body, is it therefore not of the body? If the ear shall say, because I am not an eye, I am not of the body; is it therefore not of the body? If the whole body were an eye, where were the hearing? If the whole were hearing, where were the smelling? But now God hath set the members every one of them in the body, as it has pleased him. And if they were all one member, where were the body? But now are there many members, yet one body. And the eye cannot say unto the hand, I have no need of thee: nor again the head to the feet, I have no need of you.

Adisa Franklin

Nay, much more those members of the body, which seem to be more feeble, are necessary; and those members of the body, which we think to be less honorable, upon these we bestow more abundant honor; and our uncomely parts have more abundant comeliness.
For our comely parts have no need: but God hath tempered the body together, having given more abundant honor to that part which lacked: that there should be no schism in the body; but that the members should have the same care one for another. And whether one member suffer, all the members suffer with it; or one member be honored, all the members rejoice with it. Now ye are the body of Christ, and members in particular." 1 Corinthians 12:14-27

*

For by one Spirit are we all baptized into one body, whether we be Jews or Gentiles, whether we be bond or free; and have been all made to drink into one Spirit. 1Co 12:13

WE INDEED "ALL" NEED EACH OTHER! SO LET US COME TOGETHER NOW, LET THE BLACK CHURCH UNITE AS ONE EVEN AS GOD IS ONE!

"Among the many things the race needed (and badly too) were self respect and self reliance. Henceforth they must think for themselves and of themselves, only relying on their own initiative and ability to right the wrong done them." No More Lies About Africa, Chief Musamaali Nangoli, pg. 10

We Must Think For Ourselves, the Battle is for the Mind

Again we must remember that the battle is for the mind. We must regain control of our own minds. The only way to control our minds is to begin to think for ourselves. To do so, we must abandon and reject the learned tendency to depend on others to think for us. We can no longer rely on others to define our existence, our identity, or our God. We can reclaim "the African Mind" and liberate ourselves from these current conditions. It all depends on our willingness to take back our minds. The motivation to do so depends on our understanding of the true nature of the problem. It is our hope that *"THE LIBERATION OF THE AFRICAN MIND": "The Key to Black Salvation"* has contributed to that understanding.

222

To be considered equal, Blacks must learn to stand on their own two feet intellectually and spiritually. The problem is the long history of dependence has made it habitual. **Blacks have become mentally lazy. For too many, dependency has become comfortable. This attitude of dependency is a carry over from centuries of being treated like boys and being made to act like boys in the presence of Europeans.** Yet in order to be treated like men, Black men will have to assume the mental responsibility of men of working out their own system of ideology.

> "It is unfortunate that we are but perpetuating our own sorrow and disgrace in failing to appreciate the first requisite of all peoples-organization'. 'No African' he went on 'shall be truly respected until the race as a whole has re-emancipated itself, through self-achievement and progress, from universal prejudice." (Marcus Garvey). *No More Lies About Africa*, Chief Musamaali Nangoli, pg. 97

Whenever freedom or "liberty" is the goal, Truth must be the vehicle that gets us there. But to hear the Truth and not do what the Truth would teach us to do is vain and fruitless and makes one wonder if you have actually heard the Truth. Who could hear the Truth and not want to live by it? You must "live" the Truth to be set free by the Truth.

Don't Buy the "Last Days" Hype

Many of the followers of Christendom are prophesizing about the significance of the new millennium. Most believe that the New World Order will be a time when Satan and the forces of darkness will wreck havoc and bring total chaos. **Many are hoping and expecting Jesus to come bursting through the clouds to take the faithful few up into heaven to be with the Father.** This hype is no different from the Y2K hype, which depleted much of our capital resources. **African American Christians need to understand that in the allegory of Christ coming in the clouds, the clouds represent their ignorance, that which hides the light of truth. We must abandon the hold on, hold out, and wait for Lord Jesus to return attitude. We have become so Heavenly bound that we are no earthly good.**

According to all scriptures relating to the Last Days: the Last Days where during the times of the first apostles. In at least three of the Gospels: Matthew, Mark and Luke, Jesus refers to his coming back before the death of those present during his lifetime. All the so called "last days" signs refer to the times of Jesus. Therefore, anytime preachers point to current affairs

as evidence that Jesus if soon to come back they are being deceptive and it is a ploy.

"Now as he sat on the Mount of Olives, the disciples came to him privately saying, 'Tell us, when will these things be?
And what will be the sign of your coming, and of the end of the age?
And Jesus answered and said to them: 'Take heed that no one deceives you.
"Assuredly, I say to you, this generation shall not pass away till all these things take place." **Matthew 24:34**

Wars and rumors of wars are not new. They occurred during the times of Jesus. Nations were also rising against nations. There were famines in the land then. The period in which Jesus spoke of was the time in which the disciples lived. The generation that was living then was the generation that would not pass away before Jesus was to return.

The one truth to be gleaned from this passage is that it was the end of an age that was being referred to and not the end of the world. We live in such a time. That much is true. This is the end of the age of the carnal man. The violence, alienation and chaos created by the natural man being in control must be replaced with a life of spirituality. Eventually this nation of material consumption ruled by the god of gold must become a nation where spiritual matters take priority. The crisis we face is one of spiritual identity. It is time for the spirit of man to be resurrected from the ashes of the natural man. He is the real lord from heaven that is to return. It is his time to reign in the world. This is why we need a new spiritual paradigm or matrix.

I predict that the new millennium will be a time when the African American Priest/king/gods of this world will rise up, take a stand and subdue the dark forces with the light of truth. Taking a stand for truth; means first atoning within ourselves then taking responsibility for keeping the garden (our community). The principles that govern the spiritual realm must become common knowledge. In that way, we will insure peace and harmony in the village.

The Black Church is the Key

Carter G. Woodson made us aware of the miss-education of African Americans in the Institution of Education. The purpose of this writing is to make the reader aware of the miss-education of African Americans in the Institution of Religion or more specifically, in Euro-Christianity. As it is today, realistically, we cannot expect anymore from our Church, our only Black institution. Without radical and fundamental change in doctrines, beliefs, practices and attitudes the Church will continue to fail to deliver Spiritual Freedom and deliverance to Africans in America.

[handwritten: teach the truth to the Black]

The "Key to Black Salvation" is for the African American Clergy that are sincere to be humble enough to admit they have been in error and to take the responsibility of correcting those errors. A call to humility is a call to glory. Did not scripture say *"If my people would humble themselves and turn from their wicked ways….then would I hear from Heaven?"* **Ultimately, this is where we must take our stand! Though infested with corrupt preachers I believe that there are many sincere and spiritually sound African American Pastors.**

"There is an established foundation on which every premise and every problem must be based. It is the fixed reality that is uncompromising, unyielding, and unchangeable. It is the thing that is, the only thing we can know, the criterion by which every act and feeling and condition is measured. We speak of it glibly as Truth, but when we are asked to define it, we find ourselves sympathizing with the bewilderment of Pilate when he asked the immortal question, 'What is truth"? *Know Thyself,* Richard Lynch, pg. 1

"We shall never understand the meaning of Truth until we come to know what God is, because it is the vision we perceive through soul insight. It is the ultimate, infinite power pervading all existence. It is the hidden harmony of life; the single thread of meaning that runs through and connects all things; the unchanging principle that controls the universe". *Know Thyself,* Richard Lynch, pg. 2

"We become free from the ignorance that binds and hampers us only in proportion to our knowledge of Truth. False thinking makes our way hard, but Truth is always liberating". *Know Thyself,* Richard Lynch, pg. 7

This is where we must take our stand. It is the Truth that must be lifted up today. The African American Church must take the responsibility of dispensing the Truth throughout its ranks nationwide. It must be a concerted effort. **The key to liberating Black minds from spiritual ignorance and falsehood is the Black Church.**

The foundation for a greater tomorrow and for the Spiritual, Economic and Social development of African Americans can be, should be and must be laid by the Black Church. The Black Church is financially independent and therefore is essentially controlled by Black people. It virtually has a representative in every home in the Black community. It is therefore in a position to disseminate information effortlessly throughout the community. Mobilizing millions of African Americans would be a simple matter.

God's Storehouse

The millions of dollars controlled by Black churches, their financial investments, including real estate and real property, could be combined to create a Mega-trust fund for entrepreneurial, educational and institutional corrective initiatives. This fund could be called "God's Storehouse". From this fund new paradigm K-12 schools could be built from the ground up. The Church could guarantee all of our children a college education, trade or business endeavor for generations to come. The Church could also address the issue of the neglect of widows and orphans. These are tragic oversights of too many Churches.

> "All of us may not live to see the higher accomplishment of an African Empire-so strong and powerful, as to compel the respect of mankind, but we in our life-time can so work and act as to make the dream a possibility within another generation". *No More Lies About Africa*, Chief Musamaali Nangoli, pg. 140

Lastly, in order for any substantial progress to be made the Black Church must address the issue of the institution of the family. The family is the foundation of the nation. There will be no strong communities without strong families. **Children must be taught how to find their place and fulfill their role in the greater whole. They must once again learn the sanctity of life by precepts and examples. Once again they must be taught that a crime against another person is a crime against God our Creator and themselves. This is the job of the Black Church. We cannot blame the parents. The parents are suffering from institutionalized racism. This is what the Church must rescue it from.** There should be no church without a daily ministry to families. Without such a ministry such extravagant edifices are totally absurd and unjustified.

Church facilities could be open during the week to address the crisis in drug trafficking, prostitution, and homelessness. It could provide parenting classes. As a unified people, the Black dollar could be leveraged to increase its purchasing power.

Most important, the church could be more effective in addressing the lack of spiritual understanding and awareness of Black people. Freeing the African Mind is equivalent to freeing the African Man, because *"Whatsoever a man thinks, for him it is so"*.

"But exodus does not mean a short cut. No theory or philosophical system can change human beings overnight. They cannot suddenly become perfected beings and transform the world's chaos into paradise. It has to be remembered that the generation which began the Exodus lasted forty years, but it was only a beginning on the path of learning to live in harmony with the laws of life, of nature and of the cosmos. Only through the cumulative influence of many people over many generations can a real exodus for humanity be accomplished".

Malcolm X and Martin took a stand. Nat Turner, John Brown, Frederick Douglas and Sojourner Truth took a stand. David Walker, Martin Delaney and Carter G. Woodson took a stand. Harriet Tubman, Noble Drew Ali, and Fannie Lou Hammer all took a stand. Most of them gave their lives and died taken the stand! **Did they die in vain? Was their stand for nothing? Will we not honor their lives for real by taking our stand? Your answer to this question will determine whether we just survive or live victorious in the new millennium.**

"Where can we find in this race our real men? Men of character, men of purpose, men of confidence, men of faith, men who really know themselves? I have come across so many weaklings who profess to be leaders, and in the test I have found them but the captives of a nobler class. They perform the will of their masters without question". *No More Lies About Africa,* Chief Musamaali Nangoli, pg. 141

"Only we can free ourselves from mental slavery, we must set our own minds free" Bob Marley

"The time has come for those of us who have the vision of the future to inspire our people to closer kinship, to a closer love of self, because it is only through his appreciation of self will we be able to rise to that higher life that will make us not an extinct race in the future, but a race of men fit to survive". *No More Lies About Africa,* Chief Musamaali Nangoli, pg. 141

"Men of the black race, let me say to you that a greater future is in store for us; we have no cause to lose hope, to become fainthearted. We must realize that upon ourselves depend our destiny, our future; we must carve out that future and that destiny". *No More Lies About Africa,* Chief Musamaali Nangoli, pg. 142

"IF NOT NOW, WHEN?"

The people who "know God" must rise up to subdue the earth. Carnality and materiality must be shown to be the failures they are. These values and their offspring; racism, sexism and violence must be challenged and addressed at their root levels; the very institutions of our society. This is where the spiritual ignorance is fostered. This is where we must make our stand. The Western way has not worked and will not work. It must be replaced with the "kinder, gentler" and wiser African way.

"By choice, Europeans at their mother's knees have learned to hate Africa and never had to respond to them as people with a legitimate leadership, especially apart from slavery history. Such a perception must be confronted if humanity is to humanize politics. For Africans to expose the mindset of those who de-humanize them they must fly as the Sankofa bird. Accepting Africa's past is the beginning to our liberation." *Dr. Syrulwa Soma*

Blessed and holy God, Creator of the Heavens and the Earth, grant my people, according to the riches of your glory, to be strengthened with your might through your Spirit in their inner man, that the Christ may dwell in their hearts through knowledge of You, that they being rooted and grounded in love and spiritual wisdom, may be able to comprehend with all saints, what is the width and length and depth and height of knowing the Christ within, that they may be filled with all the fullness of God.

"Up you mighty people, rise up and take your stand!"

Now, unto Him who is able to do exceedingly abundantly above all that we might think or ask, according to the power which works in all of us. To the Creator be the glory, for it is the Creator that will present us all faultless before His throne filled with exceeding joy. Thy will is done, forever and always. Amen

About The Author

Adisa became a Baptist minister in 1983. He has over fifteen years of ministerial experience including time spent serving as an Assistant Pastor. He served as Director of Education for a Ministerial Alliance. He is a dynamic lecturer and teacher. He has researched for over twenty five years in preparation for writing this book. This book, the first of a three volume series is for him a labor of love and part of a ministry of reconciliation. He is a veteran social activist. He believes that God's sons and daughters must be reconciled to God in spirit and in truth.

His vision: A powerful united Black Church working to build new institutions that will restore a race and empower Black families and communities for generations to come. In Adisa we see a combination of visionary, missionary, and teacher.

In his words; **"For Blacks Christianity is a badge of dishonor. It is the religion of the conquerors. By confessing to be Christians, African Americans dishonor their ancestors and demonstrate to the world that they willingly accept the position of servant given them by the framers of Christian dogma and doctrine"**

Made in the USA
Columbia, SC
03 January 2021